pigeon pie,
this one's for you.
with love and linguine.

xxx

Make me joyful, make me strong
Eating without thinking is just plain wrong
All animals are creatures too
Thank you, thank you, thank you, thank you

H. E.

Harry Eastwood

CARNEVAL

A celebration of meat, in recipes

BANTAM PRESS

LONDON · NEW YORK · TORONTO · SYDNEY · AUCKLAND

TRANSWORLD PUBLISHERS
61–63 Uxbridge Road, London W5 5SA
www.transworldbooks.co.uk

Transworld is part of the Penguin Random House group of companies
whose addresses can be found at global.penguinrandomhouse.com

Penguin
Random House
UK

First published in Great Britain in 2016 by Bantam Press
an imprint of Transworld Publishers

A CIP catalogue record for this book
is available from the British Library.

ISBN 9780593069950

Photography by Laura Edwards

Food styling by Annie Rigg

Prop styling and art direction by Tabitha Hawkins

Typeset in Century Schoolbook
Printed and bound by Printer Trento, Italy

Penguin Random House is committed to a sustainable
future for our business, our readers and our planet. This book
is made from Forest Stewardship Council® certified paper.

MIX
Paper from
responsible sources
FSC® C018179

1 3 5 7 9 10 8 6 4 2

contents

introduction

I was a vegetarian for four years. I didn't like the idea of eating animals.

Then I got seduced by the smell of frying bacon and yearned to eat sausages. That's when I decided that if I was going to eat meat again, I wanted to learn as much as possible about the subject first. I delved headlong into butchery. That was 14 years ago and since then I have done a nocturnal spell at Smithfield Market, working and learning from wholesale butchers there, dressed in white overalls, a hard helmet, a chain-mail apron and gloves. I went to the Australian Outback to work on a cattle farm. I have butchered (and killed) venison in Scotland and lamb in France. And I dreamed of writing this book the whole time I was learning, researching and living out my passion for meat alongside my real job, working as a food stylist.

Carneval is a collection of (mostly) meat recipes that celebrate the glory and joy of eating great meat. I have tested and researched every recipe meticulously over the course of the last decade, travelling to Europe, Asia and all over the US in the process. My recipe for Bolognese is from Bologna, Kung Pao Chicken is from China, Baby Back Ribs from Memphis. You won't find any shortcuts here: a proper Bolognese is a 4-hour affair and to make your ribs truly sticky and fall-off-the-bone they need to be marinated overnight and then slow smoked. Being a busy city dweller, though, I have included recipes that are also quick by their nature and easy to make. My aim here has always been to honour the meat first and bring

out the best in that cut. The reason that this matters to me so much is because an animal's life went into making that dish and I take that thought seriously. It is with respect and a great deal of gratitude that I cook and enjoy meat. I tend to eat a wide variety of cuts, which is why you will find recipes for brain fritters, beef cheeks and shin, as well as the more common shoulder and leg joints. This is a great book to cook from if you are feeling a bit unsure about obscure cuts of meat because I explain why those require slow cooking as opposed to a quick sizzle. The recipe introductions are also full of helpful tips. On top of these, you will find MEAT GEEK pages peppered throughout the book. Each one is an investigation into a particular area of the meat world – subject matters range from bacon to veal, hanging and resting, to brining and marinating. The MEAT GEEK pages are there to answer questions you may have such as: Is buying organic always better? What is that white shite in my bacon pan? Is it ever ethically acceptable to eat foie gras? How do I cook the perfect steak? Why should I bother to rest my meat? How can I turn my backyard barbie into a smoker? These are all questions that I have been asking myself over the last decade and a half and wished that someone had explained to me in words that I could understand. In addition to the MEAT GEEK pages, I have included a **Turkey Day Countdown** which you can photocopy and put up on your fridge to help you weather the holidays and nail Christmas dinner. It's the only way I know of to cook everything right and wind up at the appointed hour with a cocktail in my hand and a kitchen full of food that is piping hot and ready to go!

For the MEAT GEEK pages, I have relied on the patience and trust of experts such as Peter Hannan, butcher and general meat wizard, to fact check my writing. The meat that he produces and sells is some of the very best quality available in Britain today. You can find him at www.themeatmerchant.com. His dry-aged beef is absolutely out of this world.

Speaking of Pete, here's a quick thought on butchers: spend some time finding a good one, someone you can trust. He or she will be a really important person in your quest for great meat. And good butchers are longing to show us what amazing stuff they have sourced, aged and cut. If they're not, then find a butcher who is. I promise you that he or she is out there, not far from home or online (and there's a list of these fine folks at the end of the book). A butcher you can trust is the first step on your journey towards enjoying and respecting the meat you eat.

what is good meat? how was it raised? why does it matter?

What should I be asking for at the butcher's? What labels should I be zoning in on and which ones should I avoid?

There is a plethora of different (and at times, frankly meaningless) terms used to describe meat – from 'organic' and 'free-range' to 'select farm', amongst others. The meat industry specialises in confusing and even misleading language. In the States they are particularly culpable, describing meat that has been injected with a cocktail of salt, sugar, flavourings and chemicals as 'enhanced' or their worst-quality beef as 'select'. But we do it in the UK, too. According to the literature, the British 'Select Farm' ranges refer to the following conditions: the chickens enjoy 30kg/m of space, live in barns in numbers that don't exceed 30,000 animals, enjoy up to 6 hours of darkness, 40 days of life, and access to daylight.[1] This doesn't sound very 'select' to me. I just want to highlight the confusing nature of the wording. 'Select farm', in ordinary English, suggests a high-end product, a cosy set-up. Clearly this isn't the case. Similarly, 'free-range' and 'organic' come with built-in expectations, a mental image that isn't necessarily accurate. So what should you be looking for, what language can you trust when you want to find an animal that has led a happy life and will provide good-quality meat?

when the packaging says nothing

Avoid it. The welfare of the animal and the quality of the feed are in question. If there is no mention of what the animal

1 *Farmer's Weekly*, 28 May 2008

has been fed or of the conditions in which the creature was raised, it is very likely that the meat comes from the worst farming conditions. To this end, if it says nothing on the sandwich packet, on the takeaway menu, on the fancy burger joint menu, or on the ready meal – you can be sure that it comes from the lowest meat category out there. That silence is ominous. Put it back on the shelf.

free-range

This is the next step up and implies that the animals have had access to the outdoors. It does not, however, say anything about the feed or the time the animals were given to grow naturally to slaughter weight. What's more, 'free-range' can be overstating the freedom aspect, since a label can stipulate 'free-range' when the animals have had restricted access to the outdoors. Throughout the book I have stipulated free-range chicken because something better isn't always available. I would always recommend you buy the best-quality chicken you can afford.

organic

This is another label that needs clarification. 'Organic' implies that the creature in question was given a diet that qualifies for the certification. But this could be all that it implies. Or it can mean that the animal has been raised on completely organic ingredients – both labels will just read 'organic'. Although the term 'organic' doesn't refer to the way in which the

animals were raised (i.e. how much access to the outdoors, how much space they have), it does imply that the creature in question was not intensively farmed, by which I mean that it has grown slower than the battery equivalent.

the best meat you can buy

This is where the **breed**, **feed** and **animal husbandry** come in. If you go for heritage or rare breeds, you are dealing with an animal that isn't genetically designed to grow quickly and will guarantee better flavour and texture. The magic words that you hope to hear from the mouth of your butcher are: '**outdoor reared**' and '**slow grown**'. All farmed animals were designed to spend the majority of their lives outdoors and fed a natural diet. An animal that has led a good life will reward you with very good meat. All meat benefits from being aged and, depending on the species, the time can vary. In the case of beef, in particular, you want to see 'dry-aged' (at least 21–28 days) to really make the most of what it has to give you, but there is more about this subject in **Hang in There** on page 214.

how

How an animal was raised, what it was fed and the conditions in which it was farmed have an enormous impact on the meat. That is what I am referring to when I talk about '**breed**, **feed** and **animal husbandry**'.

In simple terms, heritage breeds are what you're looking for when it comes to pigs. These include Gloucester Old Spot, Tamworth and Saddleback, amongst others. Native and traditional breeds are better for sheep and cows. For beef, these include Angus, Shorthorn, Hereford and Belted Galloways, again amongst others. These are also known as 'old breeds'. If you start with the right breed, you're already on the right track.

Using pigs as an example, choosing a heritage breed is a reliable way of making sure that the animal not only has enjoyed a natural life, but that the anatomical structure of the animal is not amenable to being forced to grow quickly through industrial farming. Those wretched animals often live in horrible conditions because time and therefore space are expensive. They don't roam or enjoy any of the behaviours that are natural to them because moving around means they are spending (wasting) precious energy that could be converted into meat mass. They are slaughtered after 6–8 months instead of the 12 months of outdoor living enjoyed by a heritage breed – in order to achieve the same final weight.

We've talked about **breed** so here's the lowdown on **feed**: it's unsurprising to hear that if an animal was raised on industrial rubbish that was intesively produced (and sometimes flown halfway across the world), it will proudce poor-quality meat. The feed is closely linked to the life that the animal has had – if it's free to roam, there's a good chance that it has had access to natural feed, the most obvious example being grass.

Husbandry is a term that refers to everything else: the living conditions, the time it takes to grow to slaughter weight and, at the end, the expert hands that will treat it with the reverence it deserves (including slaughter, hanging and butchering). When I spoke to Pete about this subject, he put it like this: 'To respect the process of breed, feed and animal husbandry is to take responsibility and let that animal shine, give it the best chance possible to provide what it was intended for.' In other words: the best-quality meat you can buy.

We've spoken about cows, sheep and pigs but this scenario is also true of chickens. Intensive farming is now so commonplace that most people don't actually know what proper chicken tastes like… Properly farmed chicken has a strong taste: it has a savoury, profoundly chicken taste that is akin to what really excellent chicken stock smells of. And the meat is not meant to be bouncy under your tooth. Good chicken has a little tug to it, even in the breast meat. If it's indistinguishable from faintly chicken-flavoured industrial mozzarella, you've got a problem chicken on your hands. Don't eat it. Not only is it full of unknown chemicals, it's also the result of a miserable existence for the animal.

why

Not only does the notion of eating long-suffering, intensively farmed animals make me feel sad and angry, but the impact on the planet is devastating.

Cheap meat is not only bad for the animals and bad for the consumer from a taste and health point of view, but it also has frightening consequences for the Earth. I delve into this subject in **The Environmental Implications of Eating Meat** on pages xiv–xviii.

It may seem like I'm demonising industrial farmers here. What I want to make you realise is that they are only producing this cheap meat because WE are asking them to. Every time we buy industrially produced meat whether it's fresh or in the form of ready meals, we're asking the retailer to refill that shelf with the same junk. Business is not personal: if it sells, they're going to keep on producing it. The equation is as simple as that.

What we seem to have forgotten is that *meat is a luxury product*; it's not meant to be eaten every day and it's not meant to be cheap.

The only way to effect any real change is for us to amend our habits, demand better-quality meat and be prepared to pay for it. If that means eating a lot less of it, then that's what we need to do to. Because, as J. S. Foer points out, 'To do nothing is to do something.'[2]

The chicken and the egg

Please buy the best-quality eggs you can afford, i.e. free-range and organic, or straight from a farm, if you're lucky enough to live near one. As for chickens, all the recipes in the book state 'free-range' but please choose the best-quality available to you. As with all the other meat in this book, outdoor-reared and

slow-grown will give you the best meat – and ensure the best farming conditions.

The last thing to talk about is the most important: I wrote *Carneval* as a collection of truly wonderful meat recipes because I wanted a book that I could rely on to deliver sensational and original recipes from all over the world. This is a book that celebrates the joy of a plate of crispy, hot and sour Buffalo Chicken Wings, as well as a perfectly pink rib of beef or a basket of steamed Chinese dumplings. And the reason it matters so much to get it right every time, to nail these recipes in order to deliver long-lasting pleasure, is because I hardly ever eat meat. As a general rule, I eat meat twice or three times a week, which is to say that I'm vegetarian at least half of the time. And when I do eat meat, I refuse to waste my meat meals on soggy chicken sandwiches from the petrol station or a BLT on the go. Never forget that the white space on the packet where the words outdoor-reared, slow-raised or the name of the breed DON'T appear is actually telling you a lot.

Carneval has been the most challenging and rewarding of the books that I have written so far and I hope that, like me, it provides you with the kind of lasting joy that comes from appreciating great meat, carefully sourced, expertly butchered and cooked with love.

Finally, overleaf are a handful of practical notes and general tips to help you on your meat journey. Enjoy, enjoy, enjoy!

Harry Paris, 2016

a word on freezing meat

My general advice to you is to prioritise freezing cooked, rather than raw meat. There are some exceptions to this rule and one of them is high fat meat such as streaky bacon. I regularly cure my own bacon and freeze it. I don't find that it affects the texture much and the flavour not at all. When you eat meat as seldom as I do, I tend to buy meat on the day or day before I eat it and use it up there and then. I feel particularly strongly about any meat that requires fast cooking or contains small amounts of intramuscular fat, by which I mean beef steaks, pork chops, chicken breasts, lamb cutlets – I never freeze them because I find that they take on too much water and this interferes with their ability to achieve a crust and stay juicy inside once cooked. Slow-cooked dishes or high-fat, raw but prepare-ahead recipes, such as meatballs, sausage rolls and kibbeh, on the other hand, are good candidates for the freezer. And stock is great frozen. If you are going to freeze lean, raw meat like steak, then I advise you to wrap it first in clingfilm, then bag it before freezing. This will prevent ice crystals forming. And always put a date on it so that you make sure you eat it within 3 months.

Bones for stock are also perfectly fine stored in the freezer; it's a good place to keep them until you have enough for a really rich, strongly flavoured stock.

As far as thawing meat goes, the fastest and safest way is to immerse the sealed meat (also a good reason to use two layers of plastic) in cold water. If the cut you're dealing with is too big for immersion, then I recommend thawing it in the fridge, on a plate with a lip to catch the water. As the trusted Harold McGee points out on page 147 of his chapter on Meat: 'The simplest method – leaving the meat on the kitchen counter – is neither safe nor efficient.' In other words, when it comes to thawing meat, think ahead.

a word on quantity

I can't tell you what to do for your health, apart from urge you away from processed and industrially produced meat. But as far as the environment goes, there are very clear guidelines set out by the United Nations Environment Program on the quantity of meat that is deemed responsible: 'Scientists agree that in order to keep GHG [greenhouse gas] emissions to 2000 levels the projected 9 billion inhabitants of the world (in 2050) need to each consume no more than 70–90 grams (McMichael et al. 2007, Barclay 2011) of meat per day.' In Western countries, we are currently far off that mark since 'The USA leads by far with over 322 grams of meat per person per day (roughly the equivalent of three hamburgers), with Australia and New Zealand close behind. Europeans consume slightly more than 200 grams of meat; almost as much as do South Americans (especially in Argentina, Brazil and Venezuela) […]. China consumes 160 grams per day, India only 12 grams.'[3] If you want more information on this important subject,

3 UNEP Global Environmental Alert Service (GEAS) report entitled 'Growing Greenhouse Gas Emissions Due to Meat Production', October 2012, p.2

see **The Environmental Implications of Eating Meat** on page xiv.

a word on salt

Like setting meat out of the fridge an hour or more before cooking it to bring it up to room temperature, salting it before cooking is essential. In the case of good-quality meat (and this is the only category of meat I'm talking about in this book), salt the meat when it comes out of the fridge. The salt will act as a very quick cure and will help lock moisture (and a savoury flavour) deep into the meat muscle. It was long said that salting meat drew out the moisture to the surface thus encouraging it to dry out during cooking but good meat shouldn't have excess moisture in the first place so this theory is academic. And removing the meat from the fridge an hour before cooking for small cuts or two hours for bigger cuts means that it won't shrink in the oven or the pan, so this is also a step not to be overlooked. The less difference there is between the temperature of the meat and the heat source it's going to be cooked in or on, the juicier and more tender the results. Pepper afterwards, if using. For more information on cooking steak see **Steak Masterclass** on page 45.

a word on equipment

I don't, as a rule, use thermometers for meat, except in the case of smoking meat, as in Southern barbecue (see **Smoking Hot** on page 146). As such, I haven't included the temperatures for cooking meat and the recipes are clear and well-tested enough that you don't need one. Having said that, I've done my due diligence on the subject, having tried out a bunch of different kinds, ranging from the cheap to the most expensive ones on the market. I can recommend a brand called Thermapen. They have excellent products that are extremely reliable, both if you are testing the temperature out of the oven (they have a product called Superfast Classic Thermapen that starts at £48) and if you cook your meat with a thermometer inside its centre with a wire that comes out of the oven (this product is called Chef Alarm and can be bought through the US website). If you're more comfortable cooking meat with the help of a thermometer, then this is the one to get. Their website is www.thermapen.co.uk. As always, if you're going to rely on a thermometer, make sure you stick it into the thickest part of the muscle, which corresponds to the centre of a beef, pork or lamb joint and the thigh in the case of chicken, turkey and game birds. Le Creuset are the best cast-iron pans and casseroles for slow cooking or for hob-to-oven cooking. I used Magimix and Kitchenaid to test my recipes at home, and a Weber to barbecue meat both smoked and not.

a word on garlic

Whenever I mention garlic in my recipes, I'm assuming the green stem found inside the clove is removed as it can taste slightly bitter when cooked.

the environmental implications of eating meat

No cute title, no little pun here. This is a serious matter. My research on this subject has been the toughest of the whole book, mainly because the concepts at hand are not simple ones to grasp. What are the environmental implications of farming and eating meat? How do they apply to the different animals we farm? Why is it urgent to sit up and take notice?

what

In order to simplify matters and give you an overview that includes several perspectives, I will put forward the figures I have found most pertinent. If you want to look into this issue more, please do (see page 250 for a recommended reading list). Before we delve into the meat-related numbers, though, it's worth noting, as a point of comparison, that **all transportation worldwide is alleged to produce 13 per cent of greenhouse gas emissions**, according to the UN Environment Program (UNEP).

My first source definitely gives one pause for thought before reaching out for that weekly jumbo pack of beef mince. Alex Renton is the author of a very interesting book entitled *Planet Carnivore: why cheap meat costs the earth (and how to pay the bill)*. Taken from Chapter 5 of his book, the following stats and figures colourfully illustrate his point, which is that we must cut back on eating meat generally but especially on eating industrialised meat. Beef is by some margin the most expensive meat – in terms of cost on the environment – to produce and Renton recounts a story about how he used to take his teenage son out for a steak once a week, a sort of father and son bonding session. After starting the research for his book, they decided to cost what it took to put two 250g beef steaks, grown in the UK and fed on a normal mix of forage and imported feed on the table. Here are his findings:

❛ *...our steaks had been brought to us by using 60 morning showers' worth of water, enough grain to make 20 large loaves of bread, the energy to drive our car 35 miles and* the unpleasant outputs (in faeces and carbon dioxides) entailed in the rearing of our 500g of steak weighed as much as my 8-year-old daughter. *

Other soundbites I found relevant include the following:

❝ *The meat industry today is using up 40% of the world's grain supply.* ❞

❝ *The huge destruction of the Amazon and other forests for livestock has been as big as all of the agricultural clearances of previous human history put together.* ❞

❝ *The strain on the planet is immense. Seventy per cent of water use goes to agriculture. On the basis that nearly half of all grain crops are fed to animals, it's fair to say that livestock accounts for half the planet's water use.* ❞

UNEP has written extensively on this subject in a document entitled 'Growing Greenhouse Gas Emissions Due to Meat Production' (here is the link **www.unep.org/geas**). In this paper, they state that:

❝ *Agriculture, through meat production, is one of the main contributors to the emission of*

greenhouse gases (GHGs) and thus has a potential impact on climate change... Most studies attribute 10–35% of all global GHG emissions to agriculture... Large differences are mainly based on the exclusion or inclusion of emissions due to deforestation and land use change. [page 4] ❞

I warned you that these figures were punchy. Having now read extensively on this subject, it's not easy to pin down an exact number that corresponds to how much GHG emissions are directly linked to animal farming but it highlights a common problem that is tangible, that is real – eating as much meat as we are currently doing is a problem for the Earth, whether it's because it's putting pressure on our water supply, on space and therefore precious planetary resources, like the rainforest, or resulting in abject pollution and greenhouse gas emissions.

which animals are the most expensive on our resources?

According to Harold McGee: 'It takes much less grain to feed a person than it does to feed a steer or a chicken in order to feed a person. Even today, with advanced methods of production, it takes 2 pounds of grain to get 1 pound of chicken meat, and the ratios are 4 to 1 for pork, 8 to 1 for beef.'[1]

These figures are corroborated by Alex Renton, who agrees that, by some margin, beef is the most expensive meat to produce. Measuring how expensive cattle is to rear is difficult to estimate but these figures help us understand the size of the problem: 'The rearing and feeding of 1.65 billion cattle takes up to 60% of the world's available land, though their products provide only 2% of our calories.'[2]

The UN's report is very clear on this subject, too: 'In an analysis of the EU-27 countries, "beef had by far the highest GHG emissions with 22.6KG CO2-eq/KG" (Lessen et al. 2001) in comparison to other products such as pork (2.5), poultry (1.6) and milk (1.3)' or in an interesting comparison that makes it easier to understand: 'The consumption of 1kg of domestic beef in a household represents automobile use of a distance of 160KM/99M.'[3]

The message is clear: cut back on eating meat, especially beef. But why is this matter urgent and is it really true that industrially produced animals are worse for the environment than 'traditionally' farmed ones?

1 Harold McGee, *On Cooking: the science and lore of the kitchen*, p. 123

2 Alex Renton, Planet Carnivore , chapter 5

3 UNEP Global Environmental Alert Service (GEAS) report, 'Growing Greenhouse Gas Emissions Due to Meat Production', October 2012, p. 6

why

The main reason this subject matters so much is because it's getting so quickly so much worse. Given that we now know without a doubt that meat production is a major factor in the emission of GHGs, it stands to reason that we need to reduce the amount of meat we eat. But instead of cutting back, 'the FAO (Steinfeld et al. 2006) expects that global meat consumption will rise to 460 million tonnes in 2050, a further increase of 65% within the next 40 years.'[4]

When I spoke to my mum on the phone recently and urged her to switch to locally raised, slow-grown chickens (she already buys free-range), she asked me why industrially produced animals are worse for the environment than 'traditionally' farmed ones. *Great question*, I thought, and, at the time, I couldn't put it into words that were quick and easy to understand. There are obvious taste and ethical reasons for buying the highest welfare meat, but what are the environmental incentives to do so?

Here's the UNEP report with a brilliant, succinct answer to that question:

4 UNEP Global Environmental Alert Service (GEAS) report, 'Growing Greenhouse Gas Emissions Due to Meat Production', October 2012, p. 3

❛ *In many parts of the world 'traditional' forms of animal agriculture have to a certain extent been replaced by a 'landless', high density, industrial-style animal production system, exemplified by the phenomenon known as Concentrated Animal Feeding Operations (CAFO). Those 'factories' hold hundreds or thousands of animals, and often buy and import animal feed from farmers far away. The feeding of livestock, and their resulting manure, contributes to a variety of environmental problems, including GHG emissions [...].*

High-energy feed is based on soya and maize in particular, cultivated in vast monocultures and with heavy use of fertilizers and herbicides. It is then imported (at least in Europe and most parts of Asia) from countries as far away as Argentina and Brazil [...].

This has serious consequences in terms of land-use and change in those feed-for-export production countries. Furthermore, this manure is generated in huge quantities. In the USA alone, operations which confine livestock and poultry animals generate about 500 million tonnes of manure annually, which is three times the amount of human sanitary waste produced annually (EPA 2009). Insufficient amounts of land on which to dispose of the manure results in the runoff and leaching of waste into and the contamination of surface and groundwater. [...]

Grass-fed meat and resulting dairy products may be more environmentally friendly than factory-farmed or grain-fed options. Labeling of products, indicating the type of animal feed used, could allow consumers to make more informed choices (FOE 2010). ❜

Interestingly, in all the research that I have done at the time of publication, there is no mention of lamb. The only places I was able to get information on lamb were websites such as www.ewg.org (this stands for *Environmental Working Group*) and this last source suggests that lamb is worse even for the environment than beef.[5] Having so little information on the subject, I'm hesitant to include anything definite but urge you to research this for yourself, if you're interested or consume a lot of lamb.

5 Lamb has the greatest impact, generating 39.3kg (86.4 lbs) of carbon dioxide equivalents (CO_2e) for each kilo eaten – about 50 per cent more than beef. While beef and lamb generate comparable amounts of methane and require similar quantities of feed, lamb generates more emissions per kilo in part because it produces less edible meat relative to the sheep's live weight.

in short...

If you're living in a rural idyll where excellent quality beef and meat is abundant, these figures may seem crazy to you. But it's worth remembering that these numbers are representative of the big picture, they apply to the whole world put together. The reason that this should be a concern to everyone is because this is not an issue that's getting better with time, it will continue to get worse if we don't understand what's at stake (sorry) and cut back on eating so much cheap meat.

The solution to the ethical and environmental problem of meat today is simple: consume less meat, of better quality.

And please ask questions, whether it's to your butcher about where the meat you buy comes from (what breed, what rearing conditions) or of the packet at the supermarket, if that's where you choose to shop. If the plastic carton in your hand doesn't give you any information on what it contains, put it back. If it has anything positive to say about the origins and quality of the meat inside, it will be written in big, **bold** letters. For the environment, as well as from a welfare, health and food-quality perspective, industrially produced, cheap meat must be avoided.

I adore eating meat, and this book is a clear testament to that fact. As a general rule, though, I eat beef no more than once a month. And I don't eat meat more than 3 times a week, at the most.

chicken

Chicken Liver Pâté with Port and Prunes

If you're unsure how to make pâté or have never tried, this is a good place to start. Chicken Liver Pâté is by far the easiest pâté to make at home. There is only one golden rule that needs to be observed: the liver must be fresh, both in terms of using on the day you buy it and also avoiding defrosted livers, which can be grainy and release water later on. I can really taste the difference when using the very best quality livers. Even with more expensive livers, this remains a really great and affordable dish to feed a crowd. I've chosen to add a glossy ruby-coloured jelly to go on top but you can just as easily replace this with the usual clarified butter if you can't be bothered to make the jelly or don't like Port. You can also make this recipe for 7–8 – I've tested a half batch and all was well. The prunes are optional but I think they work really well with the slightly metallic edge that liver often brings. And when you come to serve the pâté, there's no substitute for the snap of a homemade Melba toast (see Cook's Tip on page 224)!

Serves 12 as a starter or aperitif

FOR THE PÂTÉ

10 plump prunes, finely chopped

150ml ruby Port, + 2 tbsp for soaking the prunes

30g goose fat (or you can use butter for a milder flavour)

800g fresh chicken livers

40g butter

2 onions, peeled and very finely chopped

4 garlic cloves, peeled and minced

4 bay leaves, crushed in the palm of your hand (if using dry leaves, don't crush)

½ tsp ground allspice

a few scratches of fresh nutmeg

1 tsp salt and freshly ground black pepper

100ml crème fraîche (at least 30% fat)

Soak the prunes in 2 tablespoons of Port and cover with clingfilm. Set aside for later.

Heat the goose fat in a large frying pan over a high heat and brown off the chicken livers. Do this in batches if you don't have a really big pan as it's important that they fry (and colour), rather than sweat. Once browned on the outside and barely pink in the middle, remove from the pan and set aside – there's no need to clean the pan.

Lower the heat and add the butter, onions, garlic, bay leaves and spices to the pan. Cook gently until the onions are softened.

Add the 150ml of Port and simmer for 5 minutes to burn off the alcohol and intensify the flavour. There should be no more liquid in the pan at this stage. Remove the bay leaves and set them aside.

Put the livers, salt, crème fraîche and warm onion mixture into the bowl of a food processor. Mix until smooth and season with more salt and some black pepper to taste.

Carefully spoon half of this mixture into the bottom of a terrine mould or non-stick loaf tin. Spread the chopped, soaked prunes over the pâté

Ingredients continue

Recipe continues

Chicken Liver Pâté with Port and Prunes *continued*

FOR THE RUBY JELLY
100ml ruby Port
30g caster sugar
1 tbsp water
2 leaves gelatine

cook's tip You can use butter instead of goose fat but the flavour is better with goose fat (there's a surprise!). The reason I do include some butter, though, is because butter sets harder than goose fat, which is useful for giving the pâté a firm body once it's cold.

and then top with the remaining pâté. Set aside for 20 minutes to cool and then refrigerate while you make the jelly.

Heat the Port and sugar in a saucepan over a medium heat, until the sugar has dissolved and simmered for 30 seconds. Add the water and set aside.

Soften the gelatine in a small bowl of water and then remove and wring out the excess water with your hands. When the Port mixture is still hot but cool enough for you to put a finger in, add the gelatine and swirl it around to dissolve. Set aside to cool slightly (it's not a good idea to put hot jelly on cold liver pâté).

Pour the ruby jelly over the pâté and garnish with a sunken bay leaf. Place back in the fridge to set for at least a further hour – 24 hours is best. Eat within 4 days of making.

Salade Verte

You just can't beat a really great green salad – it's one of life's greatly undervalued pleasures. The dressing is key: it needs to be sharp but not too aggressive, the leaves need to be peppy and lively. I like this kind of salad to be both refreshing and entertaining, which is why I add radish and an aromatic handful of herbs to the bowl. All in all, this is the salad that marks a green pause on the side of a meat meal. Or at the end. Or before. Or for breakfast with fried eggs. It's awesome. When I talk about serving a green salad in the book, this is pretty much the one I'm thinking of. Flavour variations are at the end of the recipe.

Serves 4

FOR THE SALAD

1 unwaxed lemon

1 small, ripe avocado, stoned and sliced

salt and freshly ground black pepper

1 garlic clove, bashed and peeled

3 large handfuls baby mixed leaves, washed and spun dry

6 medium radishes, washed, topped, tailed and sliced into thin coins

2 spring onions, finely chopped (including the green bit)

1 small handful of basil, leaves plucked from the stem and roughly chopped

1 small handful of coriander, leaves plucked from the stem and roughly chopped

FOR THE DRESSING

1 tbsp lemon juice

2 tsp coriander seeds, toasted in a dry pan and bashed in a mortar and pestle

1 tbsp white wine vinegar

1 tbsp mustard

a pinch salt

2 tbsp extra virgin olive oil

Zest a quarter of the lemon and set aside. Squeeze half of the lemon over the cut avocado and season generously with salt and black pepper. Set aside.

Rub the garlic around the inside of the salad bowl you plan to use, then discard.

For the dressing, combine the lemon juice and zest with the toasted coriander seeds, vinegar, mustard and a good pinch of salt in a clean jam jar and give a good shake. Add the olive oil and shake again.

Pour half the dressing into the bottom of the bowl and then top with all the salad ingredients, except the chopped basil and coriander. Give it a good toss. If all the leaves are glistening, that's enough. Save the rest of the dressing for another day. If you think they need a little extra, go for it. The important thing is to make sure that the leaves are not weighed down by the dressing. It's so often a problem with salads: they are drowned by dressing. Fresh young leaves have a ton of flavour and the role of the dressing is to shine a light on them, rather than gag them.

Finish off by scattering over the chopped herbs and giving a final crunch of black pepper. Serve immediately.

cook's tip In the winter, I might add toasted walnuts and red endive, sliced lengthways, replacing the avocado, coriander, coriander seeds and basil. In the summer, I use Little Gem and add in extra herbs, like dill and mint.

stock up!

Before I did my cookery training, I remember being mystified as to why everyone always banged on about the importance of stock. To hear about stock from the mouths of chefs is to hear about an elusive elixir that makes everything possible in the kitchen. The thing is: 14 years later, I'm saying exactly the same thing. If you don't understand the importance of stock yet, this page is for you. I'll explain exactly *why* great stock is such a big deal, *what* the difference is between white and brown stock, and give you a few tips on *how* to make it at home.

why

There is a big stockpot bubbling away in every good restaurant. And by 'good' I mean an establishment that cooks the food it serves from scratch, as opposed to reheating things in the microwave. Where there is cooking, there is stock.

A good stock is the base for countless sauces and it imparts flavour wherever it is used. The more care and love you put into your stock, the more X factor in your cooking. And the good news is that you can make it on a Sunday when you have some time, cool it and freeze it to use later on. In my freezer, I stockpile stock. I do! Just as I feel insecure when I run out of lemons (something is very wrong when a kitchen lacks a lemon), I feel a bit twitchy when I've used up all my stock. Once you've tasted the difference between really great stock and a stock cube, a subtle but fundamental change will have taken place inside you and you won't be exactly the same person you were before.

what

In simple terms, white stock comes from raw bones and brown stock is made from roasted bones. The flavour in both comes from slow-cooking the bones with any bits of meat scraps that may be attached. It's usual to add vegetables and herbs to help flavour the stock and the classic French flavourings include carrots, celery, onion and a bouquet garni with bay. I like to add leek and garlic. Black pepper is essential. If you're making an Asian-inspired stock, add ginger, star anise and perhaps a few Sichuan peppercorns.

You get a purer, more subtle meat flavour with white stock because the stock cooks the scraps of meat and bone and therefore all the flavour is trapped in the liquid. White stocks work well with chicken and turkey. My favourite poultry stock is a mixture of raw and roasted bones, though – see

Chicken and Matzo Soup for the Soul on page 10. I tend to peel the onions and garlic before putting them in a white stock, in order not to colour the stock too much. This is particularly important if you are using the stock for a risotto and you want it to be pale.

Brown stocks, meanwhile, are made when the bones have been roasted before you simmer them in water. The flavour from these bones is deeper and richer, which comes from the caramelisation of the meat scraps and the sugar in the vegetables. Brown stocks are particularly wonderful when made from lamb and beef. If you reduce brown stock until there is barely any liquid left, you end up with a very precious substance called *glace de viande*, which is basically an umami-loaded, meat Marmite. It's what the very best restaurants in France use as the base for most of their sauces and it takes hours to achieve.

how

The only challenge is that stock takes time. It is wonderfully low maintenance, though, and will happily simmer away on its own, which is why it's such a Sunday activity for me. It is crucial to cook it over a very gentle heat – small, simmering bubbles coming to the surface but by no means any boiling, big ones.

In terms of timing, a stock is ready anywhere between 1½ and 2½ hours

of very, very gentle cooking. Cooking it for longer won't give your stock any more flavour – the ingredients will have given you all they have to give and it will only make the stock cloudy. You can reduce it down to concentrate the flavour but take the ingredients out before you do this, once they've done their job. If you don't want to have a pot of the stuff bubbling on the stove (it does tend to steam the kitchen and impart a pleasant smell of broth and aromatics), you could cover it and 'cook' it in the oven at 120°C overnight, or for around 10 hours.

Once you have made your stock, strain out the bones and vegetables, and either use it straight away or leave it to cool in a glass bowl. I like to use glass so that I can see the layers and what is happening to the stock as it gets colder. Place the cool stock in the fridge and within a few hours, it will have turned to jelly with a layer of fat on top. You can either scrape off the fat (and save it as dripping), or keep it on. I pretty much always leave it on because it adds texture and taste to soups and sauces. Divide the stock into measured Ziploc bags or ice cube trays (cover these with clingfilm) before storing in the freezer for later use. You can keep stock in the freezer for 3 months – I suggest annotating it with the date and a description of what it is.

The best and most common uses for homemade stock, whether white or brown, are: risotto, soup, sauce or gravy.

Chicken Stock

Probably the most useful and versatile recipe in the whole of this book, a really good chicken stock is a fabulous way of using up a chicken carcass and any leftover bits of bone and skin from a roast chicken that you would otherwise probably throw away. If you don't have two carcasses, simply freeze one and save it until you have a pair (you can bash it flat to save space in the freezer). Stock made from one carcass is much less flavourful so it's worth waiting. The only things that are crucial to the success of this recipe are 1) a large stockpot or saucepan and 2) roughly two hours of your time. If you want to make this stock even richer, add some raw chicken wing tips, as I do in Chicken and Matzo Soup for the Soul on page 10.

Makes around 2 litres

2 free-range chicken carcasses, with skin and any leftover bones from the plates

2 large onions, peeled and quartered

5 garlic bulbs, bashed and peeled

3 medium carrots, peeled, topped, tailed and cut in half lengthways

5 bay leaves

1 tbsp black peppercorns

3 sticks celery, washed and roughly chopped

4 litres water

cook's tip Remember to sprinkle the stock with salt when you come to use it as it hasn't been seasoned.

Place everything in a very large pan over a high heat and bring up to a boil. Immediately turn the temperature down to a gentle simmer. Simmer uncovered for 2 hours, spooning away any scum or froth which appears on the surface and discarding it.

Strain the liquid into a large glass bowl and set it aside. When it's at room temperature, place it in the fridge.

After a couple of hours, the fat will have separated from the rest of the stock – spoon off and save to use as dripping.

Keep the stock in the fridge for 3 days or freeze in smaller quantities for later use.

Chicken and Matzo Soup for the Soul

This is probably the most famous Jewish dish of all and this version is loosely based on a recipe given to me by my good friend, Allison Task – a native New Yorker who knows a thing or two about Jewish cooking (and food generally!). This soup is renowned for being a warming and fortifying dish that nourishes and heals when you're under the weather, and is associated with lowering blood pressure and boosting the immune system. Although I'm sure there's truth in these claims, to me it's as much about the love and time it takes to get this soup just right that makes it so good for the soul.

If you want to be authentic, choose kosher fine egg noodles, otherwise I like to use vermicelli or tiny alphabet pasta shapes, which are especially popular with the little ones (or adults who like to spell out words in their soup, like me).

Serves 6

1 free-range chicken

1 carcass from a roasted free-range chicken, with all the leftover bones and skin scraped from the plates

6 raw free-range chicken wings

3 medium onions, peeled and quartered

1 clove

6 garlic cloves, peeled and smashed

1 small handful of parsley

2 sticks celery (including tops), washed and finely cubed

a few sprigs of thyme

4 bay leaves

½ tsp Sichuan peppercorns

½ tsp black peppercorns

3.5 litres water

3 large organic carrots, peeled, topped, tailed and sliced

50g fine vermicelli, kosher noodles or alphabet pasta

salt and black pepper

a small bunch fresh dill

Ingredients continue

Remove the fat from the whole chicken cavity and reserve for the Matzo balls.

Place the whole chicken, the carcass, wings, onions studded with the clove, garlic, parsley, celery, thyme, bay and peppercorns in a very large stockpot over a high heat. Add the water and bring to the boil.

As soon as it boils, reduce the heat and simmer very, very gently (so the meat will be tender and the soup will not get cloudy) for 30 minutes without the lid. It's important to skim off any scum that appears on the surface of the broth.

Add the carrots and simmer for a further hour.

While the soup is cooking, make the Matzo balls by combining the beaten eggs, cooled liquid chicken fat or butter, Matzo cracker crumbs, salt, dried onion and garlic granules, ground cayenne or ginger and dried parsley with a fork. You may need to add a little of the simmering stock to reach the consistency of dough. Cover with clingfilm and set aside to rest for 30 minutes.

When the dough has rested, make balls the size of large marbles with your hands, using a little water to prevent sticking. They will expand as they cook so don't make them too big.

Recipe continues

Chicken and Matzo Soup for the Soul *continued*

FOR THE MATZO BALLS
(MAKES 18)

2 large free-range eggs, beaten with a fork

fat from the chicken – this is known as 'schmaltz' – (rendered in a small saucepan until liquid – you should have around 2 tbsp) or use butter or goose fat

100g Matzo crackers, whizzed to a powder

1 tsp salt (kosher to be authentically Jewish)

½ tsp dried onion granules

½ tsp dried garlic granules

a pinch cayenne or dried ginger (this is especially good if you have a cold and need decongesting)

½ tsp dried parsley

cook's tip I add Sichuan peppercorns to this recipe because they give the soup a really aromatic, almost medicinal, quality and are awesome for a cold. They are not traditional, by any means, so replace with black peppercorns if you don't fancy them, or if you're already fit as a flea.

When the stock has been simmering for 1½ hours, remove the whole chicken and put to one side. Strain the rest of the broth through a sieve. Fish out the carrots and put them back into the now-empty stockpot. Add the strained stock and the Matzo balls. Simmer gently for 15 minutes with a lid on, and then add the pasta. Simmer for another 5 minutes until the Matzo balls are tender and the pasta is cooked through.

While the Matzo balls and pasta are cooking, shred the meat off the whole chicken (with gloves or using forks, if it's still hot). Discard the skin and bones.

Finally, divide the shredded chicken between your serving bowls and pour over the stock, carrots, Matzo balls and pasta. Season with salt and pepper and scatter over some dill fronds. Serve piping hot.

Teriyaki Sauce

The gloop you buy in supermarkets that calls itself teriyaki is so erratic in terms of taste and quality, I've given up on it. 'Teriyaki' loosely translated from the Japanese refers to the double action of glossing and grilling. In other words, this is a sauce that's brushed on during or added *after* grilling. Because of the sugar content, this is not a sauce that works well as a marinade – I find that it tends to burn before the piece of meat or fish is cooked through. Whereas brushed on at the end of the cooking time, it's magic. And it works particularly well with barbecued items that are slightly charred around the edges. Makes my mouth water just thinking about it! Also, this is one of the most versatile sauces in the book – in other words: it goes with everything. I love it over thin pieces of grilled pork, chicken and even beef. It's amazing with big, white, flaked fish, such as halibut, haddock, turbot or bream, as well as with the oily fish family that includes mackerel, eel and salmon. It's wonderful with stir-fried rice, vegetables and tofu (smoked, tempura, grilled – you name it). I usually have a jar of the stuff in the fridge at all times since it lasts for months.

Makes 150ml (roughly enough for 6 servings as it's fairly intense)

120ml dark soy sauce

60ml mirin or rice wine vinegar

60ml sake (basic quality is fine for this)

100g soft brown sugar

5 garlic cloves, peeled and crushed

5cm piece of ginger, peeled and thinly sliced

cook's tip If you want to have some left over for the fridge, just double the quantities (as I say, this is an addiction about to start because teriyaki enhances everything it comes into contact with).

Combine all the ingredients in a saucepan and bring to the boil. Turn down the heat and simmer gently for about 20 minutes or until the sauce has reduced by half. It should be thick enough to lightly coat the back of a spoon.

Remove the ginger and garlic and allow to cool before using. Store in the fridge.

Crispy Buffalo Chicken Wings

These wings are a favourite bar snack all over the States and they're always coated with a spicy sour glaze. It has a dry, hot flavour with a chaser of vinegar that is reminiscent of Korea and is particularly moreish on these crispy little wings. Most recipes for Buffalo wings require deep or shallow frying but I have discovered a technique that does away with that. The coating of baking powder and salt and the gradual temperature mean that the wings dry out gently in the oven and then get really, really crispy towards the end of their cooking time. If you want to try them with a different glaze, brush over a little Teriyaki Sauce instead (see page 13).

Serves 4

1kg free-range chicken wings
    (roughly 10 whole ones)
¼ tsp salt
1 tbsp baking powder

FOR THE GLAZE
50ml sunflower oil
2 tbsp red Tabasco
2 tbsp green Tabasco
1 tbsp cider vinegar
1½ tsp Worcestershire sauce
1 garlic clove, peeled and minced
1 tbsp runny honey or Agave
    nectar
a pinch salt

cook's tip These are a marvel as canapés at a party and will remain crispy. Just remember to eat them within 2 hours of cooking (this won't be a problem!), as you would with any other chicken recipe.

Preheat the oven to 120°C/fan 100°C/gas mark ½.

Cut the very tips off the wings and reserve them for stock (you can freeze them). Cut the remaining wing in two at the joint.

Mix the salt and baking powder in a large Ziploc bag and add the wings. Shake to coat evenly.

Line a large oven tray with tin foil and place the wings skin side up on a metal rack on the oven tray. Cook at the bottom of the preheated oven for 30 minutes.

Without opening the door, crank up the heat to 220°C/fan 200°C/gas mark 7 and roast for a further 40 minutes.

During this time, make the glaze by mixing all of the ingredients together in a clean jar and giving it a good shake – if you think it's going to be too hot for your taste, replace the red Tabasco with more green.

After they've had their cooking time, take the wings out of the oven and shut the oven door. Brush some glaze on to each wing, not forgetting the underside, and place back in the oven for 5 minutes. Keep an eye on them as they will colour quickly now they have honey on them.

Remove from the oven and glaze again with any remaining sauce. Serve straight away with a big green salad and a pile of napkins for your fingers.

Heirloom Tomato and Onion Salad with a Sherry and Garlic Dressing

This salad makes a refreshing side to any smoked barbecued meat recipe or a summery roast chicken. Heirloom tomatoes (sometimes called heritage) have become so much easier to source than they used to be and their vibrant colours and bumpy shapes are a wonderful reminder of what real fruit looks like, as opposed to the picture-perfect specimens that taste of nothing. You can't beat a multicoloured carnival of yellow, orange and green tomatoes on a summer's day. I suggest dressing the salad about half an hour before serving so the garlic has time to perfume the tomatoes.

Serves 6

1 garlic clove, peeled and minced

2 tbsp sherry vinegar

½ tsp caster sugar

plenty of salt

2 tbsp olive oil

6 medium tomatoes, or the equivalent amount of smaller ones, washed under the tap then sliced thinly through the waist

1 small sweet, white Spanish onion, peeled and very finely sliced

1 small handful of fresh oregano leaves

freshly ground black pepper

cook's tip This salad is also really delicious with crumbled feta cheese.

The sweetest of all the tomatoes are the yellow and orange ones.

Mix the garlic, vinegar, sugar and salt in a clean jar and give it a good shake. Once the sugar has dissolved, add the olive oil and shake again.

Arrange the tomato slices and onion rings on a large plate and drizzle over the dressing. Let the salad stand before serving with a little oregano and freshly cracked black pepper sprinkled over the top.

Beer Can Chicken

This is one of the recipes that I remember from my six months spent in Sydney about 10 years ago. The science behind it is really interesting: the toughest part of the chicken (legs) are nearest the heat (coals), while the leanest (breast) is furthest away. In addition, the beer can heats up inside the cavity and steams the inside of the bird, infusing the breast with flavour and keeping it moist. Ingenious. The beer-can method also ensures that you get crispy skin all the way around when cooking in a fan oven, as below. You will never cook roast chicken the old way again. The only word of caution is: make sure you use a small or medium chicken as a large one might topple over.

Serves 4

1 × 330ml can of beer – your choice, as long as it's the short and fat kind of can

6 garlic cloves, bashed

a few sprigs of thyme or rosemary

1 free-range chicken (no more than 1.4kg)

olive oil

salt and freshly ground black pepper

cook's tip I tried cooking this without a fan and the results were pretty average. Don't bother trying this recipe until you have access to a fan oven since this is how the skin gets really crispy crunchy.

If you are cooking a bigger bird, go for a 580ml can instead. The risk of toppling over is the only drawback to this method but it won't happen if you match the chicken to the size of the can.

Preheat the oven to 200°C/fan 180°C/gas mark 6.

Crack open the beer and take three large gulps.

Drop the garlic and herbs into the beer. Ease the bird over the can and lift carefully on to an oven tray. You can stabilise the chicken by spreading its legs to form a tripod with the can.

Rub olive oil generously over the whole of the bird and sprinkle with a little salt and pepper.

Place the chicken in the oven and cook for 45–60 minutes, or until the skin is crispy all over.

Rest for 15 minutes on the can. This will relax the chicken meat and also enable the can to cool enough to handle. Make sure to pour the juices from the oven tray (which will include some of the beer!) over the chicken as you serve.

Blonde ou Brune – It's All Gravy

This is a basic recipe that can be served with either chicken, turkey, pork or lighter-flavoured meats (Blonde) or with beef and lamb (Brune). The success of the gravy relies almost entirely on the quality of the stock that you use. It's worth buying fresh but best of all is homemade. If you've just made a roast, transfer any pan juices to a small bowl. Make this recipe in the bottom of the tin that you used to roast the meat (providing it can be put on the hob) and add the pan juices at the end of the cooking. If your roasting tin can't go on the hob, then warm some of the stock (300ml is enough) until it's boiling and pour it in the roasting tin to deglaze it (lift up any bits of flavour lurking at the bottom). Add these in with the rest of the stock as per the recipe below. Speaking of pan juices, I tend to keep the top layer of liquid fat as dripping and just add the bottom layer of intense pan juices for gravy but it's up to you. The fat gives the gravy added richness and silk, but it also slightly muffles the flavour.

Makes 750ml

800ml chicken stock (Blonde) or beef or lamb stock (Brune)

250ml dry white wine (Blonde) or red wine (Brune)

1 large onion, peeled and cut into quarters

2 garlic cloves, peeled and cut into halves

1 medium carrot, peeled and cut into quarters

bouquet garni – 2 bay leaves, a few thyme sprigs and a small bunch of fresh parsley tied with string

30g unsalted butter at room temperature, or dripping (from bacon, goose, duck, chicken or beef)

2 level tbsp cornflour

salt and freshly ground pepper

1 tbsp Dijon mustard (Blonde) or redcurrant jelly (Brune)

100ml double cream (leave out with Brune)

Heat the stock, wine, onion, garlic, carrot and bouquet garni in a medium saucepan until boiling. Turn down the heat and simmer for 10 minutes to intensify and reduce. Remove the onion, garlic, carrot and bouquet garni with the help of a slotted spoon.

Blend the fat and cornflour in a bowl with a spoon until you have a paste. Whisk this into the stock mixture with the help of a balloon whisk. Simmer for a further 10 minutes to thicken and intensify the flavour.

If you're making Brune gravy, this is when you taste and adjust the seasoning with salt, pepper and redcurrant jelly.

If you're making Blonde gravy, season and add the Dijon mustard. Remove from the heat and stir in the double cream, if using.

Leek Confiture

I started making this wonderful little condiment as a way of using up leeks that lingered in the bottom of my veg box. I like to use it as a last-minute sandwich filler (it's particularly good with thick-cut ham or corned beef); stirred into penne and sprinkled with walnuts, lemon zest and Parmesan; folded into mashed potato to accompany roast pork or beef or chicken; or as a dip warmed up with a little crème fraîche and some snipped tarragon, served with toasted baguette and a glass of white wine. Leek Confiture also goes wonderfully well with hard cheese, chutney and crackers, or with pâtés – especially the coarse ones. It's an all-round star and you won't believe how jammy and intense it becomes: like pale green, fragrant, vegetable caviar.

Makes 500g

60g butter

2 tbsp olive oil

600g leeks, cleaned and finely
    chopped

1 large onion, peeled and finely
    chopped

2 garlic cloves, smashed, peeled
    and finely chopped

a few scratches of fresh nutmeg

1 tsp salt

4 bay leaves

a few sprigs of thyme

4 tbsp water

Melt the butter and olive oil in a very large frying pan over a medium heat. Add the leeks, onion, garlic, nutmeg, salt, bay leaves and thyme to the pan and toss to coat. Turn the heat right down and cook gently for 45 minutes without a lid, stirring occasionally to prevent catching. Add the water during the cooking process, if and when you think the leeks are looking a little dry. It's best to use a large frying pan because, although they will shrink to a quarter of the original volume once they're done, the raw leeks and onion take up a lot of space so you need to prepare for that.

Once the leeks have had their cooking time, either spread on to warm toast and eat straight away with a little extra fresh thyme sprinkled on top or you can decant into a sterilised jar and keep for up to a week in the fridge.

Sunday Chicken and Tarragon Pie

This recipe has a real Sunday feel to it: clear out the fridge, change the bed, make chicken pie. Grown up comfort food. What I love about this recipe is that it does its thing in the background, which means you have time to get on with something else. Another great bonus is that you end up with a lovely, light chicken stock, which you can either cool down and freeze, or turn into soup for the coming week.

Serves 4

FOR THE POACHING CHICKEN

5 chicken legs (drumsticks and thighs – total weight roughly 1.2kg)

1.5 litres water

1 large onion, peeled and roughly chopped

3 garlic cloves, smashed and peeled

2 carrots, peeled, topped, tailed and cut in half lengthways

1 bay leaf, 1 handful of white peppercorns, a few sprigs of thyme, some parsley stalks – all or some of these

FOR THE PIE FILLING

1 leek, white part only, halved, cleaned and finely chopped

1 large onion, peeled and finely chopped

3 garlic cloves, peeled and finely chopped

3 tbsp olive oil

2 tbsp roughly chopped fresh (or dried) tarragon leaves

10 scratches of fresh nutmeg

200ml full-fat crème fraîche

salt and white pepper

Start by poaching the chicken legs in the water with all the aromatics. Bring to the boil over a high heat with a lid on, then remove the lid and reduce the heat to a simmer. Remove all the foam that rises to the surface. Simmer slowly like this for an hour.

Roll out the pastry on a lightly floured clean surface to the size of your pie dish, then place on to a baking tray in the fridge to rest.

Once the chicken stock is simmering away contentedly, turn your attention to the filling. Sweat the leek, onion and garlic with the olive oil in a large frying pan over a medium heat. As soon as you start to smell the garlic and onion, turn down the heat and put a lid over the pan. Sweat very slowly for the remaining time that the chicken has to cook, stirring occasionally to make sure that the mixture doesn't catch. If the contents of the pan look a little dry, add a small ladle of the chicken stock and continue as before.

Preheat the oven to 180°C/fan 160°C/gas mark 4.

Strain the finished stock through a sieve – you don't need this for the pie but it will taste amazing so pour it into a container and save it for another day. Like all stocks, it can be used within 3 days of making or else cool it and freeze it for later use. When the chicken is cool enough to handle, peel the meat gently off the bone with your hands, remembering to keep the chicken pieces more or less whole. Discard the skin and bones.

Ingredients continue

Recipe continues

Sunday Chicken and Tarragon Pie *continued*

FOR THE TOP

300g all-butter puff pastry
  (or shortcrust, see page 186)

1 medium egg, beaten

Once the leek mixture has had its time, it should be really soft, slightly see through and even jammy. This is when you add the tarragon, nutmeg and crème fraîche. Season generously with salt and ground white pepper before adding the chicken pieces. Allow to cool for 10 minutes. (If you top with the pastry when the contents are hot, you will end up with slightly soggy pastry.)

Paint a little bit of beaten egg around the rim of the pie dish. This is much easier if your dish has a lip, but it's still possible otherwise (see Cook's Tip below).

Tip the chicken and leek mixture into the pie dish and top with the pastry. Paint the surface of the pie with some beaten egg and create two slits in the middle of the pastry to let the steam out.

Bake the pie in the preheated oven for 30 minutes, until it is golden and piping hot. Serve with steamed green vegetables, like broccoli or beans.

cook's tip Using legs and thighs in this recipe is important because breast has a tendency to tighten up and become rubbery in a pie, or else shred and dissolve. What's more, you get a much more fragrant stock from legs because this is where the lion's share of the cartilage lies and therefore is also where all the flavour and silk are hiding.

Pies of this kind (and fruit pies, too) are best baked in a glass, enamel or ceramic pie dish that has a flat rim around the edge. This is because you can 'glue' the pastry to the rim with a little beaten egg, whereas a dish without a rim doesn't give you much to work with.

If you only have the latter at home, I suggest you use a strip of pastry about 1cm wide and, using a little beaten egg, place it on the thin rim of the pie dish. It will be sitting precariously but that doesn't matter. Next, brush more beaten egg on to the top of the strip of pastry and adhere the pie top to this. You're basically making a ledge on which to glue the sheet of pastry. This will help prevent the pastry from shrinking during cooking and pulling away from the edges. Also, I prefer to use larger, shallower dishes as it's important the mixture comes up to the edge of the pie dish and provides a resting place for the pastry.

Nena's Mashed Potatoes

I thought I knew a thing or two about mashed potatoes… Well, I was stumped recently during my Christmas visit to the States by being served the best mash I had ever had in my life. The secret: a little bit of butternut squash had been added in with the potatoes. What you end up with is a light, fluffy, slightly sweet mash that is out of this world and simple as anything to make.

Serves 4–6

1.2kg floury potatoes, such as King Edward, peeled

400g butternut squash, peeled and cut into large chunks

125g salted butter

salt and white pepper

cook's tip You can pass the mixture through a sieve after you've mashed it if you want a really fine, superlight texture. I do this when I'm making a special effort (or if the Queen is coming to dinner).

Cut the potatoes in half so that they are all about the same size.

Bring a large pan of water to the boil over a high heat then add the potatoes. Boil for roughly 15 minutes before adding the squash. Cook for a further 10–15 minutes or until all the vegetables are soft enough to insert a knife.

Drain and place back in the pan to let the steam rise off and dry them. Next add the butter and mash by hand until there are no lumps left. Transfer to a large bowl and whip the mash for a few minutes with the help of an electric whisk.

Season with salt and white pepper, if needed, and serve piping hot.

Pommes Anna – *for G & G*

It's a mystery to me why certain dishes make it into popular culture and others, that are just as delicious and easy to make, don't. This is the case with Pommes Anna, which is a potato recipe that's halfway between a Gratin Dauphinois (without the cream) and a potato Tarte Tatin (without the pastry). Neither one of these two descriptions does justice to the layers of potato, glued together with butter and starch to create a millefeuille effect that's both delicate on the inside and crispy golden on the outside. Your mouth watering yet? Thought so. If you've never tried this, give it a go. Serve on the side of any meat roast.

Serves 6

250g unsalted butter

1.2kg waxy and slightly sweet potatoes, such as Désirée or Charlotte

salt and freshly ground black pepper

cook's tip For those of you surprised by the amount of butter that goes into this dish, bear in mind that about 50g is poured away at the end of the process. It's needed to moisturise the potatoes during cooking but not needed for the final taste. This is also where using a waxy variety of potato is handy – it means that the spuds won't soak up all the butter like a floury variety would. Also, you lose about one-fifth of the butter when you clarify it. Finally, my view is that this is the potato equivalent of eating a sensational pastry, so I really enjoy it – just only once in a while…

Clarify the butter by melting it in a saucepan over a gentle heat and, once it's liquid, set it aside to cool. The white calcium solids will drop to the bottom – make sure you only use the clear top layer and discard the rest.

Preheat the oven to 220°C/fan 200°C/gas mark 7.

Brush a little of the clarified butter into the bottom of an ovenproof dish. Avoid using a metal dish as this will colour the base too much.

Peel and finely slice the potatoes one at a time (if you slice all the potatoes at once they will discolour), placing the rounds at the bottom of the dish in roughly even layers of thickness. I use a potato peeler to get the layers really, really thin but a mandolin would do a good job, too. After a couple of potatoes have been sliced and layered, brush over some clarified butter and season with salt and pepper. Continue until all the potatoes have been used and the last of the butter is gone.

Place the dish on a metal baking sheet in the middle of the oven for 45 minutes. Turn down the temperature to 200°C/fan 180°C/gas mark 6 for a final 15 minutes.

Remove from the oven and place a sheet of tin foil over the top of the dish, and then put a plate on top of this. Tilt the dish and pour off any butter into a small bowl – save for another day or discard.

Meanwhile, place the potato dish to one side to set for 10 minutes, before serving hot and cut into slices at the table.

Kung Pao Chicken

This is a recipe I jotted down on the back of a napkin (literally) after having interrogated a very patient Chinese friend in Beijing called Henry Daye, who makes a smashing version of this at home. And that's the good news: this is home food, which means it's quick and easy. Kung Pao Chicken originates from the Sichuan Province in southwestern China and is usually quite spicy (Sichuan pepper is that amazing hot and cold, anaesthetic pepper flavour) and very aromatic. If you're not a fan of this kind of heat, replace with fresh or dried chillies. As always with authentic Chinese recipes, you'll find the ratio of meat to other ingredients is lower than we might expect in Europe. This is how it should be: a little bit goes a long way.

Serves 2

FOR THE MEAT MARINADE

2 free-range chicken thighs, skinned, boned and cut into very small strips

2 tbsp cornflour

1 tbsp water

FOR THE KUNG PAO

4 tbsp sunflower oil

50g unsalted peanuts (without skins is preferable)

6 spring onions, sliced on the bias in 1cm lengths (including the green bit)

1 garlic clove, peeled and very finely minced

2cm fresh ginger, peeled and minced

2 tbsp rice wine vinegar

2 tbsp caster sugar

1 tbsp soy sauce

1 tbsp water

2 tsp Sichuan peppercorns, ground to a powder in a mortar and pestle

a little fresh coriander, to garnish (optional)

Toss the tiny strips of chicken in the cornflour. When completely coated, add the water and mix with your fingers to make sure that the chicken is evenly covered with the paste.

Heat a wok to smoking point over a very high heat then add the oil. First, fry off the peanuts until just starting to colour. Remove them promptly from the pan with a slotted spoon (they will catch quickly) and set aside.

Next, add the marinated chicken and fry for a minute until cooked through and starting to colour. Quickly add the onions, garlic and ginger and toss again. Fry for another minute, until the onions have started to wilt a little.

Finally add the vinegar, sugar, soy sauce, water and ground peppercorns. When the sauce has become sticky and glossy, return the peanuts to the pan and taste to check seasoning.

Serve straight away with a little chopped coriander and a bowl of steamed rice.

cook's tip The spring onions in Beijing were bigger than ours in Europe and they make up about half of the dish. If you have tiddly little onions or you want to up the quantity of veg, then add in some finely sliced leeks at the same time as the chicken (leeks need a few minutes longer than spring onions to cook).

White Wine, Garlic and Fresh Herb Marinade

This is a French-inspired marinade and perfect for a summer barbecue lunch served alongside a bright green salad, a bowl of olives and some really good bread. It's fresh and lively and very easy to put together. I recommend that you don't marinate the chicken breasts for more than 2 hours as they are quick to 'cook' in the marinade and could become pappy if left too long. If you're dealing with large chicken breasts (good-quality, outdoor-reared chickens tend not to have massive watermelon breasts), butterfly them to halve their thickness and make them easier to cook quickly.

Serves 4

4 free-range chicken breasts, skinless

FOR THE MARINADE
150ml white wine (medium dry is best)
150ml olive oil
½ tsp finely grated lemon zest
3 large garlic cloves, peeled and minced
1 tbsp finely chopped fresh rosemary leaves
1 tbsp finely chopped fresh sage leaves
1 tbsp finely chopped fresh parsley leaves
plenty of salt and freshly bashed pink peppercorns

TO COOK AND GARNISH
melted butter or olive oil
a pinch paprika

Preheat the barbecue or grill to hot. You're ready to go when you see white ash – this takes around 45 minutes. If you're using a grill, you should be good to go in 10 minutes, tops.

Put each chicken breast between two sheets of clingfilm and bash them gently so they end up half their starting thickness.

Whisk together the wine and olive oil so that they emulsify. If they stay separated, the flavour of the wine will be too strong. Add all the remaining marinade ingredients and combine well. Marinate the meat for no more than 2 hours. I like to use a Ziploc bag and expel all the air.

When you're ready to cook, remove the breasts from the marinade and dry them with kitchen paper. You will notice that the flesh is slightly paler than before. This is the effect of the wine on the muscle and is how you know the meat has been tenderised. Discard the marinade.

Brush each breast with plenty of melted butter or olive oil before placing under the grill or on the barbecue. Cook through – this should take roughly 6 minutes on each side for a medium chicken breast (timings will vary depending on the temperature of your grill and the thickness of the meat).

Serve hot, garnished with paprika and a bit more salt and crushed pink peppercorns.

beef

Always Pink Rib of Beef

If you're like me, you probably only have rib of beef once a year – twice at the most. Not only is it an expensive cut of meat but the pressure is on to get it just right… Perfectly pink in the middle, in other words. Ten minutes too long in a hot oven and the whole thing is ruined. All in all, I tend to avoid making it because I find it quite stressful! That is, until I tested this recipe to hell and back, and figured out that the best way to cook this cut of meat is *slowly*. This doesn't mean it ends up being shredded and surrendered, it's just a technique that ensures the meat comes up to temperature very slowly and is therefore as tender as it's ever going to be when cooked. Once you've sourced a beautiful piece of meat (dry-aged and marbled), the hard work has been done for you; this recipe will take care of everything else (see Hang in There on page 214 and the Introduction on page vii).

Serves 6 with leftovers

2.5kg rib of beef on the bone
– this will have about 3 bones to it (look for a rib with a dark colour, a nice layer of fat on it and plenty of marbling)
salt and freshly ground black pepper

cook's tip I like to take the meat off the bones to carve by slicing along where the bones are. You will end up with a roundish cut of meat, which you can then slice across the grain in whatever thickness appeals to you. I then like to cut between the bones and gnaw on them – this is the best part of the whole roast, to be honest.

The night before cooking the rib, remove any paper or clingfilm and lightly score the fat. Salt generously all over and keep uncovered in the fridge overnight, fat side up.

Remove from the fridge 2 hours before cooking. Pat with kitchen paper to remove any surface moisture that the salt may have drawn out.

Preheat the oven to 120°C/fan 100°C/gas mark ½ and place a roasting tray in the bottom of the oven.

Heat a large frying pan over a high heat and brown the fat cap on the top of the rib. Once golden brown, work your way round so that the underside is also brown. It is important to get good colour on the meat at this stage, especially on the fat cap. Do *not* sear the ends of the meat (the circular-shaped sides on either end).

Place the rib in the warmed roasting tray, fat side up. Liberally sprinkle over salt flakes and freshly ground black pepper. Cook in the bottom of the oven for 2 hours exactly.

Remove the rib from the oven and leave to rest in its tray for 20 minutes, loosely covered in foil. This cooking plus resting time will give you rare beef. If you want medium, cook for an extra 20 minutes (2 hours 20 minutes total oven time) and rest for 20 minutes, just don't cover it with foil.

Serve with your favourite sauces and Yorkshire Puddings (see facing page).

Yorkshire Pudding (via Japan)

Yorkshire puddings can be tricky little things and I have come across people who, whatever they try, can't seem to get them to rise. It's for those folks that I've added a little Japanese twist to my recipe: a bit of fizzy water gives the puddings extra lift off… I know it's not traditional but it works. Other tips I have to ensure a golden, puffed pudding include the following: 1) Fill your moulds no more than two-thirds of the way up. Muffin moulds come in varying sizes and mine might be bigger than yours. Even if this means doing another two stragglers while lunch is going on – if you fill them more than this, they will be too doughy and sink. 2) The moulds need to sit *on a hot oven tray*. The contact with the heat gives you extra oomph. 3) I whisk the batter with an electric whisk before adding to the water. This ensures no lumps and also gives it a little more jazz and bubbles during cooking. 4) Lastly, these little beauties do not benefit from sitting around, so make sure that you cook them and eat them in quick succession. It's pretty much the last thing I do when the rest of roast lunch is ready.

Makes 12

40g beef dripping
240g plain flour
½ tsp salt
a pinch of black pepper
200ml full-fat milk
3 large free-range eggs, beaten
100ml fizzy water

Preheat the oven to 230°C/fan 210°C/gas mark 8.

Put a small lump of beef dripping into each of the 12 moulds and place on a metal baking sheet in the middle of a hot oven.

Sift the flour into a large bowl with a little salt and pepper.

In a jug, blend together the milk and eggs with the help of a fork.

Make a well in the middle of the flour mixture and gradually incorporate the wet with the dry ingredients, whisking with an electric whisk as you add. Once you have an even batter, transfer to a jug that contains the fizzy water. Give a final brief stir to combine the water and batter but try not to knock out too much of the air.

Take the tray out of the oven. The dripping should be smoking hot by now. Pour enough batter to come two-thirds of the way up each muffin hole and quickly put back into the hot oven.

Cook for 20 minutes, or until the puddings are puffed up and golden. Eat immediately!

carve it up

Carving is a big subject: you can do a one-day course on it at places like Simpson's-in-the-Strand (www.simpsonsinthestrand.co.uk) and I could write a whole Meat Geek about the what, how and why of knives. In brief, I find a chef's knife (medium long blade), a boning knife (curved a bit like a small sword), a paring knife (a tiny version of the chef's knife), and a small serrated knife (sometimes called a 'fruit knife') are sufficient. Most importantly: **keep them sharp**. You can avoid blunting your knives by washing them by hand and it's better to store them in a block or on a magnet, rather than in a kitchen drawer.

As a final word on the subject, if after years of use or a particularly stubborn jointing job, you want to give your knives a spruce, ask your butcher if he will kindly grind them down for you. But remember to be careful the first time you use either a new knife or one that has been perked up by your butcher – they are sharper and more dangerous than you think. Forgive me for stating the obvious but no matter how many years of cooking you have under your belt, a newly sharpened knife is a surprisingly treacherous tool.

Here are a few general guidelines for carving the joints in this book. Incidentally, a rested piece of meat is always easier to carve than one that's come straight from the oven. More on that in **Rest in Peace** on page 164.

whole chicken

(see Beer Can Chicken *on page 18) and* bigger game birds (see Coq au Pheasant *on page 237)*

I always joint my chickens into 6 pieces that divide into wing and tip of breast, breast and leg. Jo, who is the wonderful woman who edited this book, likes to serve chicken whole and then carve it at the table like a turkey, slicing the breast and splitting the legs into drumsticks and thighs. Up to you. When jointing a cooked bird, it helps if you carve off the legs last as this will help stabilise the bird whilst you cut off the other bits. And don't forget to fish out the oyster on the back of the leg (where the thigh joins the back of the spine) – it's the best bit of the whole chicken. As a side note, if you're jointing a raw chicken, then cutting it into eight sections (separating the drumstick and thighs) is common practice and not difficult. Check online for a visual guide.

whole turkey

(see Always Tender Turkey *on page 198)*

As this is such a feast and a magnificent sight, I always carve turkey at the table. I slice off the breast and leave the legs and wings till last, since this will help keep the bird stable. You can then either remove the legs whole and divide them into drumstick and thigh, or carve the meat straight off the carcass. In the latter case, be ready to have a good gnaw on the bones. And speaking of gnawing, the wings are always fun finger food.

whole duck

(see Cheating Peking Duck on page 216)
I deal with a whole duck the same way as a chicken: I joint it. In this case, I tend only to get four pieces – two legs (thigh and drumstick) and two breasts (with wingtip attached). Again, remove the breast first.

quail

(see Southern Fried Quail on page 226)
Basically these don't need jointing because they're just breasts with small legs attached. Serve them whole and do your best with your fingers or a knife and fork. This is fun food.

rabbit

The only rabbit recipe in this book is jointed before cooking – carved into six pieces that include the saddle, the hind legs and shoulder pieces. Again, look online if you need a guide.

rib of beef

(see Always Pink Rib of Beef on page 32)
The first thing to do once the rib is cooked is to cut off the rib bones. Don't worry if you take some of the meat with them, you can nibble them later – they are extremely moreish, especially if they have good caramelisation around the ends. Then you have a choice: either slice the rib meat thinly across the grain, which is how most people are used to carving rib of beef, or cut a thick slice between the bones and cut little sashimi-width pieces along the grain. Mankind in its instinctive, carnivorous depths enjoys chewing with the grain of the meat to achieve maximum texture and juice, but eating these little meat nuggets of roast beef across the grain is wonderful, too.

lamb shoulder and leg

(see Tandoori Butterflied Leg of Lamb on page 121 and Slow-cooked Shoulder of Lamb on page 102)
The lamb leg recipe in this book is butterflied, which means it's not on the bone any more – it's been opened up like a book. With a butterflied leg, cut medium to slim slices across the grain to serve. As for shoulder, there's no need to carve it as much as tug it off the bone

– it's so surrendered that a fork and spoon are the only tools you need.

whole ham

(see Redcurrant Glazed Ham *on page 177)*

If there is no bone, then it's easy: just cut the meat in thin slices with either a very sharp boning knife (this is best because it is a little bendy) or a long serrated one, like the one you'd use to slice cakes in half horizontally. If you do have a bone, you need to be a little bit more dextrous and cut around the bone. It may feel awkward but this is normal. And the good news is that ham is a casual kind of food and even a thickish slice is still blinking delicious.

slow-cooked baby back pork ribs

(see Smoked Baby Back Ribs *on page 148 and* Pulled Pork Tennessee *on page 174)*

These cuts lend themselves to pulling the meat from the bones with your fingers or tugging it off the bone with a fork and spoon. Makes me hungry just thinking about that…

Beef Cheeks Bourguignon

My father introduced me to the joys of eating cheeks. You might say he's been on a cheek streak recently (pork and beef) – experimenting away with all manner of recipes to see what this little-known cut has to offer us in terms of flavour and texture. It turns out that beef cheeks are the perfect vehicles for a Bourguignon since they absorb all the flavours in the pan and the meat surrenders completely. The cheeks bring such silk and softness that I won't use another cut of beef for this dish again. I recommend serving it with mashed potatoes spiked with plenty of freshly grated Parmesan cheese and a bit of Dijon mustard.

Serves 6

2 tbsp sunflower oil

1.2kg beef cheeks, cut into large chunks

200g chestnut mushrooms, wiped clean and cut into quarters

200g smoked lardons or pancetta, cut into cubes

200g baby carrots, peeled, topped and tailed

250g pearl onions, peeled and tailed

1 tbsp balsamic vinegar

1 tbsp tomato purée

2 tbsp Dijon mustard

4 garlic cloves, peeled and finely chopped

75cl bottle of red wine from Burgundy (middle of the price range)

200ml good-quality stock (beef, chicken or vegetable is fine)

bouquet garni, composed of a few sprigs of thyme, a small bunch parsley and 2 bay leaves tied with string

salt and freshly ground pepper

a dash of Worcestershire sauce

a small bunch fresh parsley, stalks removed and leaves chopped

Preheat the oven to 150°C/fan 130°C/gas mark 2.

Heat the oil in a large ovenproof casserole over a medium heat, and brown the meat until suntanned all over (you may have to do this in batches, depending on the size of your casserole). Remove with a slotted spoon and set aside on a large plate.

Cook the mushrooms, lardons and carrots in the same pan over a high heat, until golden and then remove with a slotted spoon. Set aside on a small plate.

Turn down the heat, add the onions and cook for 5 minutes or until they smell fragrant. Add the balsamic vinegar and cook until all the vinegar has disappeared. Remove the onions from the pan with a slotted spoon and add to the plate with the mushrooms, lardons and carrots.

Put the beef back into the pan (along with any juices) and stir in the tomato purée, mustard, garlic, red wine, stock and bouquet garni. Bring to a simmer and scrape the bottom of the pan to loosen any tasty bits that might be stuck. Place a lid on top of the casserole and put in the bottom of the preheated oven for 3½ hours.

After this time, add the mushrooms, lardons, carrots and onions, and put back in the oven covered for a final 30 minutes.

Season with salt, freshly ground black pepper and a dash of Worcestershire sauce. Finally, sprinkle generously with parsley and serve.

Brown Beef Bone Broth

This title's a mouthful but I'm enjoying a gentle jab at the current craze for 'bone broth'. The plain way of saying it is: brown beef stock. The joy of this is in its depth and richness of flavour, which is why I roast the bones before simmering them. My favourite combination of bones is short rib and marrow bones (after they've been roasted and the marrow has been extracted – see recipe page 93). I keep any leftover bones from a roast in a Ziploc bag in my freezer and then when I have enough, or I need to make space, I make this stock.

Makes 2 litres

FOR THE ROASTING PHASE

2.5kg bones – I prefer a mixture of raw short rib and any others leftover from a roast

2 red onions, peeled and halved

2 carrots, washed, topped and tailed

1 tbsp olive oil

FOR THE SIMMERING PHASE

3 sticks celery, washed and roughly chopped

2 red onions, peeled and roughly chopped

1 leek, cut in quarters lengthways, rinsed and finely chopped

2 carrots, peeled, topped, tailed and roughly chopped

6 garlic cloves, bashed and peeled

handful of parsley stalks, a few sprigs of thyme and a bay leaf, tied together with string

10 black peppercorns

cook's tip Once refrigerated, use the stock within 3 days or freeze for up to 3 months.

Preheat the oven to 220°C/fan 200°C/gas mark 7.

Toss the bones, onions and carrots in the oil so that they are barely glistening.

Place the ingredients for the roasting phase on an oven tray and into the middle of the hot oven. Roast for 1 hour, turning the bones once during cooking. They will come out looking brown and slightly sizzled around the edges.

Boil the kettle and measure out 500ml of boiling water.

Remove the bones from the tray and put them into a very large stockpot, along with the roasted vegetables and any other bits from the bottom of the roasting tray. Pour the fat into a jar for dripping – you might end up with as much as 300ml.

Deglaze the roasting tray with the boiling water and, with the help of a spatula, scrape the bottom to catch everything you can. Pour this beautiful, fragrant, hot water over the bones in the pot.

Add the ingredients for the simmering phase, plus another 3.5 litres of water.

Bring to the boil and then reduce the heat to a very slow simmer. Cook gently for 2 hours.

Pour the stock through a sieve and either use straight away or cool down before refrigerating. You might find a layer of fat forming on top of the broth. I like to leave it in to give a richer texture to whatever your final dish is.

Pho Bo – Vietnamese Beef Noodle Soup

It's as much a pleasure for me to make this wonderful warming soup as it is to eat it. It's a real winter day favourite for when I'm feeling in the mood for pure, detox-ish, comfort food. It's the kind of broth that's packed with vitamins; the kind of soup that loves you back. This recipe relies on a really rich, brown beef stock, such as the one opposite. Sorry to say it but shop-bought just won't cut it. If you make the stock specifically for Pho Bo, I recommend that you keep some meat on the bones when you roast them. You don't actually need to add meat if you don't want to – you'll get an almighty beef hit from just the stock. It's fun to put all the ingredients (apart from the noodles that need to be cooked) in little bowls and everyone can add what they want to their own Pho Bo.

Serves 6

250g beef sirloin, very finely sliced

salt

2 litres Brown Beef Bone Broth (see facing page), with the short rib meat pulled from the bones after roasting

10cm fresh ginger, peeled and sliced into Juliennes

2 garlic cloves, peeled and very finely sliced

1 cardamom pod

2 star anise

1 tbsp brown sugar or hoisin sauce

2 tbsp fish sauce

300g wide, flat rice noodles

1 handful of beansprouts

3 spring onions, very finely sliced

1 small handful of fresh coriander, leaves roughly chopped

1 small handful of Thai basil, leaves roughly chopped

1 small handful of mint, leaves roughly chopped

1 lime, cut into 6 wedges

1 small red chilli, very finely sliced

Take the steak out of the fridge to bring it up to room temperature and season with salt.

Bring the stock to the boil with the ginger, garlic, cardamom and star anise. Simmer gently for 15 minutes to infuse.

Season the stock with the sugar or hoisin, the fish sauce and the salt, and then remove the aromatics and replace with the noodles. Cook them in the broth according to the packet instructions (be careful – rice noodles cook quite quickly so make sure that the rest of your ingredients are out and ready to go).

Divide the broth and noodles between the bowls. Add the beansprouts, spring onions, raw sirloin strips, shredded short rib meat (if using) and all the herbs. Squeeze over the lime, garnish with a little chilli and enjoy piping hot.

cook's tip Sometimes I add shredded Chinese cabbage (called Yu Choy Sum), tofu or Julienned carrots. I know that it's not traditional but it ups the level of vitamins and works well with the Pho Bo flavours. You can also make this with chicken broth – but, again, please use homemade (see page 8).

Beef Dripping Roast Potatoes

Here I have no words… This is quite simply one of the best things I've ever made. I practically had to lie down afterwards to calm myself from the high. The beef dripping in this recipe lends the most wonderful savoury flavour dimension to this Sunday lunch favourite. I have tested this many ways and have concluded that there is one golden rule that will always deliver results that are fluffy on the inside and crunchy on the outside: cook the potatoes in a very hot oven from *frozen*. The flavour of the dripping sinks in and gives them a deeply beefy taste, whilst the hot roasting pan shocks the frozen potatoes, giving them a hard shell. If you've never quite managed to achieve perfect roasties, this recipe is for you.

Serves 4 (6 at a stretch)

1kg floury potatoes, such as Desirée, Maris Piper, Saxon, King Edward, peeled and cut into halves or quarters for the whoppers

200g beef dripping

plenty of salt flakes and crushed black pepper

cook's tip You can use goose fat instead of beef dripping. I don't recommend lard, which tastes too strong and overpowers the flavour of the spud.

If you want to make these ahead, boil and rough them up. Keep them frozen until they're ready to roast. These keep their crunch once reheated, if you have any left over (which you won't).

Bring a very large saucepan of water to the boil and add the potatoes. Cook for roughly 30 minutes, or until the potatoes are just cooked through. You're looking for a texture that will rough up around the edges but hold its shape.

Drain the water from the cooked potatoes and set them aside. Once cold, give them a little roughing up around the edges, then put them in a freezer bag and freeze for an hour minimum.

Preheat the oven to 240°C/fan 220°C/gas mark 9.

In a large, shallow roasting tray, heat the dripping until it is smoking hot. I deliberately only cook smallish batches of these potatoes so that they have plenty of room on the roasting tray, otherwise they steam and don't brown. If you are making this for Christmas or a large crowd, you could double the recipe quantities. Most average-sized ovens can take 2 roasting tins side by side.

Add the frozen potatoes to the dripping and immediately put them back into the middle of the hot oven. Turn each potato over after 10 minutes and repeat until they're crunchy and golden all over. Mine take 1–1½ hours, depending on the size of the potatoes.

Season very generously with salt and black pepper before serving.

rump steak

steak masterclass

The first thing to clarify is that I'm talking about beef, as opposed to other steaks. There is a note at the end about lamb, pork and chicken. This is about how to nail your steak every time and what to choose when you're shopping.

how to source

Sourcing the meat is clearly the first and most important step to great steak. There's nothing you can do to a piece of meat that is tight, bright red and full of moisture to make it come right in the pan. You're looking for a breed that is designed to grow slowly, ideally for up to 30 months, instead of the standard 14, and importantly, one that has spent most of its life eating grass. All native English-bred cattle are slow-growing so you know you're already starting out in a good place when choosing a traditional breed. It's common practice to supplement the grass-fed diet with some (hopefully locally sourced) protein and grain, especially towards the end of their lives, in order to lay down a little extra fat that will enable the carcasses to be hung for a longer amount of time after slaughter. For example, Tim Wilson of the Ginger Pig supplements the grass and hay he gives his Longhorn cattle with 'barley, wheat, soya or peas, topped up with molasses'.

Now that you've sourced the animal, you need to choose the cut. I rarely cook fillet, rib eye or sirloin for less than two people and the reason is that, in order to achieve a good crust whilst retaining a pink centre, the piece of meat needs to be at least 2.5cm thick – 4cm is ideal. If you're cooking steak for one, I would recommend something like onglet, bavette (which will deliver great flavour even when cut thinner), or a stout piece of rump.

Colour-wise, you're looking for a piece of meat that's dark red, brown even, in colouring and dry to the touch. Some cuts are a different colour to others. For example, bavette can look almost purple and that's totally normal. Well-hung meat is always darker in colour than fresh meat. Bright red steak should therefore be avoided or treated with suspicion. Any outer fat should be firm – another indication of extended hanging time. If you see a piece of meat with a dark, almost black crust, jump on it and ask the butcher to cut your steak from that whole rib eye or sirloin. Intramuscular fat, which is known as marbling, is highly desirable because it helps moisturise the steak and adds flavour. Lots of marbling only occurs in cuts like fillet, rib eye or sirloin – less in bavette or onglet.

As always, the only way of getting to the bottom of what you're buying is to talk to your butcher, develop a relationship so that he or she knows what you like, or lets you know when they have a particularly good-quality piece of meat, even if it's not the cut you went in for that day.

how to cook

Let the meat sit out of the fridge for at least an hour before cooking and, just before the meat hits the heat, season it with plenty of salt on all sides. The steak should be body temperature when it meets that sizzling hot pan or barbecue grill. Shrinking during cooking is a result of either the cold steak shocking against the heat of the pan or an indication that the meat is full of moisture, very likely because it's not been aged. This could deliver chewy texture and no flavour – avoid, avoid, avoid.

The amazing butcher opposite the apartment where I used to live in Paris gave me a piece of beef fat every time I bought a steak. The idea is to heat a seasoned, heavy (preferably cast iron) frying pan until it's smoking hot then rub the fat around the pan until it glistens. This is partly to prevent the steak from sticking but also to flavour the pan and therefore the meat. If you can't get a bit of beef fat, very lightly oil the surface of the meat with a high smoke point oil, such as avocado or light olive oil. Adding a small amount of dripping or butter to the pan when you flip over to the second side is a nice touch for flavour and is another way of encouraging the char.

If you're like me and you enjoy a dark crust on your steak, start the steak by cooking any visible fat: using tongs, hold the fat side in the middle of the pan where it's hottest. Once the fat is golden and has melted a little into the pan, you're ready to cook the first side. When you have achieved a really gorgeous dark crust on Side One, flip it over and do the same with Side Two. I tend to push the crust further on Side One because I like the chargrilled flavour it imparts and usually the steak isn't thick enough to get this on both sides equally. The charred crust is where the majority of the umami flavour can be found and is one of the reasons that hunter gatherer man started using fire to cook his meat. In other words, it's a very primal pleasure and is one of two reasons I enjoy steak so much on the rare occasions I eat it. The other reason is for the tender, pink flesh within.

Time-wise, it's hard to put a number on it but at white hot temperature, it shouldn't take more than 4 minutes per side to cook a 4cm-thick steak. If your heat source is very, very fierce, you might want to flip your steak every minute or so until you achieve the right doneness. At home, I invariably don't. Bear in mind that to achieve this kind of chargrilled taste, you are going to engender a lot of smoke in your kitchen: a great reason to save it for the barbecue. You then need to rest the cooked meat on a warm plate for the same time again. A beautiful steak that comes from a well-looked-after, dry-aged, rare-breed animal will hardly change shape when it's cooked. This is because there is very little shrinking or loss of moisture.

not just beef

The final thing to say when discussing steak is that the rules that apply to beef apply equally to lamb and pork, with the difference that pork isn't usually served pink in the middle. Somewhere between pink and cooked through is ideal in order to prevent drying the meat out. Pork steaks are called chops and lamb steaks refer to cuts from the leg and saddle, even though the literal translation of a rib eye or sirloin on a lamb would be the loin chops or rack of lamb along the back.

in a nutshell

1 Choose a great piece of meat and make sure it's at least 2.5cm thick.

2 Take the meat out of the fridge at least an hour before cooking. Season it all over with salt just before cooking.

3 A heavy-duty frying pan needs to be smoking hot or white ash on the barbecue.

4 Season the pan with beef fat or lightly oil the steak by rubbing all over.

5 Cook and colour any visible fat before frying the sides.

6 Cook at a very high heat for a short amount of time.

7 Rest the meat on a warm plate for roughly the same time as it was cooked.

rump steak with snail butter

Snail Butter

I'm a nut when it comes to snails. When I first arrived in Paris aged four, they were my favourite thing to eat in restaurants. Followed by profiteroles. Even if you hate the idea of snails, it's easy to see that the garlic and parsley butter is one of life's great joys. The butter that is usually served on entrecôtes calls itself Beurre Maître d'Hôtel but I find that it lacks the oomph that snail butter has, so that's what I use on my steaks instead. You can make it up in a sausage shape and keep it in the freezer – slice off a fat coin as and when you need it. Chopping the herbs to kingdom come is very important, as it means you get a lovely even texture when the butter melts. Plus it makes the stuff bright green and that's just cool. This is also amazing with barbecued seafood or smeared under the skin of a chicken before roasting.

Makes enough for 18 steaks or 4 whole chickens (use what you need and freeze the rest)

5 large garlic cloves, peeled

2 shallots, peeled, topped and tailed

a large bunch curly parsley, stalks removed (roughly 35g)

a medium bunch chervil, leaves only (roughly 15g)

2 tbsp Pernod (or replace with more boiling water)

250g chilled, salted butter, cut into cubes

2 tbsp boiling water

¼ tsp white pepper

cook's tip My favourite time of year to make this is in spring when there is fresh garlic around. I make twice the quantity and keep it in my freezer for the year ahead. And, speaking of garlic, make sure it is fresh. If you use old garlic, the butter will taste bitter. It's also essential to remove the green stalk inside the clove; again, for the same reason.

Mince the garlic and shallots using a fine grater – you're looking for a pulp. A food processor won't get it quite fine enough.

Using a food processor, blitz the parsley, chervil and garlic and shallot mixture with the Pernod until it's so fine it is almost a paste. This will ensure even distribution and green colour.

Put the butter into a bowl and beat with a wooden spoon until you have a paste. Slowly add the boiling water and swap the wooden spoon for an electric hand-held whisk. Once all the water has gone in, whisk again. The aim is to introduce air into the butter before adding the aromatics. The butter should be a couple of shades paler.

Finally, using the wooden spoon, beat in the herb mixture and pepper.

Place a sheet of clingfilm on the work surface and when the butter is thoroughly well combined, tip into the middle of the sheet and roll carefully into a sausage shape. Wrap in a further layer of baking paper to protect it and keep either in the fridge or freezer.

Cut coins as and when you need them, allowing about 15 minutes to bring them to room temperature. Melt directly on top of the hot steak or melt in a pan and pour over the steak, if the meat is no longer piping hot.

Chimichurri Sauce

I came late to the delights of Chimichurri. I love Sauce Vierge and Salsa Verde, though, and Chimichurri definitely belongs in that family. This simple sauce is a vibrant slick of bright green that marries beautifully with grilled meat, fish and is easy peasy to make. This recipe makes a medium jar of the stuff and will keep in the fridge for about a week. It's addictive and full of lively green goodness so feel free to tailor it to your taste: more chilli, take out the basil, replace the vinegar with lemon… The only thing to remember with Chimichurri is that if you want it to be authentic then it needs to be heavy on the garlic and on the parsley. And, believe it or not, I prefer it with dried oregano rather than fresh – but that's entirely personal.

Makes 250ml – more than enough for 4 steaks

4 garlic cloves, peeled (you can also use green/fresh garlic if it's in season – this is even better)

2 tbsp red wine vinegar

1 large handful of fresh flat-leaf parsley, stalks removed, rinsed and spun dry

a small bunch basil, stalks removed

1 tbsp dried oregano

150ml extra virgin olive oil

2 tsp red chilli flakes

1 tbsp lime juice

salt, to taste

In the bowl of a food processor, blitz together the garlic and vinegar until there are no big chunks. Next, add the parsley, basil, oregano and olive oil. Pulse until you have a loose mixture with no big parsley leaves left.

Finally, add the chilli flakes and the lime juice. Pulse briefly before seasoning with salt.

The flavours will develop and improve over the course of the next few hours so it's a good idea to make it a little ahead of serving. As well as a sauce for grilled meat, I love it as a salad dressing, on pasta or gnocchi with a good snowfall of Parmesan, or even as a replacement for mint sauce with roast lamb.

Sauce au Roquefort

This recipe is one of the quintessential French sauces to accompany steak. The key to this pairing is to choose a steak that is tender but lacks flavour, which is why fillet is perfect here. And I never recommend fillet… I probably have it once a year, if that. When I do, you can be sure that it's draped with a strong-flavoured sauce like this one or Sauce aux Morilles (see recipe on page 56). Alternatively, a thick-cut rump steak is a good option, if you are going for something cheaper, more boisterous, or if you enjoy a bit of a texture tussle at the end of a long day at the office. A side of freshly wilted and buttered spinach is always fun here, too. Sauce au Roquefort is also lovely on a plain, grilled chicken or turkey breast, or over fresh gnocchi with a little finely chopped chives and some toasted walnuts scattered over the top, for a vegetarian alternative.

Serves 4

2 tbsp white wine

100g Roquefort cheese, crumbled (I prefer a younger, milder Roquefort for this so look for one that is mostly white with only the odd speck of green)

200ml full-fat crème fraîche

a few scratches of fresh nutmeg

plenty of black pepper – and a little salt if needed

finely chopped fresh chives, to garnish

cook's tip Yes, Roquefort is salty. But it's actually more *savoury*, than straight-up salty. Depending on the kind of Roquefort (and the age), you may need to give it a salt nudge. Taste and see.

Combine the white wine and Roquefort in a small saucepan over a medium heat and stir until the cheese is totally melted. Crush out any lumps with a plastic spatula.

Add the crème fraîche and a little nutmeg with a few twists of black pepper. Stir to combine. Taste and adjust the seasoning – adding more nutmeg or black pepper as needed.

Serve warm with a generous sprinkling of fresh chives.

sauce béarnaise

sauce au roquefort

morels cream sauce

chimichurri sauce

Sauce Béarnaise

I judge the quality of a restaurant by its Béarnaise (and its French fries)… So many restaurants cut corners or change the original formula. Why? It's perfect as it is. A traditional Béarnaise includes an aromatic vinegar reduction, egg yolks, clarified butter and two herbs: tarragon and chervil. Once you get the hang of making it yourself, it's something you'll make over and over again because it's the most exquisite sauce to go with steak. And this is not a time to scrimp on the quality of the meat: buy the most marbled, well-hung, dry-aged steak you can find and enjoy it. I wrote this recipe to go with Always Pink Rib of Beef (page 32). In that case, you can make the sauce whilst the meat is resting. Remember to serve it still warm. Done well, this is death row dinner kind of stuff.

Serves 6–8 (this is rich: a little goes a long way)

250g unsalted butter

a small bunch tarragon

a small bunch chervil

5 tbsp white wine vinegar (you could also use cider vinegar)

2 shallots, peeled and very finely chopped

5 peppercorns, bashed in a mortar and pestle

2 bay leaves

4 medium free-range egg yolks

squeeze of fresh lemon juice

salt, to taste

Melt the butter in a medium saucepan over a gentle heat and when it is completely liquid, turn off the heat. Let it stand so that the milk solids (little white blobs) drop to the bottom of the pan.

Strip the leaves from the tarragon stalks and finely chop them with the chervil. Set to one side, under some clean, damp kitchen paper.

Put the vinegar, tarragon stalks, shallots, peppercorns and bay leaves in a small saucepan. It needs to be small so that the liquid covers the shallots and other ingredients. Bring to the boil over a high heat and simmer until half the liquid has evaporated – around 3 minutes should do it.

Strain the reduced vinegar through a sieve and set it aside. Discard the shallots and other ingredients and fill the now-empty pan with water. Bring to the boil and then turn off the heat.

Put a heatproof bowl over the boiling water and add the egg yolks and reduced vinegar. Whisk until pale, around 2 minutes with an electric whisk or 5 minutes if you use a balloon whisk like I do. Once pale and thickened, it's ready to receive the melted butter.

Gently pour the melted butter in a slow and steady stream – think mayonnaise slow – whisking as you go. You're looking for the texture of industrial custard: by which I mean, it should hold its shape but not be stiff. If the mixture looks too thick or starts to separate, add a tiny bit of the boiled water from the pan underneath.

When all the clarified butter (but not the milk solids) has been added to the sauce, stop whisking and add the chopped herbs as well as a splash of fresh lemon juice. Taste and season generously with salt. Serve warm.

cook's tip You can make this slightly in advance and serve it at room temperature instead of warm if preferred. Or you can also make it up to 2 hours ahead. In this case, place clingfilm directly on to the surface of the sauce and don't refrigerate. Before serving, reheat very gently over a pan of boiling water, giving it a good stir to break up any solids that may have formed as the butter cooled down. If you heat it more than lukewarm or heat it too quickly, the sauce will melt – the flavour will be there but none of the unctuous texture, so make sure you don't overheat.

It's worth remembering that this sauce is made with eggs that are barely cooked so avoid serving it to anyone in the 'at risk' health groups (very young, elderly or pregnant).

Morels Cream Sauce – Sauce aux Morilles

This is a *cheffy* sauce that puts the wow into a grilled piece of meat, whether it's a pork chop or a chicken, turkey or veal escalope. If you're grilling a tender but less-flavoured piece of beef such as a fillet, this is also a good way to snazz it up. Sauce aux Morilles is a French classic and is easy to make, but bear in mind that even dried wild mushrooms are fairly expensive (because they impart so much flavour, one assumes).

Serves 2

20 whole dried morel
 mushrooms

30g butter

2 shallots, peeled and very
 finely sliced

2 tbsp Cognac or brandy

200ml good-quality veal or
 chicken stock

100ml double cream

2 tsp Dijon mustard

2 tsp lemon juice

salt and white pepper, to taste

finely chopped fresh parsley or
 chives, to garnish

cook's tip If you have any left over, it's killer on fresh tagliatelle…

This recipe is very easy to multiply if you want to make for 4, 6 or 8. It doesn't freeze well, though (cream and lemon are tricky to reheat without splitting).

Put the mushrooms into a small bowl and pour over just enough boiling water to cover. Place a sheet of clingfilm over the top and allow to stand for at least 15 minutes.

Meanwhile, melt the butter in a small saucepan over a gentle heat and add the shallots. Cook until translucent.

Wring out the mushrooms with your hands and roughly chop half of them and leave the other half whole. (If you don't want to waste this mushroom liquid, reserve it for another day and use in a mushroom risotto or stock.)

Add all the mushrooms to the shallots and pour over the Cognac or brandy and stock. Turn up the heat and reduce the liquid by half. This will take around 10 minutes and is important because it concentrates the flavours.

Finally, add the cream and mustard and bring back to the boil. Turn off the heat and add the lemon juice. Taste and adjust the seasoning.

Serve poured over grilled meat with a sprinkling of parsley or chives on top.

what's the beef?

Here is a library of my favourite steaks with a brief description of their profiles.

rump

This designates hard-working muscles at the back end of the cow, which means that it tends to have lots of flavour but is sometimes tough, depending on where in the rump your steak comes from. Rump benefits from being cut quite thick so that you can achieve a charred crust and a pink centre. Because of the flavour and the fact that it tends to be quite lean, this is my favourite cut for making Steak Tartare (see page 60). It is a cut that can stand up to a robust sauce, like Chimichurri, or a rich one, like either Morels or Roquefort (see pages 50, 56 and 51).

rib eye

This cut has slightly less flavour than Rump and less fat than Sirloin but is delicious when its crust is charred to kingdom come, preferably over an open flame. The muscle tends to be fairly lean with an even grain but you can expect a little layer of fat around the eye of the meat, as well as some marbling, which will help to keep it tender during cooking. I rarely have this as a steak, preferring to roast a three-bone rib instead (see page 32). I particularly like this cut served with a rich accompaniment, such as Béarnaise (see page 54), that combines both buttery velvet and a hint of sharpness from the vinegar. Fries or super crunchy roast potatoes are also a must.

fillet

To be blunt but this cut can be downright boring. Even when the Fillet is hung inside the whole Sirloin and therefore acquires as much flavour as it can, it's not a cut that you choose if you're after a steak with character. The upside is that it is meltingly tender, in spite of being quite lean, which is why I think it is so expensive. I personally never buy it, preferring something with a little more sass. It's essential to serve Fillet with a sauce that will deliver extra flavour. You can go for pretty much any one you want. I love it with Snail Butter melting over the top when it arrives on the plate (see page 49). I don't have a recipe for it here but a peppercorn sauce would be another legitimate option: something rich and with plenty of balls is what's needed.

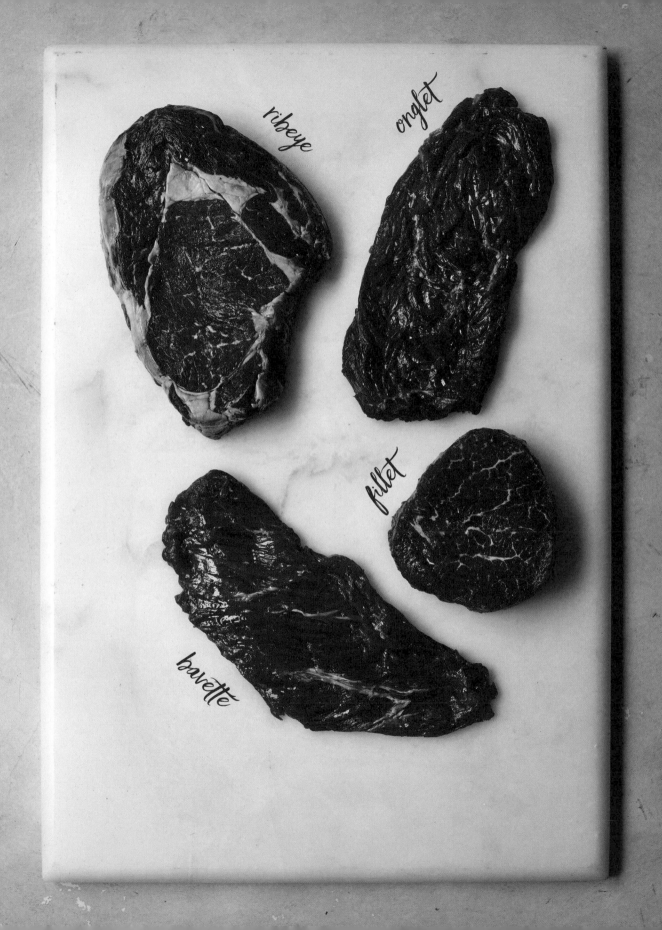

ribeye

onglet

fillet

bavette

onglet

This cut looks a bit like a darker, more fibrous version of Fillet because it comes in a long, barrel shape. That's where the similarities end. Onglet has tons of flavour and is coarse textured because of the feathering that naturally occurs throughout the muscle. I like to cook this at very high heat and not for long. I don't tend to serve any rich sauce with it, preferring something light and zippy, like Chimichurri (see page 50). Although this steak is gaining in popularity, it remains at the affordable end of the spectrum. I love the fact that you get so much flavour and texture value for the price.

bavette

I've had some life-changing Bavette steaks: succulent, tender with buckets of flavour and a juicy bite to satisfy the most demanding carnivore. I've also had rubbery, tight and stringy Bavette. The good news is that it pretty much always has flavour. You do need to talk to your butcher and ask his advice, though… If he hesitates, go for something else he can recommend. It's important that you order or cook Bavette rare and that you cut it against the grain when it's ready to eat. Don't be surprised if it puddles a little blood on the plate. This is not an indication of poor-quality meat; it's just the way the steak behaves once it's cooked. Resting will help with this. I like this topped with very finely sliced shallots flash fried in butter. Or, at a push, some Snail Butter (see page 49). I'm not a big fan of sauces with Bavette, by and large because the meat has so much of its own flavour and juice already. And fries, always with fries.

sirloin

Also known as Entrecôte here in France, this is probably my favourite cut for steak, although it's very rich and quite expensive. On a good-quality piece of Sirloin, you can expect a fair amount of marbling and a good fat cap around the outside. This fat is also what makes this cut both full-flavoured and very tender (it's usually one or the other). Always ask for a piece at least 2.5cm thick so that you can get some good colour and charring on all sides. I don't tend to serve Sirloin with a sauce, preferring the flavours of the fat and meat to express themselves.

Steak Tartare 'Coupe au Couteau'

There is a raging debate in Paris about how to cut the meat that goes into a proper steak tartare. The higher end the brasserie, the more likely you are to find it chopped with a knife, rather than minced in a food processor. The knife version takes longer and often translates into a better quality of meat. I've tested this recipe with two different cuts: fillet (expensive and commonly used in steak tartare) and rump steak (in the middle of the price range). The rump won hands down and gives a wonderful, full-beef flavour. Always buy the meat for a tartare on the day you plan to eat it and be rigorous about clean boards and knives (see I'm Not Mincing My Words on page 130). When it comes to presentation, you have two choices: the first is to mix all the ingredients together (as I have done) and serve with a raw egg yolk on top. The other involves serving the chopped meat, seasoned only with olive oil, salt and pepper, with all the other ingredients in little piles alongside. Seasoning a tartare is as personal as seasoning a Bloody Mary, so this last version is a good way to go if you're making it for tartare experts! The addition of fresh dill is a personal one – I think it brings an extra dimension to the flavour but is by no means traditionally French.

Serves 4

700g really good-quality, fresh rump steak

2 tbsp extra virgin olive oil

1 tbsp capers, drained of brine and finely chopped

3 tbsp very finely chopped cornichons or sweet pickles

1 tsp very finely chopped dill

2 tsp chopped chives, + extra to garnish

1 tbsp Dijon mustard

3 tbsp very finely chopped shallots

1 tsp Worcestershire sauce

generous pinch celery salt and white pepper

2 tsp Heinz tomato ketchup

a dash of Tabasco, to taste

4 fresh free-range egg yolks (optional)

freshly ground black pepper

To make the tartare, thinly slice the meat and cut into very small cubes with a very sharp knife. Place the meat in a bowl with the olive oil and toss to coat. Dicing the meat one slice at a time and coating in oil as you go will prevent it changing colour and is more hygienic.

Once all the meat is cut, add the remaining ingredients, except the egg yolks and black pepper. Mix together well to combine all the flavours. Taste and season, if needed.

With the help of a round pastry cutter lightly brushed with a tiny bit of oil to avoid sticking, pile the tartare on to four separate clean plates and pat down. Make a dip in the centre of the meat and remove the pastry cutter. Place a raw egg yolk in the dip of each tartare, crunch over some black pepper and sprinkle with chives. Serve straight away.

cook's tip It is even more important to source your meat from a reliable butcher when making this – always tell him/her that you are making tartare – they will sort you out accordingly.

Soul Burger

It's really difficult to put a finger on exactly what Soul Food is, except that the name originated from the American South in the 60s. By far the most important aspect of Soul Food is that it's made with love. I had one of the famous Earnestine & Hazel's Soul Burgers when I was in Memphis. The burger itself was nothing to write home about (although, here I am doing just that!) but I could definitely tell that it was cooked with lots of warm, Southern love. The Worcestershire sauce in this burger is a nod to one from Earnestine & Hazel's but the rest is my own version of a damn fine, juicy burger that's made from scratch. It may seem like a lot of extra work to grind your own beef for a burger but once you've tasted this recipe you'll know what I'm on about. A memorable burger, by which I mean one with depth of flavour, a savoury, charred crust and soft crumb inside, is one of life's great joys. As such, I've researched, tasted and tested about 12 different cuts of meat and toppings before hitting the jackpot with a combination of shin and short rib.

Serves 4

FOR THE BURGER

250g short rib beef, off the bone – you can ask your butcher to do this but you may need to call ahead, otherwise slice the meat off the bone with a sharp knife ca-re-ful-ly (keep the bones for Vietnamese Pho Bo, see page 41)

plenty of salt and freshly ground black pepper

250g ground beef shin from the butcher

4 tsp olive oil

4 burger buns, cut in half horizontally (I like the cheap ones with sesame seeds on top – brioche is too rich here)

4 thin slices Emmental, Cheddar or Gruyère (mild cheese that melts!)

a dash of Worcestershire sauce

Place the bowl of the food processor, the blade and the rib meat into the freezer for 15 minutes while you get the rest of the ingredients ready. This is to make sure that the home-ground short rib doesn't become too pasty and sleek.

To get the burger meat ready, roughly chop the short rib meat into 2.5cm cubes. Pulse in the bowl of the cold food processor until you have ground meat that is still choppy in texture, a bit like a coarsely cut tartare. Tip the beef on to a plate and remove any stringy bits that you come across with your fingers or a fork.

Season generously with salt and black pepper then pulse again very briefly with the ground meat from the butcher to combine.

With very clean hands and taking care not to handle it too much, gently form 4 patties and set aside. Rub 1 teaspoon of olive oil on to each patty to avoid sticking during cooking, then place them in the freezer to firm up for 10 minutes.

Meanwhile, place a large frying pan (cast iron is best of all) over a high heat. (If you're cooking on a barbecue, this should be prepared before you start on the meat so that it's at the white ash stage by now.)

FOR THE TOPPINGS (ALL ARE OPTIONAL BUT THIS IS WHAT I RECOMMEND)

Russian Dressing (this is the 'magic sauce' here – try it once and see what I'm talking about, page 78), or a mixture of mayonnaise (I like Hellmann's) and Heinz Tommy K, to taste

French's mustard (it's more tangy than Dijon)

1 red onion (or the sweet Spanish ones are great too, if you can find them), peeled and very finely sliced

1 large, ripe tomato (such as beef heart), very finely sliced

2–3 large dill pickles, very finely sliced

4 leaves Romaine lettuce, washed and cut into thirds

Also, if using a barbecue, you may need to press the meat together more firmly to prevent it from collapsing during cooking.

Toast the cut sides of the buns briefly to gently char the edges. Set aside and smear a generous dollop of Russian Dressing on the base of the bun, and a little mustard on the top.

Cook the meat over a very high heat on one side. When you're happy with the crust that has formed on the bottom side, flip it and add the cheese slice on top so that it has a chance to melt while the underside cooks. Just before you take the burgers off the heat, hit each one with a dash of Worcestershire sauce, which will sizzle. You can either cook the red onions in the pan alongside the burgers, or have them raw if you prefer (I do).

Place a burger on each bun base and layer with your choice of garnishes. Serve with piping-hot Shoe String Fries (see page 109), or a packet of good-quality, ready-salted crisps for an authentic Earnestine & Hazel's experience.

cook's tip For a little history on the iconic hamburger, see page 64. And for a crash course in making your own mince, see page 130.

Even though I like my steak rare, I prefer my burger medium rare – see *I'm Not Mincing My Words*, page 130.

burger off

Everybody loves a good burger, including me. Although the humble hamburger started out life as a simple, affordable solution to the growing demand for what was to become known as 'takeaway' food, i.e. food that could be eaten without the use of any cutlery, the hamburger has now reached iconic status worldwide. So what exactly is it about hamburgers that we love so much? How did this sandwich become such a big deal and why?

To rewind the clock a little, the first restaurants expressly serving hamburgers were the White Castle fast-food chain in the United States, which started with just one restaurant in Kansas in 1921. The idea behind 'fast food' was to make a small number of food items over and over again, implementing a mass-production system – thus reducing both the cost and also the waiting time. In other words, standardising the operation of making hamburgers and mimicking Henry Ford's car production assembly lines. This was the beginning of 'fast food' in America.

When hamburgers first appeared on the scene, they were aimed at the workforce who no longer went home for a midday meal and had to either pack a lunch (usually cold) or grab a cheap bite near the workplace. What could be more satisfying or appealing than a hot burger? The cost of this food was low because burger patties were made (and still are, for the most part) from offshoots of other, more valuable, cuts of meat. Ingenious! Cheap, tasty, versatile and easy to eat wherever you are – it's not difficult to see why the hamburger became such a popular sandwich.

Unsurprisingly, it has come to represent big business. According to Eric Schlosser in *Fast Food Nation*, 'The typical American now consumes approximately three hamburgers and four orders of fries every week.'

It's the business aspect of making hamburgers that I want to look into here. Meat used to be precious and rare but in the last 50 years, the proliferation of burgers, and the fast-food culture generally, have done a lot to change that. It has altered our attitudes and changed our relationship towards meat and even food itself. What was once a rare commodity is now so cheap and easy to get hold of, it is perceived to be a right in some Western cultures. It is not uncommon to find meat at the centre of the plate, two and even three times a day. Every day.

On the one hand, hamburgers are a resourceful way of using up leftover scraps of meat that might otherwise have gone to waste (the same can be said of another global meat success story: the sausage). On the other, the indistinct meat patties are a great way of hiding all manner of sub-standard ingredients of varying origins. On a side note, the popularisation of the hamburger also came about in part thanks to the fortuitous arrival of the meat grinder. According to Andrew F. Smith in *Hamburger*, it 'was a great asset to butchers, who could now use unsaleable or undesirable scraps and organ meats that might otherwise have been tossed out. It also became possible to add non-meat ingredients to the ground beef, and it was very hard for the consumer to know what was actually in the mixture.'

If it looks good and tastes good, then who cares what actually goes into it? And there are many ways of making something appealing (sugar, salt, fat and ingenious marketing campaigns targeting certain demographic groups). Frankly put, if you aren't making it yourself or getting it from a reliable source, it's anybody's guess what's in your hamburger.

The fact that hamburger meat can be produced so cheaply is widely praised, without giving much scrutiny to why this is possible and what actually goes into the nondescript patties. The ability to conceal the ingredients that make up the burger patty is also, I believe, at the heart of another modern dietary 'improvement': the arrival and proliferation of industrial food. By industrial food, I'm talking specifically about the manufacturing of large volumes of a single food item, with a view to turning as large a profit as possible. The systems put in place, initially by White Castle and then by other large hamburger chains worldwide have contributed significantly to the widespread mechanisation of food today. This, in turn, has surely had repercussions on the way that farming and agriculture have evolved to support this system of mechanised food production.

In fact, could the hamburger also be responsible for introducing the notion of 'uniformity' into our relationship with food? Food mechanisation needs a product that looks and tastes the same every time. Have we started to expect all our food products to look the same, whether they are processed or not? Is this where our rejection of 'wonky fruit and veg' comes from?

What the hamburger has done to affect our relationship with food is profound and multi-layered. It has contributed to making meat a food group that is accessible to all, a sort of 'right to meat'. What started out as an ingenious way of using up otherwise worthless cuts of meat and bringing protein to people who couldn't afford it otherwise, has become an end in itself. Factory farming has grown to support the need for hamburger, rather than hamburger being the creative way of using up scraps.

Swedish Meatballs

Although there are variations to the recipe up and down Sweden (in the north, they don't usually add pork; in the south, they do), this should be a simple dish that, dare I say it, is delightfully light on flavour. The only aromas coming through should be meat, onion, allspice and the buttery gravy. That's it. No garlic, no veal, no fancy Christmas spices. This recipe comes straight from a bona fide Swedish grandmother, Viola Johansson, who, along with making meatballs, is also an enthusiastic mushroom forager. If you can get your hands on some, serve this with lingonberry jam (cranberry sauce is the next best thing), as well as the traditional accompaniment of boiled potatoes.

Serves 6 hungry Swedes –
makes 35 meatballs

50g butter

1 small onion, peeled and very
   finely chopped

100ml whole milk

70g fresh breadcrumbs from
   a good-quality white loaf

1 tbsp ground allspice

300g minced beef (shin or chuck
   is good here, around 15% fat)

200g minced pork (shoulder is
   best, around 20% fat)

1 medium free-range egg

salt and white pepper

FOR THE GRAVY

30g butter

1 tbsp plain flour

200ml good-quality beef stock

1 tbsp double cream

cook's tip Be careful not
to over-season – my first
batch were way too salty
because I used stock that
was already quite salty.

Melt half the butter in a very large frying pan over a gentle heat and fry the onion until translucent. Be careful not to let it colour. Set aside to cool. Meanwhile, pour the milk over the breadcrumbs and add the allspice.

Tip the cooled sonion mixture into the food processor and add the minced meat, egg, soaked breadcrumbs and add a pinch of white pepper. Blend for a few minutes to combine.

Form the meatballs so that they're about 2.5cm and place on a plate. Wetting your fingers will help you roll the meatballs without them sticking.

Heat half of the remaining butter in the same frying pan until foaming. Add half the meatballs and fry on a medium heat until golden. I use a lid for about half the time so that they are cooked through and firm to the touch. Set aside and repeat with the remaining butter and meatballs until they are cooked. Keep in a warm oven while you make the gravy. Don't wash the pan.

To make the gravy, melt the butter in the pan over a medium heat and add the flour to make a roux. Cook for a couple of minutes before adding the stock, a little at a time. As you add the stock, remember to whisk to prevent lumps. Taste and season before taking off the heat. Add the cream and incorporate well before returning the meatballs to the pan to coat in the gravy.

Serve piping hot!

Ragu Bolognese – *for Rob*

I went to Bologna to taste real Ragu Bolognese and here is an extract from my diary, after the first plate was put down in front of me: 'To my surprise and delight, a plate of tagliatelle tangled in a pale meat sauce appears. The texture is soft, surrendered and subtle.' It turns out the real thing is made from white wine (not red), cooked in milk and contains very few tomatoes… Layering the ingredients, cooking really slowly and serving it with tagliatelle as opposed to spaghetti are the remaining secrets to a proper Ragu Bolognese. *Buon appetito!*

Serves 6

30g unsalted butter

3 tbsp olive oil

1 large onion, peeled and very finely chopped

3 sticks celery, washed, topped, tailed and very finely chopped

3 medium carrots, peeled and very finely chopped

1kg ground beef shin (if you can't get shin make sure that the mince contains around 20% fat)

350ml whole milk

2 bay leaves

½ whole fresh nutmeg, finely grated

salt and freshly ground black pepper

350ml dry white wine

1 × 400g can of good-quality Italian chopped tomatoes (organic tend to be sweeter)

cook's tip It goes without saying that this is a dreamboat to freeze.

This is my favourite Thermos-packed lunch on skiing hols.

First melt the butter and oil in a very large saucepan over a medium heat and fry off the onion, celery and carrots until the onion is translucent and the carrots tender.

Next nudge the 'holy trinity' (this is what Italians call the combination of onion, carrot and celery because it delivers such a tremendous flavour base) to one side of the saucepan, away from the heat. Add the meat to the hottest part of the pan and fry until brown. This will take around 20 minutes. Be careful to make sure that the veg don't burn during this time and if you feel the pan is too crowded, remove the veg and set aside.

Add the milk and bay leaves to the pan and mix the vegetables into the mince. Season generously with nutmeg, salt and a little pepper. Simmer uncovered slowly for about 20 minutes until there is no milk left, then add the wine and repeat. It's important to allow the last of the liquid to simmer away before adding the next. This is what gives the ragu its depth of flavour. When all the wine has evaporated, add the tomatoes, cover with a lid and simmer gently for 3 hours. You can expect the total cooking time to be around 4 hours.

Go back to the pan every once in a while to make sure that the bottom of the pan isn't catching and also that the ragu isn't too dry. If it is, add a splash of water.

Once the ragu is ready, taste and adjust the seasoning. Serve piping hot with fresh tagliatelle and freshly grated Parmesan.

brine me tender

It's a shame that the word 'brine' is such an ugly one because what it describes is nothing short of magic.

what

There are two ways of brining a piece of meat: one involves soaking it in a water solution made up of salt (always), sugar (often), and herbs and spices (sometimes). The other is to rub these elements directly on to the meat without bathing it in water. This last version is called dry brining or curing. Both techniques take time, and both are designed to preserve, tenderise and flavour the meat. This is what happens to bacon, ham and corned beef or salt beef. Many other meats are also brined in order to extend shelf life or artificially increase the weight but I'll come back to this later. For now, let's talk about what happens when you brine a piece of meat, whether by wet or dry curing.

how

There is a word to describe the process of what happens to meat when it's brined or cured: osmosis. Unlike brine, it's a very pretty word and, by gum, it's a powerful one. This is how Harold McGee in *On Food and Cooking* explains

the effects of brining: 'Brining has two initial effects. First, salt disrupts the structure of the muscle filaments [...] Second, the interactions of salt and proteins result in a greater water-holding capacity in the muscle cells, which then absorb water from the brine.'

So the muscle absorbs the flavoured salt water (brine), which then rejigs the meat proteins deep within the muscle and helps them retain the brine. This means that the flavour of your brine is now locked deep within the meat itself and is acting on the muscle and tenderising it from the inside out. This exchange of fluid is what the term 'osmosis' refers to.

why

Brining applies particularly to poultry (chicken and turkey), beef and pork. Fresh belly of pork needs to be cured (whether wet or dry) in order to become bacon. You can then smoke it afterwards but it's not bacon unless it's brined – it's just pork. The same applies to legs of pork and ham. Beef is wonderful brined to make **Mighty Salt Beef** (see page 74). If you smoke it, this turns into pastrami. You can also dry cure topside of beef to make bresaola. Cured beef is easy to make at home and quite delicious.

You don't need to brine chicken or turkey, especially if they are from really

71

good-quality birds, but it's sometimes a fun thing to do anyway. I often brine chicken for a few hours if I want to smoke it on the barbecue because it really helps to avoid the meat drying out during the smoke. And a Christmas turkey that's brined is never going to let you down.

The effects of brining meat are profound – if you've ever brined a turkey, you'll know exactly what I'm talking about. It totally changes the texture of the meat and means that you can cook the bird long enough so that the legs are perfectly cooked and yet the breast remains juicy. I don't want to tempt fate by writing this, but it's very difficult to overcook or dry out a brined bird. There, that's a secret worth knowing.

Preserving meat in salt (and vegetables – they become pickles) has been around since the dawn of time, along with other techniques like smoking, which also extends the shelf life by some staggering margin.

As we've seen, there's a lot to recommend brining as a means of tenderising and flavouring meat. 'Brine' may be an ugly word, but it's not a dirty one. Until fairly recently, brining was an honourable way of treating meat because it took time. When I dry cure my own bacon at home, it takes around 7 days, if I include the drying-out time in the fridge. To make ham, it can take 7–10 days. Same with salt beef. Dry curing charcuterie can take up to two years.

The problem comes when manufacturers who care about making money and little else use brining as a way of *a*) adding weight to the meat in order to make it appear bigger than it actually is and *b*) disguising miserable quality meat by artificially adding flavour and a tender texture to it. And it's true that you can get away with cheap meat for ham and bacon because, once it's brined, who's to say? When you look at it, the colour is pink and appetising, the rashers look plump and dewy inside their plastic containers. It's only when you cook it that the bacon or ham shrinks and releases all its juice – along with a dose of white shite that puddles in the bottom of the pan or roasting tray (see pages 191–2). Scarily, this kind of industrial brining is done using large needles so the brine penetrates deep into the meat muscle. What should take a week can be done in a matter of hours, 2 days at the most. So what is, in the right hands, a marvellous technique for treating meat becomes, in different hands, another way of duping the customer into buying something that is not what it appears to be.

Finally, I want to talk about saltpetre because it's important to follow the recipes carefully and respect the quantities you use. In small doses, it's harmless but it can become dangerous if you ingest too much. If you don't want to use saltpetre, you don't have to. It's only there for colour and doesn't affect the taste.

Beef Brine

Brined beef is a marvel. I adore it. I have tested this recipe with topside, brisket and chuck. Although I love the shredded texture of brisket once cooked, chuck also delivers a pleasant texture so go for that if you can't find brisket. Topside was downright dry so avoid it. Not only does brining the meat tenderise it and give it a melt-in-the-mouth texture, I also love the slightly sweet and salty pickle flavour that comes from handling beef this way. There are two technical points to bear in mind: the first is that saltpetre, which is a preserving agent and ensures that the meat turns a pretty pink colour rather than brown, is safe only when used in tiny amounts so do please respect the dosage here. The other is that it's important to brine the meat in a vessel that won't react with the salt – see Cook's Tip. Aluminium, copper, cast iron and bin liners are not food safe and must be avoided.

Makes enough to brine 2.5kg

2.5kg beef brisket (look for well-marbled brisket point with a layer of fat and wrap it in string to keep the thickness even)

2.5 litres water

300g salt

50g saltpetre (optional – see Brine me Tender, page 71), or increase the quantity of salt to 350g

4 bay leaves

2 shallots, peeled, topped, tailed and halved lengthways

1 star anise

1 clove

250g light muscovado sugar

2 tbsp cider vinegar

INGREDIENTS TO BE SMASHED IN A MORTAR AND PESTLE

4 garlic cloves

1 tbsp black peppercorns

1 tbsp dill seeds

½ tsp chilli flakes

1 tbsp coriander seeds

Start by piercing the rolled brisket all over with a wooden skewer – this will enable the brine to go all the way inside the meat faster.

Warm 1 litre of the water in a large pan over a gentle heat with the salt, saltpetre, bay leaves, shallots, star anise, clove, sugar and all the smashed-up ingredients from the mortar and pestle. Simmer very slowly and stir until all the sugar and salt have dissolved. Add the rest of the cold water and the vinegar and transfer to a very large glass bowl or sturdy giant Ziploc bag before adding the beef.

Once the beef is safely trapped in the brining ingredients and there is no air getting to it, place in the fridge to brine for 7 days.

After the beef has had its brining time, remove from the fridge and cook according to the Salt Beef recipe overleaf. Or, for a different vibe, you could slow roast it with a pepper crust to make a cheat's version of pastrami (see page 79).

cook's tip The best vessel for brining larger cuts of meat, in my experience, is a giant plastic bag that you can suck the air out of – like the ones you use to store winter duvets during the summer.

Mighty Salt Beef

There's nothing like a Salt Beef craving. For me, it's accompanied by a yearning for sweet and sour pickled flavours and lashings of dill. I make Salt Beef once every six months when the urge for it is strong enough to overcome the inconvenience of pickling a chunk of beef in my fridge for a week. It's not difficult but the waiting can be a drag. If you can't be bothered with brining it yourself, it's now fairly easy to get hold of brined brisket, especially if you look in the kosher section of the supermarket or get in touch with a kosher butcher. Once brined, the good news is that Salt Beef is cheap and a great way to feed a large number of people with something unusual, delicious and totally stress free. And the best thing of all? The Reubens you can make for days to come (see page 77)! I like it served warm so keep it in the cooking liquor when it goes back into the fridge and heat it up in its juice to keep it moist. Although Salt Beef is also associated with Ashkenazi cooking traditions, we've been enjoying it in Great Britain for centuries, not least because it keeps so well and is economical.

Serves 10 with leftovers

2.5kg brined brisket of beef, rolled with string to keep it tidy (see page 73 for recipe to brine the beef)

1 onion, peeled and quartered

2 large carrots, peeled, topped and tailed

3 sticks celery, washed and roughly chopped

2 bay leaves

1 tbsp black peppercorns

8 garlic cloves, bashed and peeled

enough water to cover the meat

cook's tip Salt Beef will keep in the fridge for a week in some of the poaching liquid, like mozzarella. To warm up and retain its moisture, heat the amount of meat you want in some of the poaching liquid.

Rinse the brined beef under cold water and put in a large saucepan with the rest of the ingredients. Cover and bring to the boil. Once boiling, reduce the heat to a very slow simmer and cook for 4 hours with the lid on. Check during the cooking process and remove any white foam that forms on the top with the help of a slotted spoon and discard.

Once cooked, remove from the water and slice across the grain.

Serve with Russian Dressing (see page 78) and Dill Pickle Fries (see page 229) or straight up dill pickles, beetroot salad or potato salad spiked with horseradish. Or my personal fave – Latkes (see facing page).

Latkes

These little potato pancakes look a lot like the French *pommes paillasson* (literally translated as 'doormat potatoes') because of all the frayed crispy bits that look ideal for wiping one's muddy boots on. The difference with this version is that it includes egg, onion and a bit of flour. Latkes are a Jewish potato pancake that are associated with Hanukkah celebrations. They are served with sour cream and chives or smoked salmon and lemon (savoury versions) or with apple purée and cinnamon (sweet version). I love them with Salt Beef. They are also a delicious accompaniment to steak or Always Pink Rib of Beef (see page 32). They are not difficult to make and can be made ahead and reheated in a hot oven so are very user friendly. They tend to be served in the colder months but, honestly, I'm up for a good latke whatever the weather.

Makes 12

2 tbsp plain flour

½ tsp bicarbonate of soda

a pinch salt and pepper

1 medium free-range egg, beaten with a fork

3 big floury potatoes, peeled and grated

1 medium onion, peeled and very finely chopped

150ml sunflower oil

cook's tip If you're not eating them straight away, let them cool and then put them into a hot oven later.

Preheat the oven to 180°C/fan 160°C/gas mark 4.

In a little bowl, mix the flour, bicarbonate of soda, salt and pepper.

Make a well in the centre and, using a balloon whisk, add the beaten egg slowly, incorporating the wet with the dry ingredients as you go.

Combine the potatoes and onion in a bowl and, using your hands, scoop up a fistful of the mixture. Wring it out over the sink to release as much water as possible. Set aside on a piece of kitchen paper until the potato mixture is as dry as possible.

Add the wrung-out potato and onion mixture to the pancake batter and mix well.

Place a third of the oil in a very large frying pan over a high heat until hot.

Using a tablespoon, measure 1 heaped spoon of the mixture into the hot oil and press down slightly to flatten. I tend to cook 4 latkes at a time but that very much depends on the size of your pan. Cook them until they're golden on both sides.

Remove from the pan with a slotted spoon and set aside on a baking tray lined with kitchen paper. Once all the latkes are golden, remove the kitchen paper and put in the hot oven for 15 minutes to cook through and crisp up (see page 76).

I Love You, Reuben

There is a deli with a diner attached in Minneapolis that serves the best Reuben I've ever tasted. If you're ever over there, look up Kramarczuk's (it's pronounced 'kamarcheck') and order your sandwich well toasted on marbled rye. A great Reuben to me is the sultan of sandwiches. Be sure to warm the meat whole in the cooking liquid and use a little of the juice to moisten the sauerkraut... Is your mouth watering yet? Mine is. Might have to make this for my lunch today. Getting back to the recipe: it's very important to use Russian Dressing (see page 78) but if you're not going to make salt beef, then you can use good-quality pastrami – just remember to heat it up a little before it goes into the sandwich. This is best enjoyed warm, with the cheese oooozing. A sandwich is often an afterthought – a way of using up leftovers – but this is one of those recipes that justifies cooking the meal in the first place. This is also a great sharing recipe – just increase the quantities, depending on how many you need.

Makes 1

2 tbsp Russian Dressing (see page 78), or replace with a mixture of 2 tbsp mayo to 1 tbsp Heinz Tommy K

2 slices of rye bread, medium thick cut (a mix of wheat and rye with caraway seeds is the best of all)

1 thin slice of Emmental cheese

120g good-quality salt beef (see page 74) or pastrami, medium thick, cut across the grain

a little French's mustard (Dijon is second best)

1 medium dill pickle (go for the sweeter variety and avoid cornichons), sliced

60g sauerkraut, drained of any brine and pressed in kitchen paper to absorb any liquid

Layer a good tablespoon of Russian Dressing on to the bottom piece of rye bread and top first with the slice of cheese, then the meat, mustard, pickle and sauerkraut. Finish with the remaining tablespoon of Russian Dressing.

Close up the sandwich and wrap it tightly in baking paper. Tie with string like you would a Christmas present to keep it whole.

Heat up a frying pan and toast the sandwich over a medium heat. Leave on the first side for 2–3 minutes until the paper is golden and the cheese has begun to melt. Flip over and repeat on the other side for another couple of minutes. You can also do this in the oven (at 200°C/fan 180°C/gas mark 6 for 10–15 minutes) if you're making more than one at a time.

Serve with French fries or Latkes (see page 75).

Russian Dressing

Russian Dressing is the unprepossessing name given to the elusive elixir which transforms an ordinary meal (two slices of bread and some leftovers) into a thing of beauty… In other words: it's the secret sauce. Once made, it keeps for a couple of weeks in the fridge because all the ingredients have a long life (unless you use homemade mayonnaise, which I don't recommend as it's wasted here, drowned out by too many other flavours). I love Russian Dressing with fish fingers or chicken goujons but it's indispensable on a beef burger or a Reuben sandwich. And it's not blinking bad in a disco-fabulous Prawn Cocktail either. Once you're hooked, the uses for this stuff become endless.

Makes 370g

100g mayonnaise (please pick full-fat Hellmann's if you have the choice)

50g ketchup

½ tsp red Tabasco (you can use green if red is too spicy for you) – try without first

½ tsp fresh lemon juice

½ tsp Worcestershire sauce

2 tsp very finely chopped fresh parsley (optional)

2 tbsp very finely chopped red onion (roughly ½ medium onion)

2 tbsp very finely chopped dill pickle (roughly 1 medium pickle)

2 tbsp creamed horseradish sauce

Combine all the ingredients in a clean jar and stir well. Taste and season with salt if needed. Store in the fridge for up to 2 weeks.

Pastrami

Upfront disclaimer: pastrami is smoked and this recipe is not. This is because I have yet to achieve a smoked brisket that isn't dry… I've tested a lot of them but I find this cut of beef particularly difficult to nail every time because the quantity of fat varies so wildly, as does the smoker's temperature (unless you have a professional smoker or one with an inbuilt thermometer). Instead, I add smoked paprika to the rub and cook it in the oven – it's a cheat's trick to give you a little of the smoke but with lots of guaranteed tenderness and moisture in the meat. As with proper smoked pastrami, the rule here is low and slow so make sure you give yourself plenty of time to cook this. Why is it worth going to the trouble? Because pastrami is quite simply one of the most marvellous things you'll ever taste… The highway to heaven is probably paved with pastrami sandwiches, like the Reuben on page 77.

Makes 2.5kg

1 × raw brined brisket – see
    page 73 (unrolled weight 2.5kg)

FOR THE RUB

4 tbsp freshly ground black
    pepper

2 tbsp smoked paprika

1 tbsp whole coriander seeds

½ tsp ground white pepper

¼ tsp ground cayenne pepper

2 tbsp garlic granules

1 tbsp dill seeds, roughly
    ground in a mortar and
    pestle

1 tsp salt

1 tbsp brown sugar

cook's tip It's fairly rare to find brisket with a nice layer of fat on it (it's the best kind) but if you are fortunate enough to have a lovely fat cap, grill for 5 minutes at the end to crisp up the top before serving.

Place all the rub ingredients in a mortar and pestle and bash the heck out of them. Get as close to a powder as you can. Rub this all over the brisket and place it, fat side up and uncovered, in the fridge overnight.

Take the brisket out of the fridge about an hour before cooking to bring it up to room temperature.

Preheat the oven to 120°C/fan 100°C/gas mark ½.

Wrap the brisket first in baking paper, then in two layers of good-quality tin foil.

Place on a baking sheet in the middle of the preheated oven and cook for 4 hours.

After 4 hours, open up the parcel carefully, discard the foil and paper and any juices, and return the meat to the oven, fat side up, for a final hour of cooking. This last cooking phase is to enable the meat to dry out a little and give you a bit of a crust.

After a total of 5 hours' cooking, take the pastrami out of the oven, carve against the grain and serve. If you don't eat it all straight away, wrap tightly in clingfilm and refrigerate.

Beef and Guinness Pie

A really great Beef and Guinness Pie is hard to beat. The dark, rich centre is the perfect medicine for a cold winter's evening or afternoon. I like to make a big batch of the casserole and freeze some (with or without the pastry on top) in smaller portions. The reason for this is that it's a slow-cooked dish that requires gentle simmering – in other words: no rushing. The ale needs to surrender its malt, the meat needs to forgive and forget in order for the sauce to release maximum flavour and texture. And silk, silk and always more silk is achieved this way, too. It's up to you what you choose to put on top, whether a shortcrust or a puff-pastry lid. I like puff because it lightens up what is honestly one of the richest and deepest recipes in the book. A small amount goes a long way but it hits that particular spot like nothing else. I like to add treacle and golden syrup to round off the flavour, so make sure you have some in the house before you start cooking. It's not what you expect in a beef recipe but it works wonders on the Guinness's distinctive metallic finish.

As for the cut of meat, I tested this with oxtail, short ribs, shin and chuck. I hardly ever recommend chuck because it's ubiquitous in slow-cooking meat recipes nowadays (and is not always the right cut for the recipe in my view) but here is a good time to use it.

Serves 8

FOR THE PIE FILLING

3 tbsp olive or sunflower oil

1.5kg good-quality beef chuck or shin, cut into 4cm cubes

2 tbsp plain flour

30g unsalted butter

2 medium onions, peeled and finely chopped

2 carrots, peeled, topped, tailed and very finely chopped

2 sticks celery, washed, topped, tailed and very finely chopped

5 garlic cloves, peeled and finely chopped

bouquet garni made from parsley stalks, 4 fresh bay leaves and a sprig of rosemary tied with string

Place some of the oil in a very large pan (preferably a cast iron one because it's easier to clean afterwards) over a high heat and brown the meat in two or three batches. Once really well coloured on all sides, transfer the meat to a big bowl and sprinkle over the flour.

Turn down the heat and melt the butter in the unwashed pan. Sweat the onions, carrots, celery and garlic together until really softened. Scrape the bottom of the pan with a spatula or wooden spoon to make sure you lift up all those yummy beef bits that are stuck on the bottom. You may need to wet the mixture with a little splash of stock if it starts to look too dry. This softening process can take up to 20 minutes so please don't rush it – it will impart much-needed sweetness and flavour to the dish later on.

Add the bouquet garni and put the meat back in the pan. Turn the heat back up, pour in the beer and stock and bring to the boil. Turn the heat

2 × 500ml cans of Guinness

500ml good-quality beef stock

1 tbsp golden syrup

1 tbsp treacle

1 tbsp English mustard

salt and freshly ground
    black pepper

FOR THE TOP

400g all-butter, good-quality
    puff pastry or unsweetened
    shortcrust pastry

1 medium free-range egg, beaten

cook's tip I recommend
serving this with parsnips
– the marriage of parsnips
and the malt from the
Guinness is magic. I like to
sweat them with butter in
small dice over a low heat
until soft, like Pommes
Rissolées, but with that
nutty parsnippy aftertaste.
Turn up the heat at the
end to caramelise them a
tiny bit and scatter with
chopped parsley.

back down to achieve a gentle simmer, place a lid
on the dish and forget about it for 3 hours. Every
once in a while, check that the mixture is only
bubbling very slowly under the lid.

After 3 hours, add the syrup and treacle and
turn up the heat to a slightly more fervent simmer
– still no big bubbles but a bit more than the odd
lazy bubble breaking the surface. This is to reduce
and intensify the sauce. Don't worry if you taste
it at this stage and it's quite bitter – this is normal
and it will right itself soon.

After 4 hours of simmering in total, add the
mustard and adjust the seasoning. You will need
to add quite a bit of salt to get the flavour right
and a certain amount of black pepper, too. Take
off the heat, discard the bouquet garni and leave
the casserole to cool.

You can either assemble the pie once the
casserole has cooled right down (it will interfere
with the pastry if assembled while hot) or keep the
casserole in the fridge or freezer for a later date.

If you're making the pie now, preheat the oven
to 200°C/fan 180°C/gas mark 6.

Pour the filling into the bottom of a deep
ovenproof dish, roughly 20 × 24cm. Roll out the
cold pastry on a clean, floured surface and cut a
piece that fits the top of the dish with a little left
over. Brush the lip of the pie dish with a little
beaten egg and place the pastry lid down on
top of it. Press the edges down with the help of
a fork. Make two steam holes in the middle
of the pie and brush the whole surface with
beaten egg.

Cook in the centre of the preheated oven for
20 minutes for puff and at least 30 minutes
for shortcrust – until the top is golden and the
middle is steaming hot. Serve with parsnips and
something green – a salad, or some steamed,
buttered, long stem broccoli.

Holy Guacamole

A far cry from most of the green smooth pastes you can buy in the supermarket, this version is textured and fragrant. I prefer my guacamole to be mildly hot (I enjoy the way it cools down dishes like beef chilli) – a green tapestry spiked with lime, coriander and sweet red onion. You can add finely diced tomato flesh (no seeds as this makes it watery), as well as more coriander for garnish, if you like a bit of extra colour. Something about avocados is almost noble. They are so nourishing and pure that I think it's a shame to overload this recipe with too many weird and wonderful flavours: they're not needed when the avos are in peak condition and just want to be themselves.

Serves 6

juice of 1 lime (if it's dry, you may need to up this to 1½ but taste it and see)

3 ripe Hass avocados, stoned and cut into small cubes

1 whole red chilli, very finely chopped with seeds left in or out, depending on how hot you like it

1 garlic clove, peeled and minced

1 small red onion, peeled and very finely chopped

1 tsp salt (add more if needed – the lime means you'll need more than you think)

a small bunch coriander, finely chopped

cook's tip This keeps in the fridge for 24 hours max covered in clingfilm (only garnish at the last minute) but is best served within a couple of hours of making.

Put the lime juice in a bowl and add the diced avocados, chilli, garlic and red onion. Give it a good stir with a fork, making sure not to break up the avocado too much.

Add the salt, three-quarters of the coriander and mix again. Taste and season with more salt if needed. Serve sprinkled with the remaining coriander.

Bowl o' Red – *for Matt*

This recipe hails from Texas but the simplicity of the method reminds me of some of the best French or Belgian casseroles. 'Chilli', as it's also known, is a textural masterpiece and therefore the cut of meat you use is crucial. I tried to make it with brisket, which is the traditional cut of choice in Texas, and, despite coaxing and cajoling, it lacked silk and generosity, even after hours over a slow fire. For consistently succulent and surrendered results, I recommend using diced shin. If you're lucky enough to have access to beef cheeks, tackle the butcher to the ground to get them. Some versions of this recipe call for ground meat and, if you feel like trying that, there's a note at the end of this recipe to guide you through the process.

I wouldn't be doing my job properly if I didn't mention the other ingredient that can take this dish to the next level: the chillies. Buying whole dried chillies and pounding them yourself will give you a totally different flavour to using ready-ground and also means you can hand pick the variety of chilli, too.

Makes enough for 6 hungry mountain men

1 or 2 whole Mexican and/or Californian dried chillies, such as guajillo or pasilla

30g butter

3 tbsp sunflower oil

1.2kg beef shin or cheeks, cut into 4cm cubes

2 tbsp cornflour

5 large garlic cloves, peeled and minced

1½ tsp cumin seeds

a pinch salt

1 large onion, peeled and finely chopped

1 × 400g can of peeled tomatoes (organic are sweetest)

2 tbsp strong coffee

400ml beef stock

1 × 400g can of kidney beans, drained of water but not rinsed

1 tbsp cider vinegar

1 tbsp soft brown sugar

Toast the chillies in a large frying pan over a low heat until they start to smoke and your nose tingles with the heat. Open the windows and make sure you don't do this with children around – it's too potent for little noses. If you have a cold when you do this, guess what? Cold's now gone. Blasted out. Put the toasted chillies in a bowl and cover with a little boiling water, soaking them for about 15 minutes while you get the rest of the ingredients ready.

Melt half the fat (butter and oil) in a large casserole over a high heat and fry off half the beef cubes until they have a deep tan on all sides. It's important not to crowd the pan or you won't get a good colour, hence doing it in two batches. Once all the beef is coloured, set aside in a bowl and sprinkle the cornflour over the browned meat pieces. Toss to distribute the flour evenly.

Drain the water and pound the softened, toasted chillies in a mortar and pestle along with the garlic, cumin seeds and salt until you have as close to a paste as you can get.

Using the same pan (don't clean it yet, Matt), add the onion, chilli, cumin and garlic paste. Reduce the heat and stir with a wooden spoon

TO SERVE

sour cream

lots of chopped fresh coriander

a lovely big green salad for afterwards – go for crunchy leaves like Bibb, Little Gem or even, dare I say it, Iceberg – and serve it with a simple dressing of lime juice, olive oil, finely chopped shallots and plenty of salt

plain tortilla chips (no funky flavours here, please)

homemade Guacamole (see page 83) or chopped avocado tossed in fresh lime juice

1 red onion, peeled and finely chopped

lime wedges

cook's tip This recipe freezes like a dream and you can easily double the quantities and save half for later.

I'm going to say this in a whisper in case anyone in Texas can hear me: if you can't be bothered to do that whole chilli bit at the beginning, buy chilli flakes and start the recipe with the browning of the meat. Add the flakes in small quantities until the heat is right for you. It won't be a proper Bowl o' Red, but sometimes life's too short for toasting and soaking chillies.

until the onion has absorbed all the browned bits of beef from the bottom of the pan and has become see-through.

Add the beef to the pan, along with any resting juices, the tomatoes, coffee and stock. Bring up to a simmer with the lid on, then reduce the heat so that the liquid in the pot barely bubbles. Cook over this low temperature for about 2 hours, making sure to give the mixture a stir and a scrape to avoid burning on the bottom. If you're using a non-cast iron saucepan, check the mixture every 15 minutes as it will want very much to stick and burn.

After 2 hours, add the kidney beans and taste the sauce. Now's the time to add the vinegar and sugar. I like to add about half of each, taste and then decide whether or not to add the rest. Add a pinch or two more salt if it needs it now, too.

Cook for a further hour with no lid – you're looking for a gentle bubbling on the surface of the liquid. Remember to stir to avoid catching.

The chilli is ready after 3 hours total cooking time. Serve in a large bowl (or individual ones), topped with a dollop of sour cream and some chopped coriander, alongside a big green salad, tortilla chips, homemade guacamole, finely chopped red onion and a wedge of lime.

NOTE ON HOW TO MAKE THIS WITH GROUND MEAT:

Please make sure (again) that you use ground shin (with around 15% fat), rather than chuck or brisket, which won't give you the depth of flavour or the melting texture in the finished dish (see I'm Not Mincing My Words on page 130). Proceed with the recipe in the same way as above, including cooking times. Only difference: no need to brown the meat as thoroughly – a light tan is fine.

Ossobucco

This is comfort food at its surrendered, silky best. It's important to ask for veal bones that come from the hind leg since they have more meat and collagen than the front ones. As with all comfort food when it's really tender, time is the key ingredient, after good-quality meat. Gremolata (which is a finely chopped mixture of herbs and lemon zest) is traditionally served with this dish and I like the fresh liveliness of it as a contrast to all that velvet. As for serving it, you can't beat some creamy polenta or mashed potatoes. It's not strictly traditional but I also love ossobucco with a pile of fresh egg pappardelle. Lastly, this recipe works best with bones that are roughly the width of a cork. And make sure that yours contain the all-important bone marrow. This will give the sauce its satin. It's worth noting that many, if not most, Milanese versions include tomatoes but I prefer it without.

Serves 4

4 veal shanks (roughly 300g each)

3 tbsp olive oil

1 small onion, peeled and diced

1 garlic clove, peeled and
    finely chopped

1 medium carrot, peeled
    and very finely chopped

1 stick celery, washed,
    topped, tailed and very
    finely chopped

2 bay leaves

1 strip of lemon peel, scraped
    of any pith

1 cinnamon stick (optional)

a pinch salt

1 tbsp plain flour

200ml dry Italian white wine

200ml good-quality chicken or
    vegetable stock

FOR THE GREMOLATA

½ tsp finely grated lemon zest

¼ tsp minced garlic

1 tbsp finely chopped parsley

½ tsp olive oil

½ tsp fresh lemon juice

a tiny pinch salt

Preheat the oven to 170°C/fan 150°C/gas mark 3.

Place the bones in an ovenproof pan over a medium heat and brown in the olive oil until golden on all sides, then remove and set aside.

Turn down the heat and cook the onion, garlic, carrot, celery, bay, lemon peel, cinnamon (if using) and a pinch of salt until the vegetables are softened and the onion is translucent. Sprinkle over the flour and mix well so that all the vegetables are lightly coated. Cook for a further 2 minutes so that the flour has absorbed the vegetable juices.

Next, add the wine and stock, and stir to loosen any flour clumps that might have formed in the bottom of the pan.

Return the bones to the pan, along with any juices, and cover with a lid.

Place on a rack (not an oven tray) in the middle of the preheated oven and cook for 2 hours.

Combine the gremolata ingredients and scatter over the top of the ossobucco before serving with fresh pappardelle, mashed potatoes or creamy polenta.

the veal deal

Traditional veal calves are bred solely to provide the food industry with veal. The meat has a very pale colour and a delicate flavour, more akin to chicken than beef. This is due to the fact that the calves are mostly fed on milk and tend not to be allowed outside, which prevents them from supplementing their diet and changing the colour and flavour of the meat. They are killed as young as 8 months and the conditions in which they live their short lives sparked a number of anti-veal protests in the 80s.

what is the alternative?

There are cows bred for milk (they are built differently and tend to have rather boney, square cut back ends) and there are cows bred for meat. It's possible to eat dairy meat but it in no way compares to meat from a breed that is designed for beef production, in terms of quality of texture and flavour, because of their brand and marbling, amongst other things. By definition, in order to produce milk, a dairy cow has to have a calf. When that calf is born female, she goes back into the system and will be raised to be a dairy cow herself. When the calf is male, however, it is to all intents and purposes redundant. The male dairy bull calves are not worth growing for meat and they certainly won't ever produce any milk… These animals are 'recycled' into what is known as Rose Veal. As far as ethics go, 'outdoor-reared rose is probably the gold-standard welfare choice'[1] and, as a whole, it has been endorsed by the RSPCA's Freedom Food scheme.

The name Rose Veal refers to the pinkier colour of the meat, which occurs because their diet does not consist only of milk or milk replacement products, like most traditional veal calves. They are slaughtered comparatively later at between 12–18 months and, in terms of flavour and texture, Rose Veal is denser than its paler counterpart and has a more robust flavour, less strong than beef, but going in that direction.

I don't, as a rule, like to eat baby animals. I don't enjoy the flavour, which tends to be mild and, in my view, slightly insipid; but, more than that, I don't like eating animals that have a potential for longer lives. I don't like the thought of eating very young creatures; it doesn't sit right with me. This having been said, as someone who consumes dairy products, I appreciate that eating Rose Veal is the responsible thing to do – that calf may not have been born if my consumption of milk didn't exist. So if you do seek it out, just make sure you buy British Rose Veal and get your butcher to confirm the provenance. Pete Hannan of The Meat Merchant says that it's a misnomer to call Rose Veal veal – it should be called baby beef.

1 Xanthe Clay, *Daily Telegraph*, 20 April 2014

Veal Kidneys with Madeira and Mustard Sauce

Most people who think they hate kidneys (the taste, the smell, the name) haven't tried veal kidneys. I'm not a huge fan of lamb kidneys and I flat out don't like pig kidneys. Too strong, too *kidney*. The thing is, though, that veal kidneys are delicate and squeaky and totally out of this world. They're easy to cook, highly nutritious and very addictive (I regularly get cravings for them). My favourite way to cook them is to barbecue them so that they are charred on the outside and pink in the middle, but they also fare well in a frying pan or under the grill. High heat and not for long is the way to go here. Madeira and mustard sauce is a traditional French accompaniment but, when you love them as much as I do, a dollop of Dijon on the side and a good crunch of salt is the simplest way to enjoy them.

Serves 2

1 veal kidney 'bundle' (roughly 400g), prepared by the butcher

a little olive oil

a little flat-leaf parsley, roughly chopped, to garnish

FOR THE MADEIRA AND MUSTARD SAUCE

25g butter

2 shallots, peeled, topped, tailed and very finely chopped

50ml Madeira

2 tbsp full-fat crème fraîche

1 tbsp Dijon mustard

plenty of salt and freshly ground black pepper

cook's tip You can make the sauce ahead in a small saucepan and you should definitely do so if you are cooking on a barbecue – prepare it while the charcoal is heating up and wait until you see white ash before cooking the kidneys.

Place the frying pan over a high heat and have all the ingredients for the sauce ready to go.

Brush a small amount of olive oil over the meat to prevent sticking and fry until golden on one side and starting to go brown around the edges. Flip over and repeat on the other side. The total cooking time shouldn't be more than 5 minutes. Set aside while you make the sauce.

Using the same pan, turn down the heat and melt the butter until foaming. Add the shallots and cook until they have softened and become translucent. Stir in the Madeira and turn down the heat even further. Cook gently for 15 minutes – the texture of the shallots should be faintly jammy. Don't worry about the kidneys cooling, you will heat them up briefly in the sauce before serving.

Finally, turn the heat back up and add the crème fraîche and mustard and cook for 2 minutes until very hot. Take off the heat and season with salt and black pepper. Add the kidneys and mix to warm through.

Serve straight away with a little chopped parsley sprinkled over the top. This is wonderful with mashed or sautéed potatoes and followed by a sprightly green salad (see page 5).

Wiener Schnitzel

Thinly cut and breaded slices of meat are fairly common (goujons, chicken nuggets, veal Milanese) but it's the delicate and slightly wrinkled, crispy texture of this dish that makes it special to me. For something that's fried, it's surprisingly light. The knack, I have found from testing this recipe a number of times, is to use tenderloin of veal and cut it on the bias before maletting it very thinly. The next best option is to use a boneless chop because it will be cut against the grain. The trouble with escalopes is that they tend to be cut in the same direction as the muscle fibre and therefore don't react as cooperatively to the pounding. Shaking the pan during the cooking will also help to deliver the desired wrinkled breadcrumb shell. Done well, this is a thing of beauty. I like to serve it with a squeeze of lemon and Tartare Sauce (see page 95), even though it isn't strictly traditional. A lot of recipes call for pork. I personally prefer veal but if you do want to use pork, opt for tenderloin cut on the bias, too. It's by far the best cut for tender results.

Serves 2

300g rose veal tenderloin, cut on the bias in two even-sized pieces

6 tbsp plain flour, seasoned generously with salt and pepper

2 medium free-range eggs, beaten with a fork

100g dried white breadcrumbs (avoid the tanned, very, very fine stuff, if you can)

100ml sunflower oil

25g unsalted butter

lemon wedges, to serve

freshly ground black pepper

cook's tip If you are making more than two, I suggest you heat the oven to 170°C/fan 150°C/gas mark 3 at the start of the recipe and keep the first schnitzels warm while you make the others.

Place the first piece of tenderloin between two sheets of clingfilm, leaving plenty of space around. Bash gently all over with a meat mallet or a rolling pin until the meat has quadrupled in surface area and is now no more than 0.5cm thin all over. Repeat with the other piece.

Dredge both sides of each schnitzel in the flour, then dip in the egg and finally in the breadcrumbs. I find it helpful to have all three of these items on separate plates before starting the recipe.

Place half the oil and butter in a very large frying pan over a medium high heat. When the butter is foaming, add the first schnitzel. After a minute or so, shake the pan so that the fat from below comes over the top. Repeat until the first side is cooked (roughly 2 minutes), then flip over and do the same on the other side. This process shouldn't take more than about 4 minutes in total.

When the first schnitzel is golden and cooked, take it out of the pan and place it on kitchen paper while you cook the other one.

Serve straight away with a lemon wedge, some Tartare Sauce (see page 95) and plenty of freshly ground black pepper.

Roasted Bone Marrow with Salade Folle and Crisp Capers

This is one of the recipes that might seem scary to someone who has never had it or cooked it before; it shouldn't be. Roasting bone marrow is very straightforward and the whole recipe can be made in less than 30 minutes. This is alternative 'fast food'. Plus, bone marrow *is* silk. Once you develop a taste for it, like I have, you will seek it out wherever you can. The big daddy of bone marrow recipes is, of course, Fergus Henderson's Bone Marrow and Parsley Salad and it's been a staple on the menu at St John for over 20 years. I love the capers he has going on but prefer to roast them alongside the bones because some of the vinegar evaporates and they become crunchy as they dry out. I like pairing the richness of the bone marrow with a fresh and lively *salade folle* (this is a herb salad with a sharp vinegar dressing that is often served with foie gras). All those intensified, crispy capers and plenty of fresh herbs help balance out the satin richness of the marrow.

Serves 2

4 small to medium veal shin
    bones (roughly 150g each) –
    ask the butcher for marrow
    bones

salt flakes and freshly ground
    black pepper

4 heaped tbsp capers, drained
    of brine by wringing out in
    your fingers

FOR THE DRESSING

2 tsp red wine vinegar

2 tsp fresh lemon juice

2 tbsp olive oil

1 tsp Dijon mustard

a pinch Sumac (optional)

1 tbsp very finely
    chopped shallot

Preheat the oven to 250°C/fan 230°C/gas mark 9.

Make the dressing by whisking together the vinegar, lemon juice, olive oil, mustard and Sumac, if using, in the bottom of a bowl. Add the shallot and let it marinate while the bones are cooking. Make sure to have all the salad ingredients ready to go so that you can toss the salad as soon as the bones are out of the oven.

Place the bones on a baking sheet with a lip, to catch any escapee marrow during cooking. Salt the extremities of the bones where the marrow shows with a fine layer of salt flakes – this will help to form a crust during roasting.

Place the bones on their ends vertically on the baking tray, with the capers scattered around them. Cook in the middle of the preheated oven for 20 minutes, until soft to the touch but not running out everywhere.

Remove from the oven and rescue the crisped capers. Add them to the salad bowl.

Ingredients continue   *Recipe continues*

Roasted Bone Marrow with Salade Folle and Crisp Capers *continued*

FOR THE SALAD

2 heads Little Gem lettuce,
  washed and cut in half
  lengthways through the
  spine (oak leaf Little Gem is
  the best if you can find it)

a generous pinch whole parsley
  leaves, rinsed

a generous pinch whole
  coriander leaves, rinsed

a generous pinch dill leaves,
  ripped from the stalk

a generous pinch tarragon
  leaves, ripped from the stalk

a generous pinch whole mint
  leaves, rinsed

TO SERVE

medium-sliced sourdough
  bread, toasted so it's a bit
  scorched around the edges

a little Dijon mustard, spread
  on the toast very thinly

Pile the salad in a bowl, add the dressing and toss to coat lightly. The salad should be barely glistening with dressing – it's important not to overdress it.

Serve the bone marrow immediately. Smear a very small amount of mustard on to the toast (or not, if you like it just as it is) and scoop out the marrow on to the toast (I tend to use the tip of a knife or a teeny tiny teaspoon). Serve the salad on the side and season with black pepper. Yum. And I never say that.

Tartare Sauce

This sauce is great with breaded meat (and fish, of course!) because it has tang and herby notes that cut through fried food. For this reason, I like my tartare to be on the astringent side and include a generous dose of vinegar, as well as sour cornichons and capers. Avoid the large pickles and opt for the smaller, more viciously vinegary types. This sauce keeps in the fridge for as long as homemade mayonnaise would, which is to say about 3 days. Apart from eating with meat, this is *amazing* as a dipping sauce for chips, especially if you're like me and enjoy a side of mayonnaise and ketchup to go with hot and crispy French fries.

Serves 6

1 large free-range egg yolk

1 tsp Dijon mustard

2 tsp white wine vinegar

150ml sunflower oil (or peanut oil – avoid anything with too much flavour, like olive)

a few hits of Tabasco, to taste

1 tbsp finely chopped fresh tarragon leaves

1 tbsp finely chopped fresh parsley (curly is slightly better as it will chop up smaller)

2 tbsp finely chopped chives

1 tbsp capers, drained of brine and roughly chopped

1 tbsp very finely chopped cornichons

salt and black pepper, to taste

Put the egg yolk, mustard and 1 teaspoon of the vinegar in a bowl. Whisk for a couple of minutes until starting to become pale (either with a balloon whisk or an electric whisk), then add the oil in a slow trickle. Once it has emulsified, you can be a bit more heavy handed with the oil, but remember that this is basically a mayonnaise so be gentle to avoid splitting.

Once all the oil has gone in, add the remaining vinegar, as well as all the other ingredients. Taste and season, adding more Tabasco, if required.

Cover with clingfilm and chill until needed.

Calves' Liver with Shallot and Sage Crisps

Calves' liver is the mildest of the livers out there and is really something of a treat at home. This way of cooking it is my favourite because sage has a unique way of complementing the delicate flavour of liver. Mustard is also lovely with all liver and I prefer Dijon here. This recipe is extremely quick and easy and has a pleasant whiff of Italian life about it; just make sure that you eat the liver on the day you buy it. As with all offal, freshness and quality are imperative. I don't find that liver is a practical option if you're cooking for more than 4 people, as it's a last-minute kind of dish (like steak), so this is perfect for a weeknight dinner when you fancy something a little different.

Serves 2

30g butter

4 shallots, peeled and very finely sliced

300g calves' liver, cut into medium/thin slices (definitely not thick)

1 tbsp plain flour

salt and freshly ground black pepper

1 tbsp olive oil

10 sage leaves, plucked from the stem

a squeeze of fresh lemon juice

Place half the butter in a large (preferably non-stick) frying pan over a medium heat. Add the shallots and leave to cook until they are see-through and gold-tinged (this takes around 15 minutes), then remove from the pan and set aside.

Meanwhile, dust the liver with the flour on both sides and season well with salt and lots of black pepper. Shake off any excess flour before frying.

Using the same frying pan, turn up the heat, add the olive oil and, when hot, sprinkle in the sage leaves. Fry until crispy on one side, then turn and fry on the other. Remove from the pan and set aside.

Add the remaining butter to the frying pan and, when it is foaming, add the liver. Cook for a couple of minutes on each side, depending on how thick the slices are and how pink you like your liver. I like mine pale pink but not raw. For a slice roughly 1cm thick, I tend to cook it for 2 minutes on each side in a hot pan.

Serve with the golden shallots, the crispy sage leaves and any brown butter left in the pan. Squeeze a dash of lemon over the lot and remember to season again with salt and pepper. The best accompaniment for this dish, in my view, is wilted Swiss chard and mashed potatoes.

Homemade Mincemeat

I attempted to make mincemeat about seven years ago without following a recipe ('How hard can it be to mix together some dried fruit and booze?') and it was an unmitigated disaster. The mixture tasted of raw alcohol and the fruit was clumpy and tough. A kitchen disaster will set you back a long time, I find, and I hadn't attempted making mince pies since, until I started writing this book. Turns out: mincemeat is a doddle to make, given the right recipe, and *so* much more wonderful than the cloying, suspiciously viscous stuff you can buy in jars. The suet is absolutely essential since it mellows out the highly concentrated flavours of both the dried fruit and the rum, as well as providing a protective coating that enables it to last for months once jarred. Combined with homemade shortcrust pastry (Katie Stewart's recipe made with ground almonds is awesome), you will make some of the most aromatic and wonderful mince pies around. Half the fun of Christmas is in the preparation. Enjoy, enjoy, enjoy.

Makes 1kg – enough for roughly 45 mince pies

1 large green apple, peeled, cored and grated

finely grated zest and juice of 1 lemon

100g shredded beef suet

250g combination of raisins, sultanas and currants

50g dates, finely chopped

finely grated zest and juice of 1 orange

100g candied peel, finely chopped

50g crystallised ginger, finely chopped

120g light muscovado sugar

1 tsp each ground ginger, cinnamon and allspice

¼ tsp ground cloves

¼ whole fresh nutmeg, finely grated

small pinch salt

3 tbsp rum

150g golden syrup

Mix the apple and lemon juice in a large bowl and toss to coat. Add all the remaining ingredients except the rum and golden syrup. Mix thoroughly before setting aside overnight to macerate.

Preheat the oven to 120°C/fan 100°C/gas mark ½.

Transfer the mixture to a large ovenproof dish or saucepan with a lid and cook at the bottom of the oven for 2 hours, stirring occasionally.

Remove from the oven, add the rum and golden syrup and stir the mixture, which will be decidedly glossy at this point.

Transfer into sterilised jars and place a piece of wax paper on the top before sealing with a lid. Once cooled, use for mince pies or keep for up to 6 months.

cook's tip I've made this with both fresh suet and the dried stuff you can buy in the baking aisle (Atora is the brand name) and I found I got more consistent results from the second version so avoid the fresh stuff. I nearly never say that but sometimes it's just true!

To sterilise the jars, wash them thoroughly with hot soapy water then rinse and place in a hot oven (around 180°C/fan 160°C/gas mark 4) for 5 minutes with the lids sitting alongside them. Remove from the oven and cool for 5 minutes before filling (otherwise the mincemeat will scorch). It's also important to sterilise the spoon you use to fill the jars (otherwise you may as well not bother with the whole jar business!). To sterilise the spoon, simply dip in freshly boiled water.

To make mince pies, use a butter-based shortcrust pastry recipe with a little bit of sugar in it. Roll and cut the pastry to fill a 12-hole muffin tray with a thin layer of pastry in each hole. Fill each case with mincemeat and use the pastry trimmings to make stars or hearts to go on top. Brush the pastry with beaten egg and bake in an oven preheated to 180°C/fan 160°C/gas mark 4 until the pastry is golden, around 25 minutes.

lamb

Slow-cooked Shoulder of Lamb – 3 Ways

This recipe appeals to me because it's so versatile and simple. Here is the basic method for making melt-in-the-mouth whole shoulder of lamb and you can flavour it however you want. I'm including Middle Eastern, French and Sicilian flavourings for you to choose from but the method is the same. The French flavouring is the one I would go to naturally, but Sicilian in the summer and Middle Eastern in the winter are also good. The succulent lamb will never fail and the leftovers are spectacular in a Lamb Shawarma Kebab (see page 135) or other pitta sandwiches.

Serves 6 with leftovers

FOR THE LAMB

1 whole shoulder of lamb
  (weighing roughly 1.8kg)

2 onions, peeled and each
  cut into 6

8 garlic cloves, bashed
  and peeled

250ml vegetable stock
  (if cooking the French lamb,
  replace 100ml stock with
  white wine)

sea salt (flakes)

MIDDLE EASTERN FLAVOURING

2 tbsp ground cumin

½ tsp chilli powder (mild or
  hot, up to you)

2 tbsp harissa paste

2 garlic cloves, peeled and
  minced to a paste

1 tbsp olive oil

FRENCH FLAVOURING

2 bay leaves

5 sprigs of rosemary

a few sprigs of thyme

2 tbsp Dijon mustard

For the **Middle Eastern** lamb, mix together all the flavouring ingredients and slather over the meat. Prick the surface of the skin with a skewer to create little holes, into which the marinade will penetrate. Marinate overnight in an airtight Ziploc bag – 2 hours is the absolute minimum.

Preheat the oven to 160°C/fan 140°C/gas mark 3.

Arrange the onions and garlic at the bottom of a roasting dish that is big enough to hold the whole shoulder. Pour over the stock.

For the **French** lamb, remember to replace 100ml of the stock with wine, and add the herbs to the roasting dish. Rub the mustard all over the lamb and rest the meat on top of the herbs and veg.

For the **Sicilian** lamb, mix all the flavouring ingredients together to form a loose paste. Cut incisions into the thickest, fleshiest parts of the shoulder. Using your fingers, push the mixture into the flesh hither and thither. You will have about half the mixture left. Save this for later – you can toss the salad in it before serving.

In every case, sprinkle a generous layer of salt flakes over the meat to help create a crust. Place the shoulder on top of the vegetables in the pan and cook at the bottom of the oven for exactly 3 hours, basting occasionally.

The meat is ready when it pulls away from the bone if tugged at with a fork. Remember to serve it well moistened with the cooking juices and to remove any herbs with stalks.

SICILIAN FLAVOURING

4 anchovy fillets, very
finely chopped

finely grated zest of ½
unwaxed lemon

1 tbsp capers, drained of brine
and very finely chopped

2 tbsp very finely chopped fresh
parsley leaves

1 tbsp olive oil

1 garlic clove, peeled
and minced

2 sun-dried tomatoes, very
finely chopped

5 pitted black or green olives,
very finely chopped

Serve the Middle Eastern lamb with couscous, studded with toasted pine nuts, pomegranate seeds, finely grated lemon zest, finely cut spring onions and finely chopped coriander.

Serve the French lamb with mashed potatoes and sautéed green beans.

Serve the Sicilian lamb with new potatoes tossed in olive oil (you can roast them in the top of the same oven for an hour). Make a salad of finely chopped red onions, basil and cherry tomatoes. Add 1 teaspoon of Dijon mustard to the remaining marinade and loosen with olive oil and lemon juice to taste. Toss the tomato salad in this dressing and grate over a little extra lemon zest.

Lamb Stock

This is a lovely, richly flavoured lamb stock. I tend to find that lamb stock is overlooked. Everyone talks about chicken but lamb is so fragrant that it works beautifully as a stock, particularly a brown one, as here. It's a good idea to skim the fat off the top of this stock once it's cold – you can expect a generous layer on top of the liquid. Save the fat to use as dripping – it's particularly fabulous for roasting potatoes to go with lamb or for sweating the vegetables in Roast Carrot and Cardamom Soup on the facing page. You could also use it instead of butter or another fat when making couscous or any other Middle Eastern recipe.

Makes roughly 3 litres

2kg raw lamb bones (any kind)

2 tbsp olive oil

2 carrots, peeled, topped, tailed and cut in half lengthways

8 shallots, halved (skins left on)

1 medium red onion, peeled and quartered

1 handful of parsley stalks

5 sprigs of thyme

2 bay leaves

1 sprig of rosemary

5 garlic cloves, bashed

2 sticks celery, washed and roughly chopped

1 tbsp tomato purée

10 black peppercorns

4 litres water

Preheat the oven to 200°C/fan 180°C/gas mark 6.

Toss the bones in the olive oil and put on a baking tray, along with 1 carrot and the shallots. Roast in the middle of the oven for 45 minutes, until golden brown.

Place the roasted bones with all the other ingredients in a large stockpot and bring to the boil. Reduce the heat and simmer very gently for 2 hours. You will need to remove any scum or foam that appears on the surface.

Strain into a clean bowl and set aside to cool.

Once cold, skim the fat from the top and keep separately. Refrigerate or freeze until needed.

cook's tip The stock keeps fresh for up to 5 days in the fridge or may be frozen for up to 3 months (providing that the bones were fresh at the beginning) – see Stock Up on page 6.

Roast Carrot and Cardamom Soup with Garlic and Parsley Croutons

The reason I love roasted carrot soup is twofold. Firstly, it's the laziest way I know to deal with cooking carrots and onions for soup since you just roast them and then blitz them – no chopping faff involved. Secondly, roasting really adds caramel and depth of flavour to a soup like this. My favourite stock for this recipe is a brown lamb stock (see facing page) but you could use any richly flavoured brown stock.

Serves 4–6

FOR THE SOUP

1kg organic carrots, peeled, topped and tailed

3 medium onions, peeled and halved

2 tbsp olive oil or lamb dripping

4cm fresh ginger, peeled and finely grated – discard the very stringy centre

2 garlic cloves, peeled and very finely grated

8 cardamom pods, crushed in a mortar and pestle with husks removed

2 litres lamb stock (see facing page)

plenty of salt

a pinch cayenne pepper

FOR THE CROUTONS

1 tbsp olive oil

300g stale bread (baguette is my favourite), cut into 1cm cubes

30g unsalted butter or – even better – lamb dripping

1 tsp very finely chopped garlic

1 tbsp very finely chopped parsley

Preheat the oven to 200°C/fan 180°C/gas mark 6.

Line an oven tray with a layer of tin foil, then a layer of baking paper.

Toss the carrots and onions in the olive oil then place in the tray and roast in the middle of the oven for 1 hour until golden and cooked through.

Whilst the vegetables roast, make the croutons by adding the olive oil and the bread to a large frying pan over a medium heat. Toast until golden.

Add the butter or dripping, garlic and parsley to the pan and turn off the heat. Toss to coat in the melted butter and aromatics. Once the fat has been absorbed and the croutons are evenly coated, set aside until the soup is ready for its garnish.

To finish the soup, place the ginger, garlic and cardamom pods in the bowl of a blender with a little of the stock and whizz until you have a paste. Add the cooked carrots and onions and remaining stock and blend to a soup-like consistency.

Season thoroughly with salt and a pinch of cayenne pepper before serving piping hot topped with the croutons.

cook's tip I think you can really tell the difference between organic carrots and regular ones, which is why I recommend using them here. Also, this soup is particularly well suited to freezing. Simply freeze in batches and thaw in an airtight container in a basin of cold water. Reheat as needed.

Gourmet Lamb Burger

By and large, I'm not a fan of the word 'gourmet' – it's a bit like 'luxury': if you have to say it, it's probably not accurate. (The word 'gourmandise', on the other hand, I love – it means something between peckish and 'I really shouldn't but I'm going to anyway'.) Saying that, this lamb burger is fabulous. I've pushed the boat right out when it comes to jamming it with an array of lamb-loving flavours.

Makes 6

800g minced lamb shoulder (roughly 20% fat)

2 tbsp very finely chopped fresh mint

2 tbsp very finely chopped fresh parsley

2 tbsp very finely chopped fresh dill

1 tbsp Dijon mustard

½ tsp dried chilli flakes

4 sun-dried tomatoes, very finely chopped

salt and freshly ground black pepper

FOR THE GARLIC AND CORIANDER MAYONNAISE

8 tbsp mayonnaise

1 tbsp fresh lemon or lime juice

2 garlic cloves, peeled and minced

1 small handful of coriander, finely chopped

a pinch smoked paprika

salt and freshly ground pepper

TO ASSEMBLE

12 thin slices halloumi

6 good-quality burger buns

1 handful of baby spinach leaves

1 red onion, peeled and finely sliced

Mix the minced lamb with the herbs, mustard, chilli, sun-dried tomatoes and seasoning. Form into 6 burgers without pressing the meat too much in your hands. Chill in the fridge until ready to cook.

Make the mayonnaise by combining all the ingredients in a bowl – taste and adjust the seasoning.

Fry or grill the burgers over a really high heat until done how you like them (if you're barbecuing, you want the coals to be white hot). I tend to find that 4 minutes on each side is about right. Cook the halloumi at the same time as the meat – in the same pan if you can.

To assemble, put a generous dollop of mayonnaise on the base of a bun, then add a burger, some spinach leaves (the contact with the hot meat will wilt them perfectly), the onion rings and grilled cheese. Finish off with another dollop of mayonnaise. If you have any tomato and sweet chilli jam, this is definitely a good time to use it.

cook's tip These burgers are also really good with a homemade Flatbread (see page 118) instead of a shop-bought bun.

Shoe String Fries with Rosemary

If you've never made fries before and you want to get them right first time, this recipe is for you. In a nice way, these fries are totally novice proof – you don't need to blanch them first and chill them, or faff around with frying them more than once, as with most French fries. And they're always crispy. In France, they are called *pommes paille*, which translates as 'straw fries'. This is because they arrive piled high on your plate and look exactly like golden, crispy strands of straw. You can't beat them paired with a juicy steak or Steak Tartare (see page 60).

Serves 4

500g Maris Piper potatoes, scrubbed

1 litre sunflower oil

5 sprigs of rosemary, leaves stripped from the stalks

plenty of salt and black pepper

cook's tip Either eat straight away or else simply reheat in a hot oven for a couple of minutes before serving. The good news is that, unlike regular fries, Shoe String Fries tend to keep their crisp so are suitable to make ahead.

You will need either a mandolin or a potato peeler with little teeth, since you're looking for Julienne strips (like long matchsticks). Once all the potato is sitting in a pile of strips, take a third of them and wrap them in kitchen paper. Press hard, to absorb any potato water. Repeat with the other thirds until they are all done.

Place the oil in a large saucepan over a high heat – the level of the oil should be no more than one-quarter of the way up the pan. When the fat is very hot (you can gauge this by dropping in a few strands – when they bubble like mad and turn golden within 20 seconds it is hot enough), grab a small handful and untangle it to loosen the strands. You want a clump that isn't too packed together so that when the strands fry they form a messy bundle and end up as a ledge in the hot oil. This makes them easy to flip over. Drop them carefully into the oil and cook for about 90 seconds until golden. Flip with the help of tongs or two forks and do the same on the other side.

Once golden, remove with a slotted spoon and drain on kitchen paper. Repeat until all the fries are cooked. It's important to wait a few minutes before you repeat the process, though, as the fat needs to heat up again.

Finish by frying the rosemary leaves for 20 seconds and then removing with a slotted spoon.

Toss the fries with salt, pepper and the rosemary leaves before serving.

Kibbeh

These little meatballs are everywhere in Middle Eastern cuisine. I grew to love them when we lived in Qatar, back in the 80s, and I love them still. Apart from the nostalgia they impart, I adore the business of mixing lamb with fragrant winter spices like cinnamon and cumin. What's more, the mince can be made up from cheaper, deeply flavoured cuts of meat. And if those aren't enough good reasons to make Kibbeh at home, then there's something festive and wonderful about a feast of little bits and bobs to be shared. I serve Kibbeh with homemade Hummous (see page 116), Roasted Garlic and Aubergine Moutabel (see page 115), Tabbouleh (see page 114), Griddled Flatbread (see page 118), olives and I also sometimes add a Roast Carrot and Cardamom Soup (see page 105) – although not strictly a Middle Eastern recipe, this soup is an invention of mine that adds a little extra colour and some vegetables to the table.

Serves 4 as part of a mezze or 2 as the main event

FOR THE STUFFING

2 tbsp olive oil

300g minced lamb breast (or shoulder if breast isn't available – 20% fat at least is important here)

salt and white pepper

1 large white onion, peeled and very finely chopped

2 garlic cloves, peeled and finely minced

30g pine nuts, toasted

2 tsp ground cinnamon

1 tsp ground allspice

½ tsp ground cumin

finely grated zest of 1 unwaxed lemon

Make the stuffing first – place 1 tablespoon of the olive oil in a large frying pan over a medium heat and fry the lamb. It doesn't need to be browned but it does need to be cooked through. Taste and season well with salt and pepper. Remove from the pan with a slotted spoon and set aside in a large bowl.

In the same pan over a medium heat, sweat the onion and garlic with the remaining tablespoon of olive oil until translucent. Once cooked, add to the lamb and stir in the pine nuts, spices and lemon zest. Mix well and set aside whilst you make the outer shells.

Put the bulgur wheat in a large bowl and pour over the hot vegetable stock. Let it stand for 15 minutes, covered with clingfilm, whilst you put together the rest of the shell mixture.

In a food processor, blitz together the remaining raw meat, allspice, onion and a pinch of salt until smooth. Check that all the liquid has been absorbed by the bulgur wheat. If it hasn't all been absorbed, strain off whatever is left over and discard it. Add the soaked bulgur wheat to the food processor and blitz again briefly. Transfer to a clean bowl.

Take a snooker-ball-sized amount of the shell mixture and flatten it into an oval, concave shape

FOR THE OUTER SHELLS

200g fine bulgur wheat

500ml vegetable stock, boiling

400g minced lamb breast (use the same as above)

1 tsp ground allspice

1 onion, peeled and very finely chopped

a pinch salt

TO FINISH

a little plain flour, to help seal the kibbeh once made

1 litre sunflower oil

cook's tip If you have any kibbeh left over, simply freeze them once cooked and cooled in plastic freezer bags. To use, simply defrost and reheat in a hot oven until piping hot in the middle.

A note on why I'm using breast of lamb for this recipe – because of the high fat content this is a really moist cut of meat that also has tons of flavour. If you can't find breast, choose shoulder. The kibbeh will fall apart if you use any cuts of lamb (like leg) that are leaner than that.

in the palm of your hand. Next take roughly 1 teaspoon of the filling and place it in the middle of the shell. Cradle the filled shell in your hands and pinch the sides together, going from top to bottom. Fill in the middle gap with more shell mixture. You will naturally end up with a rugby ball shaped kibbeh that looks a bit like a fat, baby banana. Set aside on a plate, whilst you repeat this with the rest of the mixture. Once all the kibbeh are made, sprinkle a little flour over each one and pat the outsides gently in the palm of your hands until they are smooth.

Place in the freezer for 10 minutes to chill whilst you heat up the oil.

Heat the oil in a medium-sized, deep pan over a very high heat until it shimmers (this means it's very hot), then cook the kibbeh in batches of 2 or 3 for about 6 minutes, or until they are a rich, golden brown colour. Remove with a slotted spoon and drain on kitchen paper.

Serve warm. If you don't want to serve them straight away, simply reheat in a hot oven for 5–10 minutes until piping hot.

Tabbouleh

I love this parsley salad and as an accompaniment to lamb it is wonderful (especially with Middle Eastern-style recipes, such as Kibbeh on page 110). The citrus, slightly peppery quality that it brings to the table cuts through the richest of meat dishes and the spices deliver a warming, aromatic hit that is welcome in an otherwise cold dish. I sometimes serve it on the side of lamb burgers or an Indian-style leg of lamb. Where there's lamb, tabbouleh belongs. And if you are used to tabbouleh where there are a few sparse flecks of green in what is otherwise a bowl of bulgur wheat, you're in for a treat. Tabbouleh is firstly a herb salad, with a little wheat thrown in, not the other way around.

Serves 4

50g fine bulgur wheat

10 cherry tomatoes, cut into quarters

4 spring onions, very finely chopped

1 tsp ground allspice

¼ tsp ground cloves

juice of 1 lemon

300g flat-leaf parsley, leaves removed from the stems and very finely chopped

50g fresh mint, leaves removed from the stems and very finely chopped

4 tbsp olive oil

salt and freshly ground black pepper

seeds from ½ pomegranate

Tip the bulgur wheat into a bowl and pour over enough boiling water to cover it plus a little bit more. Cover with clingfilm and a clean tea towel. Set aside for 15 minutes, until all the liquid has been absorbed. If there is any liquid left in the bowl after this time, just drain it away. You want the wheat to be puffed up but not too wet.

Combine the tomatoes (and any juices that come from chopping them), spring onions, spices and lemon juice in a bowl and add the bulgur wheat. Cover with a clean tea towel and set aside for 10 minutes.

Stir in the parsley, mint and olive oil and toss to combine. Season generously with salt and black pepper.

Scatter over the pomegranate seeds just before serving (see page 112). The tabbouleh will keep in the fridge for a day or two.

cook's tip It took me about 20 minutes to chop the herbs for this (otherwise very straightforward) recipe so make sure you factor in the time that takes.

Roasted Garlic and Aubergine Moutabel

Wow, I love this stuff. For those of you who don't know this dip, it's a smoky, silkier version of hummous and is made from my sister's favourite vegetable: aubergine. It's smokiest when made over a gas ring but in my kitchen I only have electric so I'll show you how to use an oven to achieve a similar effect. Moutabel goes blissfully with all Lebanese food and especially lamb and beef dishes.

Serves 6 as part of a mezze

2 medium aubergines
3 garlic bulbs, tops cut off to reveal the cloves
120ml olive oil
salt flakes
juice of 1 lemon
3 tbsp tahini paste
a pinch cayenne pepper
1 tsp cumin seeds, toasted
a few roughly chopped coriander leaves
pomegranate seeds, to garnish (optional)

cook's tip If you are lucky enough to have a gas ring, then place the aubergine directly on to the open flame, turning it every 5 minutes with tongs until it's totally charred all over. I know it sounds crazy but you'll see that the skin holds the fruit together until the last moment. Once charred, proceed as detailed right. As for the garlic, simply turn the oven to 180°C/fan 160°C/gas mark 4 instead of using the grill and cook for 45 minutes until soft and roasted.

Preheat the grill to its highest setting.

Place the aubergines on a baking sheet near the top of the oven.

Place the garlic on a separate baking sheet and drizzle with 1 tablespoon of the olive oil and a sprinkling of salt. Wrap each bulb in tin foil with the cut side facing upwards. Slide the garlic into the bottom of the oven – make sure they are underneath the aubergines' baking sheet to prevent them getting too much direct heat – they should roast, rather than grill.

Grill the aubergines for 10 minutes on each side (assuming that an aubergine has 3 sides), until charred and smoky all over. Remove them from the oven and wrap in a double layer of foil. Place back in the hot oven and cook for a further 20 minutes wrapped in foil, or until they feel floppy and squishy to the touch. Take both the aubergines and the garlic out of the oven and let them cool off for a further 10 minutes inside the foil.

Being careful not to burn yourself, unwrap the aubergines and cut in half. Scoop the smoky flesh into the bowl of a blender. Pop each garlic clove out of its shell and add to the blender. Pour in the lemon juice, the remaining olive oil, tahini and plenty of salt and blend to a paste. Taste and season again if necessary.

Sprinkle with the cayenne, cumin, coriander and pomegranate seeds before serving at room temperature (see page 112).

Hummous

Everyone makes hummous in a different way and I've been honing this recipe for about six years (and enjoying the testing/tasting process enormously!). I like a goodly hit of garlic in my hummous and a texture that is not as chunky as some of the versions I've tried. I also love a sprinkling of za'atar over the top and some extra toasted sesame seeds to give it a bit of crunch. A great all-round dip, this is particularly well suited to lamb dishes. I urge you to try it with the cinnamon, which is my own personal addition, but you can leave it out or replace it with ground cumin, if you like. I prefer to use canned or jarred chickpeas, rather than soaking dried ones, which can give a drier result. Do try to get organic chickpeas – you can taste the difference and they tend not to have any weird, artificial ingredients but use only onion and salt in their preserving.

Serves 8 as part of a mezze

2 × 400g can of organic chickpeas, drained of water and rinsed under the tap (or 520g drained weight)

4 garlic cloves, peeled and roughly chopped

6 tbsp tahini paste

juice of 1 large lemon

200ml virgin olive oil

1 tsp ground cinnamon, + extra to garnish

1½ tsp salt

sprinkling of za'atar (this is a mixture of toasted sesame seeds, thyme leaves and Sumac and is available in some supermarkets or Middle Eastern shops) or toasted sesame seeds

Take out 2 tablespoons of the drained chickpeas and set aside.

Blitz together the remaining chickpeas, garlic, tahini and lemon juice in a food processor until you have a paste. Add 150ml of the olive oil along with the cinnamon and whizz until combined. Taste and adjust the seasoning with salt and a little extra cinnamon if needed.

Tip into a bowl, scatter over the remaining chickpeas, drizzle the rest of the olive oil and sprinkle with the za'atar and a pinch of cinnamon. This will keep covered in clingfilm in the fridge for up to 4 days.

cook's tip If you have any leftover hummous that isn't quite enough to save for another day, simply add some lemon juice, shake it, then some olive oil and salt and shake it again for a lovely, creamy dressing to go over a spinach leaf salad. If you have some leftover lamb as well, then bingo – add this to the salad, along with some chopped red onion, roasted butternut squash and toasted pine nuts for a fabulous leftover dinner.

You can also use wholegrain tahini for a slightly nuttier version.

Griddled Flatbread

This recipe is easy to make, even if you've never made bread of any kind before. There is something totally wonderful about a kebab served with homemade flatbread, and it will turn leftovers and even shop-bought dips into a feast. Eat the flatbreads quickly after they are cooked, though – they benefit from not hanging around too long. This recipe is perfect for the Rue des Rosiers Lamb Shawarma on page 135. You can also cook them straight on the barbecue – which makes this a wonderful, versatile little number to have up one's sleeve.

Makes 4

130ml hot water

7g active dry yeast

1 tbsp olive oil

230g plain flour

1 tsp caster sugar

1 tsp salt

cook's tip Make sure the water is hot but not boiling – you should be able to dip your finger in. Yeast is a delicate old thing.

Transfer the hot water to a jug and add the yeast. Stir to dissolve, then let it sit for 2 minutes until there are no lumps. Add the olive oil.

In a medium bowl, combine the flour, sugar and salt and form a well in the centre. Slowly add the yeast and oil water, incorporating as you go.

Knead the dough for 10 minutes, then place a sheet of clingfilm and a clean towel over the top and leave to rise in a warm place for an hour, or overnight in the fridge.

Once the dough has proved (don't be surprised if it doesn't rise much), turn it out on to a lightly floured surface and knead for a minute. Divide into 4 pieces and flatten each one with your hands until roughly the size of a side plate.

Cook in a dry griddle or frying pan over a medium heat, or on a barbecue on the edge of the grate, where the heat is not at its hottest. Once puffed and golden on one side, flip over and repeat with the uncooked side. It shouldn't take more than about 2 minutes on each side. Serve straight away (see page 117).

Cumin, Chilli and Garlic Chuanr Rub

Chuanr (pronounced 'chwar') is one of the most common street foods in the old part of Beijing, although I believe it originated from Xinjiang in the northwest of China. If you're wandering around the hutongs that surround the Lama Temple, it's almost impossible not to stumble across tiny little street stands where men are tending to charcoal troughs lined with skewers of delectable smelling meat and sprinkling over some version of this rub. They are then repeatedly dusted with the rub before being handed out to eat there and then, preferably with a very cold beer. When at home, I like to use either lamb breast or tiny little lamb cutlets from the first few chops of the best end, like they do in Spain (called *chuletas de cordero*) – applying the rub before, during and after cooking. Either way, Chuanr is at its best when the meat is barbecued over a flame. The original version I had in China is good and spicy but you can use more or less chilli powder – it's up to you.

Makes enough for about 20 skewers or cutlets and serves 4

3 tbsp cumin seeds

2 tsp ground chilli powder (this will make it really hot)

2 tsp garlic granules

2 tsp fennel seeds

2 tsp salt

500g lamb breast, cut into 2cm cubes (leave the fat on), or 20 tiny cutlets

cook's tip If you don't have a barbecue, use a pan that is very hot but not smoking, or you can cook them under a hot grill to achieve a similar effect.

Light your barbecue. The correct temperature to cook the meat is white ash, i.e. once the flames have all but died down. This is much hotter than a flame and will not scorch the rub on the meat.

Using a spice grinder or a mortar and pestle, blitz all the spices with the salt to a fine powder.

If using breast, spear the lamb on to pre-soaked bamboo skewers, threading them closely together so that they form a stripy lollipop, alternating layers of fat and meat. If using cutlets, the bone acts as a natural skewer. Sprinkle most of the rub liberally over the meat and set aside to marinate for at least 15 minutes. The salt will tenderise the meat during this time.

When the coals are white hot, place the marinated skewers and/or cutlets on the barbecue to cook. You're looking for the meat to get a lovely charred aspect and the fat to become translucent. Turn the meat frequently and sprinkle with more rub when you turn to cook the other side. I usually cook the breast meat for about 8–10 minutes and the cutlets for about 4–6 minutes, depending on their size and how done I want them. Eat straight away.

Tandoori Butterflied Leg of Lamb

I've made this recipe as kebabs cooked on skewers from lamb leg or lamb steak squares, which is good, too. In both cases, the advantage of marinating in yoghurt is that it produces the most incredibly tender meat imaginable. I often fill a flatbread with the leftover lamb the next day (see page 118) and, even when reheated, the meat retains its extraordinary tenderness. This recipe is perfectly suited to the barbecue since you will get a lovely chargrilled effect from its contact with the open fire, a bit like cooking it in a tandoor oven. The fact that the outside is charred and blackened is totally what you're hoping for, so don't worry about the burnt look – the middle stays beautiful and pink.

Serves 8

2kg leg of lamb, boned and butterflied

sunflower oil

1 handful of coriander, roughly torn

3 spring onions, very finely sliced

FOR THE MARINADE

10 cloves

2 tsp whole black peppercorns

3 tsp coriander seeds

3 tsp cumin seeds

10 large garlic cloves, peeled and minced

generous piece of fresh ginger (roughly 10cm), peeled and finely grated with all the stringy bits discarded

2 tbsp sunflower oil

2 tsp ground cinnamon

2 × 125ml pots full-fat natural yoghurt

1 tsp chilli powder, or more if you like it hot

2 tsp salt

Heat the spices for the marinade in a dry frying pan over a medium heat until they smell fragrant. Blitz them in the bowl of a food processor (or mortar and pestle), along with the garlic, ginger and oil. When you have a uniform paste, add the ground cinnamon, yoghurt, chilli powder and salt and mix again. Pour this mixture into a large Ziploc bag and add the lamb to marinate. Twenty-four hours is ideal but at least 2 hours is fine.

To make the raita, wring the grated cucumber juice out using a clean tea towel over a bowl. Please don't throw it away! Cucumber juice is fantastic (see Cook's Tip on page 122). Mix the cucumber together with all the remaining raita ingredients, apart from the olive oil and cayenne, and season to taste with salt and pepper. Top with a few extra mint leaves, drizzle with the olive oil and a pinch of cayenne. Cover with clingfilm and set aside until the lamb is ready.

To cook the lamb, preheat the grill to very hot, or heat the barbecue to white ash stage. Remove some but not all of the marinade from the outside of the meat and brush over a little sunflower oil to prevent sticking. Place on or under the grill and cook for about 15–20 minutes, depending on the thickness of your meat. Remember to turn it

Ingredients continue   *Recipe continues*

Tandoori Butterflied Leg of Lamb *continued*

FOR THE RAITA

½ large cucumber, grated

3 × 125ml pots natural yoghurt

1 handful of mint leaves,
    finely chopped

1 garlic clove, peeled and
    minced

1 tsp olive oil

a pinch cayenne pepper

plenty of salt and pepper

over halfway. To check the doneness, make a cut in the middle of the meat and take a peek. It's very important to rest this cut of meat and I like to give it a good 15 minutes.

To serve, cut across the grain into thin slices about 1cm thick and scatter with chopped coriander and spring onions. I like to serve it with the raita and either some steamed basmati rice (scented with bay and cardamom and a little butter) or else with Flatbread (see page 118).

cook's tip Best ever cucumber martini. If you're looking for the perfect cocktail to have before serving this, mix the cucumber juice (½ cucumber will give you roughly 1 martini's worth of juice) with a little vodka or gin, an ice cube, a couple of sprigs of mint and give it a good shake to cool the cocktail right down. Serve straight up, garnished with a cucumber slice… If you want to sweeten it, add a little elderflower cordial before shaking.

the marinade brigade

what

1 Wine/vinegar – see White Wine, Garlic and Fresh Herb Marinade on page 30

2 Lactic acid (yoghurt) – see Tandoori Butterflied Leg of Lamb on page 121

3 Salt – see Smoked Baby Back Ribs on page 148

4 Citric acid (lemon, lime, pineapple, tomatoes, papaya and kiwi) – see Hawaiian Pineapple Pork on page 159

5 Cornstarch – see Pork and Vegetable Chinese Stir Fry on page 166

When you use any of the above marinades, you're altering the muscle structure in a similar way to when meat is cooked with heat. Think of what happens to a raw egg yolk when you sprinkle it with salt, or what happens to fish in a ceviche. In the case of the yolk, little white flecks appear where the salt has effectively 'burned' the yolk. In the case of ceviche, the fish goes from clear to opaque as it 'cooks' in the lime juice. It wasn't until I spent time in China that I appreciated what an amazing marinating ingredient cornflour is, though. When frying small meat strips over very high heat (which is what happens in a stir fry), the cornflour not only coats and protects the meat from drying out or shrinking, it also seals in the juices and provides a crispy edge. As if that wasn't enough, cornflour also goes on to form the base for the sauce. As far as I'm concerned, it's the most surprising of all the marinades and one of the most exciting to use.

how

Think ahead – marinating implies at least 2 hours (except in the case of cornflour).

If marinating meat for more than 2 hours, do so in the fridge and not at room tempature.

Marinate meat in airtight environments to increase the effect on the flavour and the texture. A Ziploc is ideal. Adding oil to the marinades also produces good results on this front because oil effectively 'seals' the marinade on to the meat.

Don't use the marinade for other food once it's done its job because it will contain raw meat bacteria.

Don't marinate in aluminium, foil or copper because they could react with the marinade. I prefer to use large plastic food bags or glass bowls.

It's worth remembering that when using sugar or honey, there is a risk of the meat scorching, if you intend to grill or cook it over a high heat. The only way to manage this is to keep an eye on it and turn down the heat if necessary.

why

As well as flavouring the meat, the point of a marinade is to tenderise it. It does this by altering the muscle structure and breaking down the fibres. Marinades alter the structure so dramatically that it's important to respect marinating times: left too long, a delicately textured meat can turn into something gummy. Marinating for tenderising purposes isn't effective on tougher cuts that contain high amounts of connective tissue. You are better off extracting the silk from these cuts through long and slow cooking. You can use rubs and marinades for flavour only in these cases.

Moussaka

Moussaka is one of my favourite food words and I'm genuinely considering it for a dog's name down the line. My mum used to make us Moussaka when we were growing up and I have a particularly nostalgic relationship with this comforting dish. I did a fair bit of research and testing before I was happy with this recipe, which is made from lamb (some recipes call for beef, veal, pork or a mixture) and includes lots of lovely Greek and Turkish spices like cinnamon and oregano. It's very important to use a cut of lamb that is naturally moist when it cooks, so shoulder is definitely preferable to leg. And with all dishes of this kind, it always tastes better the day after so try and make it a day ahead as the flavours and textures will have softened and developed beautifully. If you've never had Moussaka, it's like a Greek lasagne, where the pasta is replaced with a layer of soft aubergines and topped with nutmeg-infused Béchamel that is enriched with egg yolk so that it goes a beautiful crème brûlée colour during cooking.

Serves 8

FOR THE FILLING

2 medium onions, peeled and very finely diced

6 garlic cloves, peeled and minced

4 tbsp olive oil

2 bay leaves

2 tsp ground cinnamon

3 tbsp finely chopped parsley

2 tsp dried oregano

½ tsp dried or fresh thyme leaves

1.2kg minced lamb shoulder or you can mix breast and leg but make sure there is around 20% fat to muscle content

200ml dry white wine

400g passata (or 1 × 400g can of cherry tomatoes – organic tend to be sweeter)

2 tbsp tomato purée

Preheat the oven to 200°C/fan 180°C/gas mark 6.

Fry off the onions and garlic in half the olive oil in a very large saucepan over a gentle heat until translucent, then add the bay, cinnamon, parsley, oregano and thyme.

Push the onion and seasonings to one side and fry off the lamb on the other side of the pan, keeping the side of the pan with the meat over the heat. When the meat is cooked through and there are no more pink bits, add the wine and reduce over a medium heat until it's almost all gone.

Add the passata and the tomato purée and repeat the reduction until there is no more liquid in the pan, only moisture from the meat and the vegetables themselves. When there is no more visible liquid in the pan, turn down the heat even further and cook with the lid on for 30 minutes. Check once in a while that nothing is sticking to the bottom and burning. The total time for cooking the meat should be around 1 hour and should not be rushed. Even if the mince is cooked after about 15 minutes, it won't be tender unless it

Ingredients continue

Recipe continues

Moussaka *continued*

2 large aubergines (weighing roughly 400g each), cut into 1cm circles

salt

3 medium waxy potatoes, such as Desirée, peeled and cut into wafer thin discs (with a potato peeler)

FOR THE BÉCHAMEL

100g butter

50g plain flour

700ml full-fat milk

1 organic free-range egg, + 1 egg yolk, beaten together

½ tsp ground nutmeg

cook's tip You can also freeze the leftovers – just remember to let it thaw at room temperature overnight before reheating.

I prefer a wider, shallower dish for Moussaka, so that all the layers are thinner. This also means that the Béchamel layer is more spread out.

cooks slowly for a bit longer. The good news is that you can get on with cooking the aubergines and making the Béchamel during this time.

Brush the aubergines with a little olive oil and sprinkle with a little salt on both sides. Lay flat on a baking sheet and avoid overlapping them. Bake in the preheated oven for 15 minutes each side, until softened and golden. Once cooked, remove from the oven and set aside.

To make the Béchamel, melt the butter in a medium pan until foaming. Gradually add the flour and cook for at least 2 minutes over a medium heat, making sure to move the mixture around the bottom of the pan. Very gradually add the milk, whisking with a balloon whisk as you go. Run a spatula along the bottom and sides of the pan to prevent catching. This will also help avoid lumps. Once you have a thickened mixture, take off the heat and add the beaten eggs. Continue to whisk for another minute. Season generously with nutmeg. Set aside.

Once all three components are ready (meat, aubergines and Béchamel) start assembling the Moussaka. Place half the meat in the bottom of a large ovenproof dish and then top with the aubergines. Spoon the rest of the meat on top and then finish with a layer of raw sliced potatoes and top with a generous layer of Béchamel. The heat from the top and bottom will cook the potatoes in the oven.

You can either cool this down and use it later or freeze it at this point. If you want to have it now, cook it in a hot oven (180°C/fan 160°C/gas mark 4) for 30 minutes before serving. If the top isn't as golden as you were hoping for, stand by whilst you grill it for 5 minutes or less.

Sweet and Surrendered Aubergine Stir Fry

This dish is one that I picked up in Beijing from a lovely local lady who takes care of my nephew and niece – little Otto and Eloise – out there. This recipe uses a traditional Chinese stir-fry method for aubergine, is foolproof and will always ensure that you end up with silky, soft and surrendered aubergine – without it swimming in oil or becoming bitter. Aubergine can be a little daunting to cook if you're not in the habit of eating and preparing it. I love it and cook it like this often. Aubergine is often misunderstood and this is a great method to get the best out of its texture and sweetness.

Serves 6

3 medium aubergines (roughly 1kg total), washed, topped, tailed and cut into 2.5cm cubes

3 tbsp sunflower oil

1 medium onion, peeled and very finely chopped (or 4 spring onions)

2.5cm fresh ginger, peeled and very finely chopped

chilli flakes, to taste (I like mine quite spicy so I use ½ tsp)

4 large garlic cloves, peeled and finely chopped

3 tbsp soy sauce

salt flakes, to taste

1 tbsp sesame seeds, toasted

1 small bunch coriander, chopped

Place the cubed aubergines in a steamer above a pan of boiling water. Put the lid on and steam for 10 minutes until softened. (If you have a microwave, place the aubergine cubes in a bowl, cover with clingfilm and blitz on high for about 8 minutes.)

Place the oil in a wok or large frying pan over a high heat. If you don't have a pan that's big enough to comfortably fit all the aubergine, I strongly suggest doing this in two batches. When the oil is shimmering, add the softened aubergine and the onion. Cook for about 5 minutes, giving it a stir, until the aubergine has started to colour on all sides and the onion is slightly softened.

Add the ginger, chilli and garlic. Toss the ingredients over the high heat for a couple of minutes, keeping them all on the move to prevent the garlic from burning.

Add the soy sauce and stir again. When the soy has reduced to nothing, add a little salt to taste. You'll know it's ready when the aubergine is tanned all over and the onion and garlic have softened.

Serve with the sesame seeds and chopped coriander scattered over the top.

i'm not mincing my words

Do you ever wonder what the word 'mince' refers to on the supermarket shelves? I do. The thing is, if your butcher isn't grinding the cut that you want to order, it's anybody's guess what's gone into the lump of mince inside that shiny, clear packet. This is why I make my own.

why make your own mince?

I also don't understand why so many recipes just state 'mince', without giving you the cut. What goes into mince is a big deal! It will affect the outcome of the dish, both in terms of flavour and texture. When I'm making burgers, I want a mixture of grassy, lean muscle meat for flavour, and rich, deeply savoury, fatty meat to provide juiciness and the ability to become crusty and charred on the outside edges. However, this is not what I look for if I'm making a Bolognese, for example, when I want the meat to impart silk and be able to cook for over 4 hours getting deeper and richer as it goes.

I'm shocked to see that supermarkets are allowed to sell meat that is simply called 'ground beef' or 'minced pork' without going into any more detail. You can be sure that if the mince is a specific cut of meat it will say so on the packet. If you don't want to make your own mince, then your butcher should be happy enough to grind up whatever you ask him or her to, given a little notice.

There are a few rules to remember when making mince and they have more to do with food hygiene than anything else:

Wash your hands meticulously with hot soapy water before you start and also any work surfaces, boards and any utensils you plan on using.

● Repeat this painstaking washing ritual after you've handled the mince.

● Wash the blade and bowl of your food processor or meat grinder until impeccably clean. I use boiling water for this because all bacteria present will definitely be killed off.

● If using a food processor rather than a meat grinder (I only have a food processor at home), put the meat into the freezer for 30 minutes before grinding. This will help give you a fine grind – any fat or sinew would otherwise be difficult to cut. It slips at room temperature and that can give you a slightly paste-like texture, rather than a good clean chop. Do the same with the blade and the bowl of the food processor, for the same reason.

● Make the mince right before you plan on cooking it. The shorter the amount of time the mince has sat in mince form, the less likely it is that bacterial content will have had time to develop.

● Avoid handling the mince too much. By which I mean, if you're making hamburgers, then bring the mince together to form a slightly rounder hamburger shape and, once it holds together, put it down. Don't fiddle and prod it.

● Cook the mince well. I know it has become unacceptable to most 'food types' to enjoy any kind of beef cooked more than pink but, as far as I'm concerned, pink is the rarest I like my hamburgers. I don't like them cooked all the way through but I don't eat them rare either.

The reason why it's so important to treat mince with caution is because bacteria only live on the surface of the meat. A steak only has two big surfaces and a side that surrounds them; mince, meanwhile, is made up of millions of tiny pieces. This multiplies the risk of bacterial presence exponentially.

Here is a rough guide of what cuts I use and for what purposes:

beef

For slow-cooking dishes like ragu Bolognese, cottage pie or lasagne, I like to use minced shin because it has a deeper flavour, and plenty of sinew and collagen that turns to silk over time and slow cooking. If you use chuck (this is what most ready-made mince is), I think it's essential to add a cut with deep flavour and crucially fat, like meat from the short rib area. The most basic rule is to have 15–20 per cent fat content for anything that you plan on slow cooking.

lamb and pork

These two can be lumped together because they behave in a similar way. Broadly speaking, use shoulder, neck and breast for slow cooking and leg, mixed with shoulder meat, for burgers or meatballs. The reason I add shoulder meat here is because anything less than 20 per cent fat will be dry.

chicken and game

Only use leg meat. I hardly ever use minced chicken unless I'm making Asian meatballs or dumplings and, even then, I'd always prefer pork. When mincing chicken, make sure you include the skin, since that will help with the texture and will give you a little extra fat which translates into moisture and flavour.

Shepherd's Pie — for Christopher (and all the Sheppards)

I don't think that it's possible to write a book honouring meat recipes without including Shepherd's Pie. It spells out Sunday night to me in warming, sloppy, rich, comforting letters. With a side of minted peas, please. I like a ratio of about two-thirds mince to one-third mash, and I include butternut squash because it sweetens the mash and gives it extra goodness. Depending on how sweet the squash is, I like to add a little maple syrup because the contrast of the sweet mash and the super savoury mince is amazing – you can, of course, leave it out if you think the mash is sweet enough. The main issue I have with Shepherd's Pie, and mince recipes in general, is that the meat lacks depth of flavour. In poncy chef terms, it lacks *umami*. The mushrooms and mushroom ketchup give this recipe a savoury boost, as do the sun-dried tomatoes. It's imperative to use a higher fat cut of meat, like shoulder, for this recipe – leg is just too dry. And it's important to slow cook the mince to coax out its tenderness. With Shepherd's Pie there's nowhere to hide – it's just mince and potatoes – so the mince needs to be outrageous.

Serves 6–8

FOR THE MINCE

2 tbsp olive oil

1.2kg minced lamb shoulder (around 20% fat content)

20g unsalted butter

1 large onion, peeled and very finely diced

1 large carrot, peeled, topped, tailed and very finely diced

2 sticks celery, washed, topped, tailed and very finely chopped

100g chestnut mushrooms, very finely chopped

2 tbsp mushroom ketchup (or 1 tbsp Worcestershire sauce)

300ml medium-bodied red wine (most Bordeaux reds are too heavy for this)

In a very large saucepan, heat half the olive oil and add half of the minced lamb. Cook over a medium to high heat. Once golden, remove and set aside (including any juice). Repeat with the other half of the oil and lamb. Remove and set aside with the rest.

Add the butter to the pan, turn the heat down and cook the onion, carrot and celery until soft, around 10 minutes. Add the mushrooms to the pan and cook for a further 10 minutes. If you add them at the same time as the carrot and celery, they will soak up all the liquid and leave the other vegetables parched and disgruntled.

Once the mushrooms have had 10 minutes to cook and absorb the surrounding flavours, it's time to add the mushroom ketchup (give it a stir), then the reserved meat, red wine, stock, sun-dried tomatoes and star anise.

Bring to a boil over a medium heat then reduce to simmer very slowly for an hour with the lid on. After an hour, take off the lid and simmer for a further 30 minutes, stirring occasionally to

200ml homemade lamb stock (use vegetable stock if you don't have homemade lamb stock)

150g sun-dried tomatoes, very finely chopped

1 star anise

salt, if needed

FOR THE MASH

½ quantity Nena's Mashed Potatoes (see page 25) (or 900g good-quality mash)

50g freshly grated Parmesan

1 tbsp maple syrup (optional)

FOR THE TOP

100g breadcrumbs

30g freshly grated Parmesan

cook's tip If you are making this ahead, allow the meat to cool and divide into freezer-to-oven friendly containers. Top with mash before cooking and serving.

prevent catching. By the end of the total cooking time (1 hour 30 minutes), there should be no liquid left in the bottom of the pan and the flavour of the mince should be very concentrated. Beware not to add salt until the very last minute because the mushroom ketchup is very salty.

During the mince cooking time, make the mash according to the recipe. Once made, add the grated Parmesan and maple syrup (if using).

If eating today, preheat the oven to 200°C/fan 180°C/gas mark 6.

Once the meat has had its cooking time, adjust the seasoning and remove the star anise. Pour into an ovenproof dish, top with the mash and sprinkle with a mixture of breadcrumbs and Parmesan.

Cook in the middle of the hot oven for 30 minutes until bubbling.

Serve with peas, a little knob of salted butter that will melt as they stand and plenty of chopped fresh mint.

Rue des Rosiers Lamb Shawarma Kebab

For about two years, I lived right next to the Rue des Rosiers, at the heart of the Jewish quarter in Paris, which is where you can find the best falafel and shawarma kebabs I've tasted anywhere. Making this with homemade Flatbread (see page 118) is the ultimate version but even a toasted pitta will give you a good idea of why I consider this to be one of my favourite lunches on the go. If you're making ahead, wrap in baking paper then tin foil and blitz in a hot oven for 10 minutes before taking it with you. It should keep warm for about 30 minutes. I should also mention that the pink salad of lightly pickled cabbage and onion is absolutely amazing and goes well with all Middle Eastern inspired food and chargrilled meats. I like to make a biggish batch and eat it for up to three days after making. It benefits from being made a little ahead – a couple of hours is perfect but anything from 30 minutes is fine.

Serves 4

FOR THE PINK SALAD

5 tbsp fresh lemon juice

1 tsp salt

2 tbsp caster sugar

1 tbsp olive oil

400g red cabbage, very
    finely shredded

1 large onion or 2 small ones,
    peeled and very finely sliced

1 small handful fresh parsley,
    finely chopped

1 small handful fresh coriander,
    finely chopped

FOR THE SHAWARMA

8 slices aubergine, fried with
    3 tbsp sunflower oil until soft

500g cooked lamb (see pages 119
    or 121), very thinly sliced

4 Flatbreads (see page 118), cut
    in half lengthways, or good-
    quality pitta, toasted briefly

4 tbsp Hummous (see page 116)

4 tbsp rose harissa paste, or less
    if you want it mild

1 tbsp raita (optional)

Make the pink salad by combining the lemon juice with the salt and sugar. Stir until dissolved before mixing in the olive oil. Add the cabbage and onion and toss to coat thoroughly. Set aside for 30 minutes before adding the parsley and coriander.

Preheat the oven to 200°C/fan 180°C/gas mark 6.

Place the aubergine and the lamb in the oven, covered in foil, until warmed through.

Smear the inside of each flatbread with 1 tablespoon of hummous on one side and 1 tablespoon of harissa on the other. Cradle the open flatbread in the palm of your hand and pile in the meat and aubergine, followed by the pink salad. Finally, top with raita (if using) and tuck in. If taking on a picnic, wrap first in baking paper and then in foil. It's meant to be really full! Because of this, I recommend serving with a fork.

cook's tip This is also wonderful made with falafels instead of lamb for a vegetarian version.

If you have any aubergines left over from the recipe on page 129, these work well as an alternative to frying slices – as seen in the picture opposite.

Brain Fritters with Middle Eastern Spices

I realise that the thought of eating brains will be too much for a lot of people. I personally think they are one of the most amazing parts of an animal (whether lamb or veal). For those of you who are unconvinced, I'm going to defer to the master of offal, Fergus Henderson, who describes fried brains as 'biting through crunch into a rich cloud'. In word game terms: brain is plain. The hit of Middle Eastern spice does wonders to bring the fritters to life and honour their extraordinarily tender texture.

Serves 4–6

4 whole lamb brains (weighing
   roughly 200g in total)
enough full-fat milk to cover
   (300ml should be enough)
1 medium onion, peeled and
   roughly chopped
1 bay leaf
1 cinnamon stick
a pinch saffron strands
3 garlic cloves, bashed
   and peeled
¼ tsp salt
20g butter
2 tbsp sunflower oil
1 lime, cut into wedges
roughly chopped parsley, spring
   onions, dill and coriander,
   and a little fresh red chilli
   (optional)

FOR THE BATTER
60g self-raising flour
¼ tsp chilli powder
½ tsp Sumac powder
a pinch saffron
a pinch salt
1 medium free-range egg,
   beaten with a fork until loose
100ml fizzy water

Soak the brains in the milk for an hour. Pat dry.

Place in a medium saucepan and pour in enough water to just cover them (500ml should be enough). Add the onion, bay leaf, cinnamon, saffron, garlic and salt. Bring to the boil, lower the heat and simmer for 5 minutes. Turn off the heat and leave to poach in the hot water for an hour.

Place in the fridge to get really cold and to infuse. Keep refrigerated until you're ready to fry them (no more than 24 hours).

When you're ready, make the batter by combining the flour with the chilli powder, Sumac, saffron and salt. Make a well in the middle and add the egg. Gradually incorporate the wet with the dry ingredients. Loosen with a little fizzy water.

Remove the brains from the water and slice or break into pieces roughly 1cm wide. It doesn't matter if they're uneven. Tip into the batter and mix with your hands to coat them.

Place a large frying pan over a high heat and add the butter and oil. When the fat is hot, drop the fritters into the pan and fry for 4 minutes on each side, or until a golden, crispy outside edge has formed. Transfer to a warm plate to garnish.

Serve piping hot with a wedge of lime squeezed over the top and scatter with plenty of fresh herbs. If using chilli, make sure this goes on last.

offally good

By its very nature, offal is mysterious. Perhaps that's why so many people are reluctant to cook it or eat it. I have always been baffled by the distinction many folk draw between muscle and organ… Why is it that eating kidney or liver is more offensive than eating back or belly?

What's more, the offal on a carcass represents around a quarter of the weight of meat on an animal. This is what they call in Testaccio, the district of Rome that housed its slaughter houses into the 1970s, the *Quinto Quarto*, or fifth quarter. This is a vast percentage that is either going to waste or being turned into dog food! I can understand that a plate of tripe might not be everybody's idea of a good time (it's not mine either) but do try some of the offal recipes in this book because they really are delicious.

Even though the UK (and almost all of the US) is only just reacquainting itself timidly with offal, the majority of the world loves the stuff. I live in France, where it's unusual not to find some kind of offal on the menu. Perhaps it's the memory of grey liver and rubbery kidneys from school dinners that puts so many folks off in the UK. Herein lies the rub: with offal there is a much bigger margin of error. When it's badly sourced or handled, offal can be

awful. It's really unfortunate that these words sound so similar. When done well, I think nothing beats a thinly cut piece of calves' liver or warm, jelly-like bone marrow piled on to sourdough toast (see pages 97 and 93).

There is a wave of brave and visionary chefs here and abroad who are putting offal back on the menu. It didn't use to be unpopular, quite the reverse. Not only has offal been enjoyed since man first hunted animals to eat, but it used to be amongst the most highly prized parts on the carcass. The other thing to remember is that it's very rich in nutrients. Indeed, as Nina Edwards points out in *Offal*, 'Kidneys are particularly rich in zinc and iron. The heart contains taurine, which in turn is good for the heart […] Liver is packed with complete proteins and with iron, needed for haemoglobin […] It also helps in the healing process and increases our resistance to infection.'

In short, offal is nutritious, inexpensive, often fast to cook, full of umami flavour and is, for the most part, delicate in texture. So why are we still turning our noses up at it? The only possible explanation is that we have managed to convince ourselves that it's too much part of the body it once came from. In other words, unlike most other meat cuts, offal actually looks like what it is.

pork

Pork Rillettes

I made a version of this recipe for the first time last Christmas as part of a live cookery segment on France 2. I was surprised how easy it was to make this super Frenchie pâté and the good news is that it keeps for about a week in the fridge. Unlike the industrial stuff you find at the supermarkets, this recipe is not a slick of fat with a few flecks of meat scattered here and there; instead, it's a meat pâté held together with seasoned fat, which is why you should expect it to contain chunks. Serve it at room temperature on some freshly toasted sourdough and be sure to have cornichons and a little dollop of mustard nearby, too.

Makes 1.5kg or roughly 5 jars

10 juniper berries

6 large or 9 small garlic cloves, peeled and finely chopped

1 tsp ground white pepper

1 tsp thyme leaves

½ whole fresh nutmeg, finely grated

1 tbsp olive oil

1kg pork belly, rind removed, cut into 2.5cm cubes

500g pork shoulder, cut into 2.5cm cubes

6 rashers dry-cured smoked bacon, cut into tiny strips

1 onion, peeled and finely chopped

½ tsp ground allspice

¼ tsp ground cloves

2 tsp salt

cook's tip If you're not eating straight away, you can freeze the jars once cooked and cooled. Just remember to always serve at room temperature.

Preheat the oven to 180°C/fan 160°C/gas mark 4. You will need 5 clean and sterilised jam jars.

Crush the juniper, garlic, white pepper, thyme and nutmeg together in a mortar and pestle.

Heat the oil in a large ovenproof casserole and add the belly, shoulder, bacon, onion, allspice, cloves, salt and spices from the mortar. Cover the casserole with a lid and place in the middle of the preheated oven for 4 hours. It's worth giving it a stir halfway through to make sure that nothing is sticking or burning on the bottom.

Remove the casserole from the oven without taking off the lid whilst you sterilise your jars. Dip them in boiling water and then place them in the hot oven beside their lids for 15 minutes.

Meanwhile, shred the meat using two forks and toss in the cooking juices to coat. Taste and adjust the seasoning, if necessary.

Remove the jars from the oven and divide the mixture between them. Close the lids and set aside to cool. Once they reach room temperature, put in the fridge for up to a week.

When you are ready to eat, roughly chop some cornichons to scatter over the top and serve with toasted sourdough and a good grind of black pepper. If you are serving as part of a picnic, pack a rug, take one jar of pâté, one of mustard and one of cornichons, along with a baguette and a bottle of chilled white wine, a knife and a corkscrew, and find the banks of a river…

Pork and Shrimp Vietnamese Spring Rolls with Sweet and Spicy Dipping Sauce

This recipe is inspired by the *nems* I have regularly on a Sunday night at Le Petit Cambodge, here in my neighbourhood. The spring rolls are delicious served hot and wrapped in a lettuce leaf with fresh mint, dipped in the sauce and eaten with crunch and gusto. Definitely not a first date dish! Sauce dripping down your arm… etc. If you want to make them ahead and reheat, replace the shrimp in the mixture with pork. Also make sure they're piping hot before serving.

Serves 4

50g thin vermicelli rice noodles

1 small carrot, peeled, topped, tailed and cut into tiny dice (save 1 tsp for the sauce)

1 very small handful of chopped coriander leaves

1 small handful of chopped Thai (or regular) basil leaves

½ fennel bulb, roughly chopped

2 garlic cloves, peeled and roughly chopped

1 small piece of fresh ginger, peeled and roughly chopped

2 whole spring onions, roughly chopped (including the green bit)

1 tbsp sugar

1 tsp salt

plenty of white pepper

1 tsp sesame oil

1 tbsp fish sauce

100g minced pork shoulder

100g headless raw prawns, peeled and roughly chopped

1 litre sunflower oil, for frying

8 large spring roll rice wrappers (you can find dry versions in the Asian food section of most supermarkets)

Ingredients continue

Start by soaking the noodles according to the packet instructions until just cooked. Drain any liquid and roughly snip with scissors so that you end up with a bowl full of short strands. Add the carrot, coriander and basil and set aside.

Make the dipping sauce by combining all the ingredients, plus the reserved carrots, in a jar with a lid and giving it a good shake. Set aside.

In the bowl of a food processor, whizz up the fennel, garlic, ginger and spring onions with the sugar, salt, white pepper, sesame oil and fish sauce. Add the pork and prawns and whizz again until combined. Tip this meat mixture into the bowl with the glass noodles and mix until combined.

Heat the sunflower oil in a medium saucepan, making sure that the oil doesn't come more than one-quarter of the way up the pan.

Meanwhile, wet a spring roll wrapper in a shallow pool of water on a plate so that it is immersed completely. After about 1 minute, it will be soft enough to handle so take it out of the water and place it on another clean plate. Place the next wrapper in the water while you stuff the first. Put a small sausage shape of the meat mixture into the middle of the wrapper and fold over first the top and bottom edges and then roll into a spring roll shape, taking care to stretch out the wrapper so that it's tightly secured.

Recipe continues

Pork and Shrimp Vietnamese Spring Rolls *continued*

FOR THE SWEET AND SPICY DIPPING SAUCE

2 tbsp sweet chilli sauce

4 tbsp fish sauce

5 tbsp freshly squeezed lime juice

5 tbsp caster sugar

2 tbsp water

½ tsp red chilli flakes (or more if you like it hot)

1cm piece of fresh ginger, peeled and very finely minced

1 tsp very finely diced fresh red chilli

1 stalk of lemongrass, bruised and very finely chopped

2 garlic cloves, peeled and very finely minced

TO SERVE

1 lettuce, broken into 8 leaves

a small bunch fresh mint, leaves torn from the stalk

When the oil is shimmering hot, carefully place the spring roll in the hot oil – the slightly wet roll is bound to spit and crackle, this is normal. Cook for 3–5 minutes, depending on how golden it looks and the thickness of the spring roll. I don't recommend cooking in batches of more than 2 or 3 at a time, as this cools the oil down too much. When you remove them from the oil, the meat inside should be cooked through when you bite into it.

Repeat the assembling and frying of the spring rolls until they're all done. Serve wrapped in a large green lettuce leaf with at least 3 leaves of mint per spring roll and the dipping sauce on the side.

cook's tip If you're making these slightly ahead, keep them in a hot oven (around 180°C/fan 160°C/gas mark 4) until needed. If they have lost their crunch, turn up the heat for a few minutes but remember to keep an eye on them. I mention this because deep frying always stinks the house out! And I usually make these ahead for that very reason and open the windows wide.

Pork and Chive Chinese Steamed Dumplings

I love this recipe. I learned how to make these dumplings in China, on one of my many trips out there to visit my sister and her family. They're really easy and tremendous fun. My nephew loves to roll out the dough himself and can eat 9 or 10 without a problem (he's only 3½ years old). Because they can be ready in just over 10 minutes from frozen (freeze the raw dumplings then fry and steam from frozen as below), they're great last-minute fast food. Mostly, though, I make these when I miss my sister and her family, and wish we were all together again.

Makes 24 dumplings

FOR THE FILLING

3 leaves Chinese cabbage (weighing around 130g), or white cabbage or fennel

½ tsp salt

1 tbsp Chinese rice wine vinegar

2 tbsp sunflower oil

350g sausagemeat, or pork shoulder mince

1 garlic clove, peeled and minced

a small bunch chives, very finely chopped

2.5cm piece of fresh ginger, peeled and minced

1 tsp soy sauce

2 tsp caster sugar

½ tsp Chinese 5 spice powder

1 tsp sesame oil

½ tsp ground white pepper

FOR THE DOUGH

250g plain flour

175ml boiling water

FOR THE DIPPING SAUCE

2 tbsp dark soy sauce

2 tbsp black rice wine vinegar (this is milder and sweeter than clear rice wine vinegar)

Very finely chop the cabbage and mix together with the salt and vinegar. Set aside for 20 minutes before adding 1 tablespoon of the sunflower oil, as well as all the other filling ingredients. Mix thoroughly.

To make the dough, tip the flour into a bowl and make a well in the centre. Gradually pour in the boiling water, incorporating it into the flour with a fork as you go. When all the water has gone in, turn out on to a floured surface and knead for 5 minutes until the mixture has come together and is elastic. Cut into quarters and cover with a clean tea towel.

Combine the dipping sauce ingredients in a shallow bowl.

Roll the first quarter of dough into a long sausage shape and cut into 6 pieces. Lightly flour a clean surface and roll each piece into a thin circle roughly 12cm in diameter. Place a heaped tablespoon of the filling in the middle of each circle and fold over the dough to form a half moon. Pinch the edges to seal and sit it on its side, pressing down to make a flat edge (the sealed edge should be facing upwards). Lightly dust a plate with flour and set each dumpling aside and refrigerate while you make the rest.

Once all 24 dumplings are made, heat the remaining tablespoon of oil in a large frying pan. Fry the dumplings on their flat base over a medium heat until golden, about 2 minutes.

Add 200ml of water to the pan and cover with a lid. Steam for 10 minutes or until the dumplings are cooked through – top up with more water if the pan dries out before the dumplings are cooked.

Serve hot with the dipping sauce.

smoking hot

what

I need to get some vocabulary issues out of the way up front: in Europe (and in many other parts of the world, like Australia and some parts of North America) we call it a barbecue when you light a fire and cook meat over the hot embers. In the American South, this cooking method is called grilling and not barbecuing. Brawls have started over much less. Barbecuing in the South is practically a religion and having tasted the smoky, surrendered, silky results, it's not difficult to see why.

Speaking of words, barbecue has an interesting etymology: it's unclear whether it originated from '*barbacoa*', which according to Harold McGee is a West Indian Taíno word that refers to 'a framework of green sticks suspended on corner posts, on which meat, fish, and other foods were laid and cooked in the open oven over fire or coals', or whether it comes from the ancient French expression *barbe à queue*, because you can cook and eat the whole animal from its beard (*barbe*) to its tail (*queue*).

Either way, the Southern obsession for 'barbecue' is legitimate and quite addictive once you get the hang of it. Cooking meat over a slow fire, infused with smoke and steam, and rubbed with spices is a spectacular way to enjoy it. It does, however, require a little bit of forward thinking and a few bits and pieces of equipment.

I wouldn't be doing the business of barbecue justice if I failed to mention dry rubs and wet rubs. Depending on where you go for your barbecue in the US, they will tell you adamantly that it's not 'real' barbecue unless you cook your meat smeared in a wet rub (in other words, sauce). If you travel even just a state over, people will swear blind that dry rub is the only way to go. And I'm not even going to go into the different flavour variations of barbecue sauce. My research for barbecue took me to Memphis and the World Championship Barbecue Cooking Contest. After I'd tried and tasted and taken reams of notes, I concluded that my favourite way of smoking meat is to rub it with a fragrant, spicy, sweet but not too sweet rub the day before (see The Marinade Brigade on page 123), then smear a little homemade Barbecue Sauce (page 155) on the cooked meat right at the end of cooking. This method means that the meat isn't scorched by the sugar in the wet rub but has been infused with tons of flavour from the dry rub. I also find that serving the smoked meat with more barbecue sauce on the side is essential. I mean: who doesn't love a good dunk?

For those of you who are planning to go deep into the subject, you should know that there are four big barbecue hotspots in the American South and they all treat their meat with slightly different flavourings; indeed the meat choice differs as well. Texas is big on brisket and spicy flavour; Kansas City is known for 'burnt ends' whether pork or beef; in Memphis they tend to cook mostly pork; and in both North and South Carolina they are known for a slightly more vinegar based sauce to accompany the meat, which also tends to be mostly pork. I tread very carefully when saying this, though, because, like all things barbecue, it's a serious business in these parts and I am making generalisations.

when and who

'When the enslaved African-Americans got pigs of their own, necessity inspired nose-to-tail consumption, as well as the ingenuity to create dishes to make the pig's least pleasant parts edible. Those culinary skills were vital after the end of slavery, when the men and women needed to go into business for themselves. "An African-American man – or woman, but less often women – could literally dig a hole in the ground on the side of the road, lay on some bed springs, shovel in coals and start a business," says John T. Edge, author and director of the Southern Foodways Alliance. "It was the food truck of the 19th century."' [1]

how to turn your backyard barbecue into a smoker

The two pitfalls of smoked barbecue are: 1) the heat won't be enough to cook the meat all the way through, especially if you're dealing with a thick piece of meat like a pork shoulder and 2) the meat can dry out when it's smoked.

If you're serious about smoking your meat, either choose a barbecue that has a temperature gauge or invest in a good-quality thermometer that you can leave in the meat during cooking (see page xiii).

The risk of the meat drying out is also why it's important to include a tray with either juice or water in it, as this will create steam and help keep the meat silky and soft throughout the long cooking process. Wood chips are another important aspect of smoking because they will flavour the smoke-infused meat. For a slightly spicy taste, go for mesquite and for a milder, slightly sweeter flavour, I like to use either apple wood or cherry wood. You can buy all of these on the Weber website (www.weber.com). There's a decent chance that your local garden centre will also stock these items, along with sturdy tin foil trays.

Once the charcoal is white ash, cover half of it with the soaked wood chips. Place the grill over the top and put the foil tray above the wood chips. Lay the meat you want to smoke on the other side of the grill. It helps if you have a bigger barbecue because you will have more space to keep the meat away from the heat but I've had good results on a small Weber, too.

1 Jessica Lussenhop, 'Black Pitmasters Left Out of US Barbecue Boom', *BBC News Magazine*, 24 August 2015.

Smoked Baby Back Ribs

Although there are many different ways to cook barbecued meat in the US, the main difference between what we do to ribs in the UK and what happens in some parts of the American South is twofold: 1) They smoke their meat over a low heat for hours; 2) They tend to only apply a smallish amount of barbecue sauce towards the end of cooking, rather than baking the ribs in the stuff. The focus there is much more on the flavour and texture of the meat itself. I have found that the problem with using a 'wet rub' (cooking with sauce on) is that the sugar in the sauce can scorch during cooking. I prefer to tenderise and flavour the meat with a 'dry rub' overnight. The wet rub is not a marinade in this recipe, as much as it is a sauce.

Serves 4

2 racks of spare ribs, weighing
    around 600g each (make
    sure you ask the butcher to
    remove the membrane)
6 tbsp Barbecue Sauce
    (see page 155), + extra
    for dipping

FOR THE DRY RUB

1 tbsp dried fennel seeds

1 tbsp dried garlic granules

1 tbsp light muscovado sugar

1 tsp fine table salt

1 tbsp smoked paprika

a pinch cayenne pepper

a pinch white pepper

½ tsp ground cinnamon
    (optional)

FOR THE BARBECUE

2.25kg wood chips (either
    cherry, apple or mesquite),
    + extra for topping up
enough water to cover the
    wood chips completely

Make up the dry rub by whizzing the fennel seeds and garlic granules in a spice grinder (or mortar and pestle) until they are powdered. Mix with the rest of the ingredients in a large bowl. Rub all over the rib racks and set in the fridge for 2 hours, overnight is ideal.

To smoke in a barbecue, soak the wood chips in water or apple juice for an hour before cooking and start your barbecue fire. (The instructions for how to create a smoking barbecue as opposed to a grilling one are on page 147.)

Push the hot coals to one side of the barbecue, so that there is a pile of coal on one side and an empty space on the other. Fill an aluminium foil tray with some water and set in the space next to the coals. Heap the soaked wood chips on to the hot coals. Place a grill over the top. Once the wood chips have started to smoke, place the rubbed racks on the grill above the water tray – avoid being directly above the smoke. Place the lid over the barbecue and cook over this low heat (roughly 140°C/fan 120°C/gas mark 1) for about 3 hours, or until the meat starts to shred away from the bones when you insert a fork. Just make sure that the meat is falling off the bone when you serve them. If it isn't, let them go for longer. They literally cannot overcook when done this way. You will need to top up the coal and the wood chips as you go to maintain roughly the same heat.

After the cooking time is up, lightly brush the barbecue sauce over the ribs and place back on the grill with the lid on for 15 minutes. Remove from the heat and wrap in tin foil to rest for another 15 minutes. Serve warm with a little more barbecue sauce, if you want (see page 151).

NOTE ON HOW TO COOK IN A CONVENTIONAL OVEN:

To cook in an oven, preheat to 140°C/fan 120°C/ gas mark 1 and wrap your marinated ribs first in baking paper then in tin foil tightly. Cook at the bottom of the oven for 3 hours. Don't be alarmed that when they come out of the oven they will be sitting in a puddle of juice as the next stage of cooking will sort this out completely. After 3 hours, take off the foil and paper and smear the ribs in barbecue sauce. Place in an oven tray and then back in the oven for 1 hour, remembering to put the ribs fat side up.

Dr Pepper Baked Beans

This is a delicious Southern twist on one of Britain's favourite staples: the mighty baked bean. The idea came to me whilst I was eating baked beans and barbecued pork off a plastic plate on the banks of the Mississippi, and was wondering what the dickens had gone into the beans to make them so dark and stickily delicious. Then it hit me: Dr Pepper! I don't actually like the taste of it much on its own, but for some reason when mixed with the spices that go into making beans, Dr Pepper really brings the party to the plate. If you've never tried making baked beans from scratch, it's a lot of fun.

Serves 4

2 tbsp olive oil

1 stick celery, washed, topped, tailed and very finely chopped

1 large onion, peeled and very finely chopped

3 garlic cloves, peeled and finely grated

1 tsp mixed spice

bouquet garni consisting of thyme, rosemary, parsley and bay – all tied with string

500ml good-quality passata

250ml Dr Pepper

1 × 400g can of haricot beans, drained of water and rinsed under the tap

2 tbsp cider vinegar

1 tsp English mustard

2 tbsp Barbecue Sauce (see page 155) or shop-bought

a dash of Worcestershire sauce

a dash of Tabasco

a generous pinch salt

Preheat the oven to 200°C/fan 180°C/gas mark 6.

Pour the olive oil into a medium saucepan and add the celery, onion, garlic, mixed spice and bouquet garni. Cook over a low heat until the onion is translucent.

Stir in the passata and Dr Pepper and boil for 10 minutes until slightly reduced.

Add the beans, vinegar, mustard, barbecue sauce, Worcestershire sauce and Tabasco and transfer to a shallow heatproof dish and into the middle of the preheated oven.

Bake for 1½ hours until jammy and thickened.

Check the seasoning before serving (see page 150) and remember to retrieve the bouquet garni!

cook's tip You can make these beans in advance – in fact they are even more delicious the second time around. Reheat in a hot oven until piping hot before serving.

Smoked Corn in the Husks

This recipe couldn't be easier or more delicious. Very simply: instead of boiling corn on the cob, simply peel back the green outer layer, remove the silks and rub butter all over it. Put its husky jacket back on and bung it on the barbecue to smoke. Each corn kernel will soak up smoke and spice, and squeak with juiciness. You can also cook it in the oven in exactly the same way and, although it will not have quite the same amount of smoke, it's still scrumptious and super tender. Corn is a staple in the American South and is a fabulous addition to a table that's heaving with fall-off-the-bone, surrendered meat.

Serves 4

soaked wood chips for the
barbecue (see page 147 for
a full explanation)

4 cobs of corn, with silks and
green husks still attached

60g salted butter at room
temperature

4 generous pinches smoked
paprika

Once the barbecue is white ash hot, put your soaked wood chips directly on to the hot coals.

Pull back the silks and husks of the cobs and discard the silks. With clean hands, rub one-quarter of the butter over each cob. Replace the husks over the buttered corn and twist at the top to secure it shut like a sweetie. If there isn't enough husk to do this, just secure with a toothpick.

Place the corn on a corner of the barbecue, away from direct flames or the husk will burn off. Replace the lid of the barbecue and smoke in this way for 45 minutes.

To serve, pull back the husks, sprinkle with paprika and eat with your hands (see page 150). Buttered corn dripping down your chin is an occupational hazard here, I'm glad to say.

cook's tip If you want to make these in the oven instead of on a barbecue, simply preheat your oven to 200°C/fan 180°C/gas mark 6 and cook for 45 minutes, followed by 5 minutes at the end under a hot grill to give them a little indoor 'smoke' – but beware of the husks catching fire under the grill. I've got distracted and set off the fire alarm at home before, which is why I mention this!

Proper Southern Cornbread

My love of cornbread started on my first visit to North Carolina, about five years ago, but I rediscovered it when I went to Memphis to investigate the barbecue scene. The key to a great cornbread is to put the tin in the oven first so that the batter hits a hot pan and starts to puff up instantly. Traditionally, cornbread is made in a skillet (a heavy duty ovenproof frying pan) and the cooking process starts on the stovetop, and is finished off in the oven. I like to use either bacon dripping or lard for this recipe, but if you're put off by that idea, you can grease the bottom of the tins with sunflower oil instead. Some people like to add chopped roasted red pepper, jalapeños, cheese or corn kernels to their cornbread, but I prefer mine plain.

Serves 8–10

45g lard or unsalted butter
200g fine cornmeal (polenta)
60g plain flour
2 tsp baking powder
3 medium free-range eggs
2 tsp caster sugar
½ tsp salt
284ml buttermilk
1 tbsp sunflower oil

cook's tip I made this recipe once with cornmeal that was medium-ground, as opposed to fine, and the difference was huge: the cornbread hardly rose at all. It's really important to use the finest cornmeal you can find to get the lightest results.

Preheat the oven to 200°C/fan 180°C/gas mark 6 – it is best to use a fan oven, if possible, as this gives the cornbread a boost as it goes in.

In a large ovenproof frying pan measuring roughly 20cm wide and 4cm deep (cast iron is best of all), melt the butter or lard.

Meanwhile, mix together the cornmeal, flour and baking powder in a large bowl.

With a hand-held whisk, beat the eggs, sugar and salt together in a separate bowl until bubbly. Pour in the melted fat and the buttermilk.

Make a well in the middle of the cornmeal mixture and pour in the liquid ingredients, stirring with a balloon whisk to avoid any lumps.

Using the same frying pan as before, heat the sunflower oil until hot.

Pour the cornbread mixture into the hot pan and keep the cornbread on the stovetop over a medium heat until you see bubbles starting to appear in the centre of the mixture, then transfer straight to the middle of the hot oven.

Cook for 25–30 minutes, until the cornbread is risen and golden.

Cut and serve straight away (see page 150). There is no substitute for warm, fresh cornbread! You can keep it in an airtight container but it won't last for more than a day or so.

Barbecue Sauce

There is a world of difference between the complex, dark depth of this sauce and the brown gloop you can buy from the supermarket. If you want to take a small step towards massively improving the quality of your summer, make a batch of this sauce at the end of the spring and keep it in the fridge for when the urge for barbecue hits. You won't regret it! Barbecue sauce is indispensible with baby back ribs (see page 151) and pulled pork. I personally like a mildly spicy sauce that has strong woody hints and a slightly acidic aftertaste.

Makes approximately 500ml

2 star anise

2 cloves

1 tsp fennel seeds

1 tsp coriander seeds

1 tsp cumin seeds

1 medium onion, peeled

8 garlic cloves, bashed
   and peeled

1 red chilli (leave in all the
   seeds if you like it hot – leave
   in half for a milder kick)

4 tbsp sunflower oil

2 tbsp ground allspice

1 tsp ground ginger

1 tsp ground nutmeg

2 tbsp smoked paprika

1 cinnamon stick

1 tbsp dark soy sauce

3 tbsp dark muscovado sugar

1 tbsp Worcestershire sauce

3 tbsp French's mustard

100ml maple syrup

200ml runny honey, + extra,
   to taste

150ml good-quality pineapple
   juice

150ml cider vinegar

400g tomato ketchup

red Tabasco, to taste

½ tsp celery salt

Bash the star anise, cloves, fennel, coriander and cumin in a mortar and pestle until you have a mixture that resembles dust as closely as possible.

Roughly chop the onion, garlic and chilli. Fry over a medium heat in a large saucepan with the sunflower oil, allspice, ginger, nutmeg, smoked paprika, cinnamon stick and the spices from the mortar and pestle until the onion is translucent.

Next add the soy, sugar, Worcestershire sauce, mustard, maple syrup, honey, pineapple juice, vinegar and ketchup and bring to a slow simmer. Turn the heat down and simmer gently for 45 minutes and adjust the seasoning with Tabasco, honey or celery salt, to taste.

Once cooked, pass through a fine mesh sieve and decant into a clean, sterilised jar.

Memphis Mustard Slaw

Coleslaw and barbecue are a great pairing: like Elvis Presley and tight, white jumpsuits. For this coleslaw recipe, I marinate the shredded cabbage briefly in vinegar, sugar and salt, which helps to soften the texture and gives the salad a delightfully acidic dimension. I much prefer this slaw when it's made with my homemade mayonnaise, which is heavy on the mustard, but if you're going to use shop-bought, then definitely go for Hellmann's and don't be shy about adding a bit more Dijon to the finished dish. They like their mustard in Memphis! This slaw keeps (and improves by doing so) in the fridge for up to three days.

Serves 8

1 small white cabbage, outer leaves removed and very finely sliced

5 tbsp white wine vinegar

1 tsp caster sugar

plenty of salt and white pepper

5 tbsp full-fat mayonnaise

1 heaped tbsp Dijon mustard

1 tsp mustard seeds

2 medium fennel bulbs, very finely sliced

1 large white onion, peeled and very finely sliced

6 spring onions, very finely sliced (including the green bit)

Combine the sliced cabbage with the vinegar, sugar and a pinch of salt in a large bowl and let it stand for 10 minutes, giving it an occasional stir.

Add the mayonnaise, mustard, mustard seeds and stir until well coated. Finally, add the fennel and white onion and give it a last stir. Set aside for 30 minutes before serving so that the flavours have a chance to mingle. Season generously with salt and white pepper and top with the spring onions for a bit of extra greenery.

cook's tip If you don't have a mandolin, you will find that cutting the cabbage with a bread knife makes your life easier. I also tend to make my coleslaw in a Ziploc instead of a bowl so I can massage the ingredients together to help the flavours develop and to encourage the vinegar to work its magic on the cabbage and break down its texture.

Ranch Dressing

This is *the* dressing that's everywhere in the United States. Particularly well suited to dipping fried or barbecue food into, it also acts as a fabulous dressing for any green salad you can think of.

Enough for 1 dip or 2 generous salad dressings

150ml buttermilk
   (shake the pot before using)

80ml sour cream

40g mayonnaise

1 tsp Dijon mustard

a dash of Worcestershire sauce

a dash of Tabasco (optional)

1 garlic clove, peeled and
   minced

a combination of fresh dill,
   parsley, chives and fresh
   or dried tarragon (tarragon
   is especially good if you're
   serving this with chicken)

salt and freshly ground black
   pepper, to taste

1 small handful of chives, finely
   chopped

Combine all the ingredients, except for the chives, in a bowl and give it a good stir. Taste and season. Sprinkle chives over the top before serving.

Hawaiian Pineapple Pork Marinade

I'm not one for pineapple on my pizza but there is something amazing about the combination of pork and pineapple. It just *works*. As such, this is a marinade you can either apply to diced chunks of pork leg or whole pork chops – destined for the barbecue or a frying pan.

Serves 4

1 tbsp strong mustard, such as Colman's English

50g light muscovado sugar

200ml good-quality pineapple juice

1 tbsp Worcestershire sauce

1 tbsp dark soy sauce

2 tbsp Sriracha or other Asian hot sauce with a mild kick and a little extra body (reduce the quantity to 1 tbsp if using Tabasco and depending on how hot you want this to be)

4 garlic cloves, peeled and minced

2.5cm piece of fresh ginger, peeled and minced

1 tbsp cider vinegar

4 × 200g pork chops (or 800g pork leg, cubed)

a little sunflower oil, to brush over the meat before cooking

1 handful of roughly chopped coriander leaves

2 spring onions, roughly chopped

To make the marinade, stir the mustard with the sugar and a little of the pineapple juice until it forms a paste. Add the rest of the juice, along with the Worcestershire sauce, soy sauce, Sriracha, garlic, ginger and cider vinegar, and stir to combine.

Place the meat in a large Ziploc bag with the marinade – take care to remove the air for better results – and leave for roughly 2 hours; 30 minutes is the absolute minimum.

Once the meat has been marinated, take it out and pat it dry with kitchen paper. Brush the sides of the meat lightly with oil.

Heat the grill, frying pan or barbecue until hot but not scorching and add the meat. Cook for roughly 5 minutes on each side, depending on how fierce the heat is. Avoid a very high heat as this could burn the chops. One of the points of marinating is to tenderise the meat, so it's not a problem to cook over a slightly lower heat – this will help preserve the flavours both of the meat and the marinade.

Rest the chops for a couple of minutes and then garnish with roughly chopped coriander and spring onions. Serve with wild rice and buttered spinach.

Garlic and Fennel Crispy Pork Belly

This is the recipe I go to if I want to make dinner ahead for a small party when the weather starts to cool down. I prefer to keep the bones in for the cooking as it adds flavour and succulence but if you can only get a boneless joint, that's fine, too – same method and timings apply. In order for the crackling to get good and crispy, it's important to prepare the meat the day before. Apart from the basic act of thinking ahead and rubbing on the salt and spices, this is a slow cook, don't-think-about-it-once-it's-in-the-oven cinch of a dish that always seems to deliver enormous pleasure to everyone. The leftovers also make the most melt-in-the-mouth sandwich filling for an Asian take on a bacon buttie (see Cook's Tip overleaf).

Serves 6 or 4 with leftovers

1.6kg pork belly, with skin on (I prefer a slightly fattier belly but this works just as well with lean)

salt flakes

FOR THE RUB

4 garlic cloves, peeled and minced

1 tsp light muscovado sugar

½ tsp salt

1 tbsp fennel seeds, smashed in a mortar and pestle

1 tbsp coriander seeds, smashed in a mortar and pestle

1 tbsp sunflower oil

a small pinch cayenne pepper or red chilli flakes (smashed in a mortar and pestle)

Mix the rub ingredients together to form a paste. Slather this all over the meat, avoiding the skin side, which you should just score and sprinkle with salt – please go for flakes, if you can, as this will draw out the moisture without over-salting the skin. The easiest tool to score a belly of pork is a Stanley knife and I like my score lines to be close together to give the best possible crackling.

Line an ovenproof dish roughly the same size as the belly with baking paper and lay the marinated meat (skin side up) on top. Place in the fridge uncovered (this is very important) overnight.

The next day, take the meat out of the fridge, wipe away the moisture from the skin with kitchen paper and sprinkle again with salt. This is to extract as much moisture from the skin as possible. Leave at room temperature for 2 hours before cooking (so this should be 6 hours before serving).

Preheat the oven to 170°C/fan 150°C/gas mark 3–4 – this works best with a fan setting.

Wipe the surface of the skin again and repeat the sprinkling of the salt flakes. Scrape the marinade ingredients away from the flesh and put the meat back into the dish skin side up. Cook for 2 hours, then turn the temperature of the oven

Recipe continues

Garlic and Fennel Crispy Pork Belly *continued*

cook's tip If you do serve it with the seaweed and mash, the good news is that you can make the seaweed before you cook the meat and the mash the day before. The seaweed doesn't need reheating and the mash can be warmed through in the microwave or on the hob.

If you have any meat left over, you can warm it up and use it to make the most gorgeous Asian twist on a bacon buttie. Warm a plain white roll and then slather some hoisin on one side and a tiny bit of Sriracha (chilli sauce) on the other. Put the warm pork in the bun and top with thinly sliced spring onions and cucumber. If you have any Watermelon Rind Pickles (see page 183), add a little of that, too. It is frankly amazing!

down to 150°C/fan 130°C/gas mark 2 – now it is best without the fan. Cook for another 1½ hours.

Once the meat has had a total of 3½ hours cooking, set the oven to grill mode. Prop up the meat with a scrunched-up piece of tin foil, if necessary, so that the crackling surface is more or less level and place the dish at the bottom of the oven to prevent burning. You want to keep an eye on it at this stage as the crackling will puff up like popcorn and can catch. Once the whole of the top is bubbly and crackled up, remove from the oven and rest in the oven dish for 10 minutes.

Cut the meat into medium slices and serve with Celeriac Winter Mash (see facing page), Crispy Chinese Seaweed (see page 242) and a little heated up hoisin sauce, or simply with Spiced Winter Jelly (see page 209) and a little Dijon mustard.

Celeriac Winter Mash

Pork and celeriac are meant for each other… Oh, and game and celeriac! How could I forget? This is a wonderful winter twist on mashed potatoes. The only trick to using celeriac in this way is to poach it in milk, as this takes away any bitterness that can sometimes develop with this vegetable during cooking. Make sure that you stir the bottom of the pan, too, as milk has a tendency to stick and burn. Apart from that, it's plain sailing. Even my father, who loathes celery with a passion (it has a hint of the same, slightly aniseedy flavour), loves this stuff.

Serves 6

700g potatoes, peeled (I like to use Désirée, which are very slightly waxy)

700g celeriac, peeled and cut into chunks (roughly 1 medium root)

2 bay leaves

10 scratches of fresh nutmeg

2 garlic cloves, bashed and peeled

enough full-fat milk to cover the veg during cooking (roughly 1 litre)

50g semi-salted butter

celery salt and ground white pepper, to taste

cook's tip As a little bonus, I strain the infused milk after poaching and make Béchamel (see page 128), which I then freeze for another day. Celeriac-infused Béchamel is pretty awesome on a *croque monsieur* or in mac 'n' cheese.

Cut the potatoes in half and put into a medium saucepan with the celeriac chunks, bay, nutmeg and garlic. Cover with milk and bring to a slow simmer. If you allow it to boil, it's very likely to bubble up over the rim of the pan and make a big mess, so please be careful to do this slowly.

Poach the vegetables on a low heat for as long as it takes for the potatoes to become tender and cooked through (roughly 20 minutes). Run a spatula along the bottom of the pan every so often to make sure that the milk isn't sticking and burning.

Once the vegetables are cooked, remove them with a slotted spoon and place in a large bowl.

Add the butter to the hot potatoes and celeriac, and then mash with a ricer. If you don't have a ricer, I suggest whipping it with an electric whisk until you have got rid of most of the lumps. If the mixture is slightly too stiff, add a little of the poaching milk.

Season thoroughly and serve piping hot.

rest in peace

We're all bored to tears with hearing chefs tell us to rest the meat we've just cooked. Why should we rest it? And what are the best ways to do so, in order to achieve maximum tenderness without losing all the heat?

Temperature has a huge impact on both texture and taste. The first thing to know is that you don't need to rest meat that has been slow cooked. Secondly, it's OK to serve steak at room temperature; in fact, it's likely to enhance the natural flavour and texture by doing so. The same applies to roasts: you'll get the best out of them by serving them just warmer than room temperature. If you like hot food to be piping, serve it on a hot plate with hot sides and sauce.

why

The primary reason for resting a piece of meat, whether a small cut like a steak or a larger cut like a roast, is to even out the temperature inside the meat. The surface of the meat reaches a much higher temperature than the centre during cooking so resting lets the centre 'catch up' with the outside and vice versa (there is a surprising amount of residual heat in a roasted piece of meat).

It makes perfect sense to rest your meat if you understand what the cooking process does to the muscle:

applying high heat to a muscle alters its structure, both in terms of its texture and flavour profiles. Muscles react to heat by shrinking and releasing moisture (a mixture of fat and water but predominantly water since meat is made up of 75 per cent water). The higher the heat, the more the muscle tightens as it cooks. It's as though it's fighting, shying away from the heat that is changing its fundamental structure. Cooking at very high heat 'shocks' the meat and it needs a period of time to 'relax' into its new form, let the dust settle, or more aptly put: let the juices and the heat (since these go hand in hand) redistribute themselves throughout the muscle. This, by the way, is also why it's so important to cook meat from room temperature: it's less of a shock when the muscle hits the heat of the oven or the pan.

By resting, you're giving the meat you've just stressed out through cooking the chance to reorganise its components and homogenise its structure and therefore texture. Having taken the trouble to source the meat and cook it beautifully, the least you can do is let it take a few minutes to gather its wits during resting, and pull itself together literally and figuratively. Moreover, most chefs actually rely on the resting period to finish off cooking their meat: they take the joint out of the oven just before the meat has cooked through completely. Or rather, they factor in the resting time as part of the cooking time since the meat continues to cook due to the residual heat, even if it's now at a much slower, gradual rate than when it was in the oven.

Finally there is another reason why resting meat is so unanimously recommended by the experts: by gently cooling the whole cut, the fibres inside the meat will relax and it will make it easier to carve. When your meat is rested (and the moisture is therefore more evenly distributed throughout), you will release less of the precious juices during carving.

how

Here is a rough guide to how long to rest different types of meats:

- Rest a steak about as long as you've cooked it (whether it's grilled or fried).

- I like to rest a 5kg turkey for 45 minutes – 60 if it's stuffed.

- For a rack of lamb, about 10 minutes is enough.

- For a roast chicken that feeds four, 15–20 minutes is good.

- For anything larger than a chicken but smaller than a turkey (rib of beef, pork roast, leg of lamb) – rest for 30–45 minutes.

These are all rough estimates and, as always, I find that the best way to tell if your meat is ready to eat is by touch. It should be tender and not spring back immediately or fight you when you prod it with your finger. If it feels tight, it needs more time on the board or in the roasting tray.

As for how to rest cooked meat, there are lots of different opinions on this subject. Some talk about a 'tent' of foil, others place foil directly on the meat. I like to rest meat on a warm plate or, better yet, in whatever container or oven tray I have cooked it in. The residual heat from the tray will ensure that it doesn't cool down too quickly, whilst allowing the resting to do its job. Secondly, I don't like using foil because it conducts too much heat and doesn't allow the meat to breathe. As it's resting and changing its internal structure, your joint will emit steam and heat. My favourite thing to cover a resting joint is: absolutely nothing. If you have achieved a crispy crust (whether it's the skin from your turkey or chicken, the fat cap layer on a rib of beef or crackling on a pork roast), covering it can wilt the crispy exterior. If it's sitting on a hot oven tray, your resting meat will come down to room temperature and you will maintain the crust. Make sure that your meat is not near an open window, though, as this would cool it down too quickly.

Pork and Vegetable Chinese Stir Fry

I spent two months in Beijing at the end of 2014 and, amongst other things, got to grips with how to make a proper Chinese stir fry. It's not difficult and the method is very straightforward but there are a few rules to follow. The first is to always use a smoking-hot wok and cold oil. This provides the right kind of heat to sauté the ingredients without burning them or overcooking them. The second is marinating the meat strips in cornflour. This is an absolute revelation and I wax lyrical about it in The Marinade Brigade (see page 123). It's a game changer. Finally, all the vegetables need to be cut roughly the same size in order to cook at the same speed and it's therefore important to have them prepped and ready to go before you start the recipe. In China, they use a vegetable that resembles lettuce root. Since I've never seen it in the UK (I'm not even sure what the word for it is), I've discovered that the closest thing in terms of texture and taste is peeled and seeded cucumber. It may seem strange but it works well and provides an unusual, mild crunch and flavour. This is therefore predominantly a vegetable dish with a little meat, rather than the other way around.

Serves 2

1 tbsp cornflour

150g pork loin, cut into very fine strips

1 tbsp water

2 tbsp sunflower oil

1 medium onion, peeled and roughly chopped

1 small red or orange or yellow pepper, cut into thin strips

2 sticks celery, washed, topped, tailed and cut on the bias (into similar-sized strips as the pepper)

100g cucumber (roughly 1/3 of a medium one), peeled, seeded and cut into similar-sized strips as the celery and pepper

a pinch chilli flakes (optional)

1 tbsp dark soy sauce

a pinch salt

Heat a wok over a high heat until smoking point.

Whilst the pan is heating up, mix the cornflour with the pork strips and massage the flour in with your fingers. When it's dry to the touch and the flour is evenly spread around, add the water and massage a bit longer. The meat should be covered in a slightly pasty coating.

Add the oil to the pan and then fry off the meat. It should colour up really fast because this is essentially shallow frying the meat. You want to toss the meat in the oil so that it's cooked through and golden on all sides for a couple of minutes. Remove from the pan with a slotted spoon and set aside.

Next add all the vegetables and chilli flakes (if using) to the pan and coat with oil. Toss until glistening and cook over a very high heat, keeping them on the move, for roughly 2 minutes. The vegetables should be getting a tan but remain crunchy and slightly undercooked.

Add the soy sauce and a small pinch of salt. Soy and salt are not the same kind of savouriness, which is why I use both.

Finally, return the meat to the pan and toss for a further minute to reheat (so 3 minutes cooking of the vegetables in total). Serve piping hot with steamed rice.

cook's Tip Optional extras – You could add a scattering of toasted cashews with the vegetables if you want to make this stir fry a little heartier. Some chopped coriander or toasted sesame seeds also make a nice garnish.

A lot of people can't stand celery (my dad and Doug, my publisher, amongst others) and if this is the case, simply replace it with more cucumber. I love the stuff but it's not a deal breaker. And you could just as easily replace the pork with chicken or beef and treat it in the same way.

Oh and this is killer with Teriyaki Sauce (see page 13). Not at all traditional but ridiculously good nevertheless.

Chinese Stir-fried Rice

Why does the stuff you get in restaurants taste so much better than the fried rice you knock up at home? And how do they get the egg to do that strand thing? Turns out there are a few tricks to making perfect stir-fried rice and one of them is to use leftover rice. If it's crispy and dried out and has been sitting in your fridge for 24 hours, it's perfect for this recipe. And I use the word 'recipe' here loosely because this is a case of adding in or subtracting whatever you have leftover or particularly fancy. The only non-negotiable ingredients, as far as I'm concerned, are: rice, eggs, peas, spring onions and peppers. The technique for cooking off whatever veg you are adding remains the same whatever you decide to put in. Remember to chop any raw meat on a separate board from where you're handling the vegetables. Also, the rice needs to be piping hot before serving. With any stir-fry recipes, there are a few rules and top of that list is: hot (and by that I mean smoking hot) wok, cold oil. This prevents the ingredients burning but gets them good and hot nevertheless. Stir frying is a quick process so make sure you have all of your ingredients ready in advance. The whole recipe shouldn't take you more than 8 minutes from start to finish.

Serves 2

2 tbsp sunflower oil

1 large organic free-range egg, beaten with a fork

1 tbsp sesame oil

100g pork loin, cut into very fine strips and sprinkled with salt

1 small red pepper, very finely diced

100g frozen peas

200g cooked rice

a pinch chilli flakes (optional)

1 tbsp light soy sauce

salt and freshly ground black pepper

2 whole spring onions, finely chopped (including the green bit)

Hot wok, cold oil. Place a wok over a very high heat and leave to get smoking hot.

Put 1 tbsp of the sunflower oil into the hot wok and tilt the wok to spread the oil around.

Pour in the egg, turning the wok so that the egg spreads and cooks very fast. A little bit of ruffling with a fish slice or a pair of chopsticks is a good idea. Add a tiny bit of salt. Flip, flip, scrape, scrape. It will puff up and become golden in less than 10 seconds. Remove from the pan and set aside on a clean board. Put the wok back on the heat to warm up again and chop, chop, chop the egg into thin strips.

Add the sesame oil to the hot pan and cook the pork scraps until golden and cooked through. Set aside next to the cooked egg.

Make sure the pan is still really hot before adding the remaining sunflower oil. Add the pepper, peas, cooked rice (which will be glued together and stiff) and chilli flakes, if using. With

cook's tip As I mentioned in the introduction, there is an infinite number of substitutions that can be made here – just follow the same method with the rice and make sure you cook the egg and meat (if using) at the start of the recipe. Ham or shrimp are great substitutes for the pork and there is no need to fry either of them in sesame oil first – just add at the same time as the vegetables.

your chopsticks, break up the rice and flip, flip, scrape, scrape again until the vegetables are turning golden and the rice is hot. I like it when the rice goes a tiny bit toasty and golden but that's up to you. Now add the soy sauce and enjoy the sizzle. Stir, stir, scrape, scrape again.

Finally, season with a little more salt (salt and soy sauce are not the same kind of savouriness) and some pepper to taste, and return the pork and egg to the pan. Toss briefly to combine and reheat before adding the spring onions.

Serve straight away.

Ham Hock Stock

Of all the ways to make stock from pork bones, hock stock is my favourite. This recipe is made from raw hock bones but read the Cook's Tip to see how to make the stock from cooked bones, such as the one you will find in a ham. Hock is an underused cut of pork but I love it because it has tons of flavour and shreds in a very satisfying way that works well in sandwiches, salads or risottos (see recipe for Ham Hock Risotto with Asparagus and Peas on the facing page). You can expect it to set slightly when cool because of the high percentage of collagen, which makes it perfect for soups, too. You can make this stock and use it straight away or leave to cool and freeze it in batches.

Makes roughly 2 litres and yields roughly 400g delicious, shredded hock meat

1 onion, peeled and roughly chopped

2 garlic cloves, peeled and smashed

1 carrot, peeled, topped, tailed and roughly chopped

2 sticks celery, washed and roughly chopped

1 small fennel bulb

2 bay leaves

a small bunch parsley

1 tbsp black peppercorns

1.2kg brined raw ham hock (also called 'knuckle')

Put all the ingredients into a large saucepan and cover with water – 2 litres is usually about right.

Bring to the boil and then reduce to a very slow simmer. Cook uncovered for about 3 hours at a slow simmer until the meat shreds easily. You will need to skim the surface of the pan occasionally to remove any foam.

Remove the hock from the stock and leave until cool enough to handle. Peel or cut off the skin layer with a knife and discard. Using your fingers, shred the meat from the bone.

Meanwhile, strain the stock through a sieve and allow to cool before using. You can expect to find a layer of fat on top of the stock when it's cold – you can remove this, if you want. I usually keep it.

cook's Tip If you have bought a cooked ham hock, as opposed to a raw one, you can still make this stock and it's totally delicious. The good news is that it will only take an hour of very gentle simmering.

If you are using only cooked bones and no meat (like the leftover bone inside your Christmas ham), then simmer for 2 hours instead of 3. You may want to save bones in the freezer until you have enough to fill the bottom of the saucepan, though.

Ham Hock Risotto with Asparagus and Peas

Although I make this risotto with Ham Hock Stock (see the facing page), you could make a vegetarian version with the water from cooking the asparagus topped up with boiling water. This is a bright green, springtime favourite of mine and is pretty straightforward as long as you understand that making risotto is like long distance running: pace yourself and don't add too much of the stock at the beginning. The method for this risotto comes from the legendary Marcella Hazan whose recipes are always reliable and who explains things in words that make absolute sense. In her seminal book *The Essentials of Classic Italian Cooking*, she defines risotto in the following terms: 'It is only through the gradual administration of small quantities of liquid, through its simultaneous absorption and evaporation, and through constant stirring, that the rice's soft starch is transformed into a clinging agent, pulling the grains together and fastening on to them the taste of the flavour base. Rice that is not stirred, that stews in too much liquid or that cooks in a covered pot, may turn into a perfectly agreeable dish, but is not risotto, and will not taste like risotto.' Amen to that, Marcella.

Serves 6

1.5 litres Ham Hock Stock (see facing page), or an alternative stock

200g asparagus, trimmed

2 tbsp olive oil

50g unsalted butter

1 small onion, peeled and very finely chopped

450g arborio rice

50g Parmesan, finely grated

200g frozen peas, run under cold water to defrost

salt and plenty of freshly ground black pepper

a little finely grated zest of 1 unwaxed lemon, to garnish

roughly chopped chervil, to garnish

Bring the hock stock to the boil in a saucepan. Drop the asparagus spears into the saucepan and, when it comes to the boil again, take them out with a slotted spoon. Slice finely on the bias and keep to one side.

Take the stock off the heat and set aside.

In a very large saucepan, heat the olive oil and one-third of the butter. Cook the onion over a gentle heat until it is translucent.

Add the rice and stir with a wooden spoon until all the grains of rice glisten and are coated in oil.

Using a measuring jug, ladle out around 100ml of the stock and add to the rice, stirring all the time until the liquid has disappeared. The heat under the pan should incite a hiss when the stock comes into contact but if it sizzles and all the stock disappears at once, it's too hot. Risotto is not difficult to get perfect – the trick is to get the right temperature under the pan so that the stock

Recipe continues

Ham Hock Risotto with Asparagus and Peas *continued*

cook's tip I love that this recipe is mainly green but if you want to include some hock meat, that would be delicious here, too.

is absorbed slowly enough to release the starch and give a creamy texture without overcooking or undercooking the rice and turning it to paste.

Continue adding the stock in 100ml increments – making sure to stir the mixture until all the previous stock has been absorbed before adding the next 100ml.

After about 20 minutes, the rice should be tender with a slight bite and the mixture should hold its rice shape and be *slightly* sloppy. Take the risotto off the heat and add the remaining butter. When melted and stirred in, add the Parmesan, peas and reserved asparagus. Season with salt and black pepper to taste.

Ladle on to plates and sprinkle over a little lemon zest and chervil. Serve straight away.

Pulled Pork Tennessee

In the American South, barbecue is synonymous with smoke. There is a smoked version of this recipe in the Cook's Tip on the facing page, in case you're in the mood for something a little different. In Tennessee, they just love pulled pork, cooked low and slow and served with a generous slick of barbecue sauce, coleslaw, beans, Watermelon Rind Pickles and Proper Southern Cornbread (see pages 182 and 154). If you're in the mood for smoke, there are explanations on page 147 on how to turn a smallish barbecue into a smoking one. If you can't be bothered with the hassle or live in a small apartment like I do, this recipe works just fine in the oven. I do recommend making your own barbecue sauce, though, to give the pulled pork a real Tennessee tang.

Serves 6 with leftovers

2kg pork shoulder, bone in with skin and fat on (ask the butcher to score it for you or do it yourself with a Stanley knife, making lines that are close together)

FOR THE RUB

5 tbsp dark muscovado sugar

1 tbsp smoked paprika

a generous crunch of black and white pepper

1 tbsp dried garlic granules

1 tbsp dried onion/shallot granules

¼ tsp cayenne pepper

1 tsp ground allspice

1 tsp celery salt

Combine all the ingredients for the rub and then cover the shoulder of pork with it. Leave to marinate uncovered in the fridge, skin side up, for at least 12 hours or up to 2 days.

Preheat the oven to 120°C/fan 100°C/gas mark ½.

Cover an oven tray first with tin foil, then baking paper (this is to protect it as the rub that slides off the meat will caramelise and become difficult to remove later on). Put the marinated meat on the tray skin side up and into the bottom of your preheated oven.

Cook the shoulder uncovered in the preheated oven for 7 hours.

Once the meat has had its time, it will be succulent and falling off the bone, which is perfect. Take it out of the oven and, using a sharp knife, remove the layer of skin and fat on top and set aside. Transfer the meat on to a warm serving platter, along with any cooking juices. Discard the crusty paper and foil.

Turn the oven to a low grill setting.

Place the skin and fat on the now-cleared oven tray and under the grill in the middle of the oven. You need to keep an eye on it or it will burn. Grill until golden, crispy and puffed up all over. Cut or break into small pieces.

Shred the pork with two forks, scatter the rind over and serve with a selection of Barbecue

Sauce (see page 155), Memphis Mustard Slaw (see page 157), Dr Pepper Baked Beans (see page 152), Watermelon Rind Pickles (see page 182), Proper Southern Cornbread (see page 154), Heirloom Tomato and Onion Salad (see page 17) – or all the above fixin's! This is meant to be a Southern feast so go ahead and enjoy! Any leftovers can go into making Po' Boys the next day (see page 189).

cook's tip The smoked version is the same as the oven version, in terms of marinating time – the only difference is that you cook the meat in your barbecue smoker (for instructions see page 149).

The timings are inevitably more approximate with a smoker so keep an eye on it to make sure it's not drying out. Here are the tools and ingredients needed to make the smoked version:

2.5kg wood chips – like apple or cherry wood
1 foil tray for the fruit juice
500ml apple or pineapple juice

A compromise that delivers silky meat and a note of smoke is to cook the meat in the oven for 6 hours and then finish it on the smoker for the last hour, having taken off the skin (grilling the skin is the best way to get crackling).

Redcurrant Glazed Ham

This recipe is a particular favourite of mine at Christmas time but you can honestly make this all year round. It's great to feed a crowd and will always be the cause of much excitement as you bring out the magnificent, lacquered ham. This is an old-fashioned recipe that is easy but does require a bit of thinking ahead, since it involves poaching the cured ham and then baking it with a glaze. This is the only way I know to achieve a ham that is cooked through but not dry. You can serve it warm or cold, or warm then cold. There are a couple of important things to remember: 1) Always ask the butcher for a cut with plenty of fat on the top so that you can score it before baking; and 2) Please, please, please don't skip the resting of the poached meat in the cooking juices before baking. This last step ensures the succulence of the ham when it's done. If you're even more intrepid and want to take the homemade ham one step further, you can brine your own 'green' ham to achieve maximum flavour (see page 71) and then proceed with this recipe as normal.

Serves 14–16

3.5kg cured, raw ham on the bone, with a good layer of fat and skin still attached

3 bay leaves

1 whole onion, peeled and halved, then studded with 2 cloves

2 sticks celery, washed and roughly chopped

1 tbsp fennel seeds, bruised with the back of a knife

40ml cider vinegar

4 tbsp redcurrant jelly

In a large saucepan, cover the ham with water and bring to the boil. Once it's come to the boil, discard the water. Add more water to the pan and bring the ham to the boil again. Now add all the other ingredients apart from the redcurrant jelly, reduce the heat and simmer gently for 1½ hours, removing any scum as it arises.

Once the meat has had its time, turn off the heat and let the ham sit in the stock until it's cool. This should take at least 4 hours. If you can leave it overnight, it's even better.

Preheat the oven to 180°C/fan 160°C/gas mark 4.

To make the glaze, heat the redcurrant jelly in a small saucepan over a medium heat until it's liquid.

Line an oven tray with a large layer of tin foil and then a layer of baking paper. Curl up the corners around the ham to create a lip so that the glaze won't escape and ruin your oven tray when it caramelises.

With the help of a sharp knife, cut the skin off the ham, taking care to remove as little fat

Recipe continues

177

Redcurrant Glazed Ham *continued*

underneath as possible. Score the fat with tight lines going from one side to the other, like stripes. Place the scored ham in the prepared tray and brush over the glaze.

Bake at the bottom of the preheated oven for 1 hour.

Take the ham out and turn the oven temperature up to 220°C/fan 200°C/gas mark 7. Brush the meat with the juices at the bottom of the pan. Once the oven is up to temperature, return the ham to the oven for a further 10 minutes, or less if it colours quickly. This final blast will ensure a delicious glossy crust.

Remove from the oven and allow to rest for at least 30 minutes before serving warm. Serve with Dijon mustard or Spiced Winter Jelly (see page 209). And this is a good time to bring out that noble ham side dish: Celeriac en Remoulade (see facing page).

cook's tip I find that I get the best results with an even cut of meat that is more 'round' than 'oblong' because the denser the meat, the less it has a tendency to dry out during the cooking. A healthy layer of fat will help with this problem too. There is more flavour if you cook the meat on the bone (which is why I do it) but it's more difficult to carve later. If you would rather have an easy-to-carve ham, go for one with the bone removed that weighs around 3kg and follow the recipe as above.

Cooking ham in this way is a colossal money saver if you're someone who (like me) is partial to having ham in the fridge as a last-minute meal option. It will keep for 3–5 days in the fridge, and of course can be frozen, too.

Celeriac en Remoulade

If you're buying a plate of charcuterie and want to make a small something to serve with it to add the homemade factor, Celeriac en Remoulade is delicious and ready in 10 minutes. I prefer mine not to be swimming in rich sauce but rather to have a slight sharpness amid all that delicate celery whiteness. And lots of black pepper is not only really pretty visually but also gives it the kick it needs. You can keep this in the fridge for up to three days and you can expect it to get slightly wetter and the initial celery hit to fade as the days go on. In France, where I live, they serve it with cured charcuterie (see page 180) as well as *jambon blanc* (cooked ham). I also like it as an accompaniment to smoked fish, such as mackerel on toast.

Serves 4 as a side or more if you're having it as part of a charcuterie, cheese, bread and salad lunch

3 tbsp mayonnaise (I like to use Hellmann's or homemade)

3 tbsp full-fat crème fraîche

¼ tsp table salt

1 tsp Dijon mustard

2 tbsp fresh lemon juice

1 medium celeriac, weighing around 250g once peeled, topped and tailed

lots of freshly ground black pepper

Mix together the mayonnaise, crème fraîche, salt, mustard and lemon juice in a large bowl.

Using either a mandolin or a potato peeler with teeth (the kind that makes Julienne strips), shred the celeriac finely. If you don't have either of these tools, the next best thing is the medium-sized grate on a Microplane or box grater.

Toss the celeriac in the mixture and season generously with black pepper.

Serve straight away, or you can keep in the fridge for up to 3 days.

1, 2, 3, charcuterie

Here's a thought – charcuterie *should* be expensive. Making charcuterie can take up to 2 years and the meat can lose roughly 30 per cent of its original, raw weight during the process. That's a long time to be holding on to stock that takes up a lot of space before you can sell it. I can't begin to imagine the cashflow issues that come with that sort of business model. But I think charcuterie is a perfect example of the pleasure that comes from slow food, made with love and from the very best quality ingredients. The flavours of really beautifully made charcuterie are so intense that you don't need to eat a lot to deliver a hit of lasting pleasure and tongue-tingling umami.

As for making charcuterie at home, I haven't done much of it except for Diana Henry's excellent recipe for bacon from *Salt, Sugar, Smoke.* The reason that I don't make salamies or other charcuterie is simply that I have access to a lot of good stuff here in Paris. Also, I live in a very small apartment, which is not conducive to curing or drying. The key ingredients in charcuterie making are time, salt and the space to house the work in progress. If you're keen to make charcuterie, however, check out the bibliography (see page 250) for a list of books that I can recommend – and the recipes will work. Nothing is worse than spending the time, effort and ingredients on curing a leg of ham for months only to find that the recipe is too salty and the whole thing inedible.

I'm a particular fan of Pete Hannan's bacon at The Meat Merchant – you've got to try his Moyallon Guanciale; – and cured meats from Cannon & Cannon.

Watermelon Rind Pickles

This recipe comes from the American South where a watermelon rind pickle is often served with barbecues. Most traditional recipes that I've come across include the use of limewater, which is neither common in Europe, nor appeals to me much because it's basically a saturated solution of calcium hydroxide. Even though I do buy bicarbonate of soda (for cakes and scones) at the pharmacy here in France, this is pretty much where I draw the line. So this is a recipe that makes the most of the wonders of watermelon without requiring any chemicals or a three-day process, just good old vinegar, salt, sugar and spices. *Vive la simplicité!* Apart from tasting delish, this is one of the prettiest pickles you can make and is, therefore, a great homemade present.

This pickle is fabulous with pork (try it with Pulled Pork Tennessee – see page 174 – and Po' Boys – see page 189) or with rich Asian-flavoured dishes like Cheating Peking Duck (see page 216) or Garlic and Fennel Crispy Pork Belly (see page 161). I also just had some with barbecued mackerel, ooh la la.

Makes approximately 1 litre

about 1.8kg watermelon (¼ large one), with the green rind peeled off, leaving just the white plus about 2cm of the pink flesh (prepared weight 1kg)

250ml red wine vinegar

130ml water

5 tsp salt flakes

220g caster sugar

1 whole star anise

1 cinnamon stick

2cm piece of fresh ginger, peeled and finely sliced against the grain

Cut the watermelon into 2cm cubes.

Combine the vinegar, water, salt, sugar and spices in a large saucepan and bring to a simmer until the sugar and salt have dissolved.

Add the watermelon and bring the mixture back to the boil. When just simmering again, transfer into hot sterilised jars.

Leave to cool and after an hour, put the lid on and refrigerate. It will keep in the fridge for up to 10 days.

cook's tip To sterilise your jars, simply put your cleaned, heatproof jars into the oven at 180°C/fan 160°C/gas mark 4 for 15 minutes. You will also need to sterilise the lids, which should go *next to* the jars and not *on* them. After 15 minutes, remove from the oven.

Serious Sausage Roll

I'm not talking about those cute little sausage rolls that are all tidy and tame and can be popped elegantly into your mouth at a cocktail party... I'm talking about a double-handed job. I'm talking about the DADDY of sausage rolls. A sausage roll that crumbles when you bite into it. I'm fortunate enough to live next to a really amazing little coffee place. It's called the 10 Belles and is at 10, rue de la Grange aux Belles, in the 10th arrondissement. My love of symmetry gets a kick out of that, especially when I've had one of their fantastically delicious coffees that wires me for the rest of the day. On Sunday I sometimes saunter over there to get a coffee and one of their killer sausage rolls for brunch. This recipe is a nod to the ones they sell there. And I love the fact that they use shortcrust rather than puff.

Makes 8 whoppers (you can freeze any extras)

FOR THE PASTRY

130g salted butter, cold, cut
    into cubes

250g plain flour

1 large free-range egg yolk,
    beaten

a tiny amount of icy cold vodka
    (or cold water)

FOR THE FILLING

1 tbsp Dijon mustard

1 small onion, peeled and
    very finely chopped

20 sage leaves, very finely
    chopped

1 small bunch parsley,
    stalks removed and
    very finely chopped

10 scratches of fresh nutmeg

3 rashers smoked streaky
    bacon, very finely chopped

2 tbsp Worcestershire sauce

3 tbsp tomato ketchup

To make the pastry, proceed as with any shortcrust by rubbing the fat into the flour in a very large bowl, using your fingertips. When you reach the breadcrumb stage, gradually add the egg yolk and start to bring the mixture together. If, and only if, you need a little more liquid to bind it into a dough ball, add the cold vodka, 1 teaspoon at a time. The reason I prefer to use vodka is that it evaporates very quickly during cooking and gives you a more crisp and flaky finish – you won't taste it, I promise. Wrap the pastry in clingfilm and press down on it so that it starts to look a bit like a rectangle. Put it in the fridge to rest for 30 minutes.

Preheat the oven to 180°C/fan 160°C/gas mark 4 and put a baking tray in the middle of the oven to heat up.

Whilst the pastry is chilling and resting, combine all the filling ingredients. If you are mad about mustard or like the idea of adding more sage, go for it. This is how I like mine but the recipe is perfect for customising.

Roll out the chilled pastry on a lightly floured surface into a long rectangle that is roughly

600g sausagemeat from good-quality, plain sausages with around 20% fat (the percentage is important in order to keep the middle of the sausage roll tender)

salt and plenty of black pepper

3 garlic cloves, peeled and minced

FOR THE GLAZE

2 free-range eggs, beaten

2 tbsp nigella seeds

cook's tip You can prepare these ahead by making them up to the point where you have brushed the raw sausage rolls with egg. Freeze them on a baking sheet with some space in between. When they're frozen, throw them in a bag all together. Defrost in the fridge overnight before cooking in a hot oven as per the recipe.

You can also make lots of little baby ones if you're doing them for a party. In this case, roll the pastry so that it's much narrower and make a tiny little meat cannon. Cook them at 180°C/fan 160°C/gas mark 4 for 15 minutes and check on them in case they need a little 5-minute blast to crisp up and make the pastry shine.

50cm long and 25cm wide. This will make one big sausage roll that you can then cut afterwards. The thickness of the pastry should be around 0.5cm.

Form a cannon shape with the meat and place it lengthways in the middle of the rectangle. Please avoid packing the meat too tightly as this will prevent it being moist and crumbly when the sausage roll is cooked.

Fold the sides back over the meat in the middle and paint the seam with beaten egg. Roll over so that the seam is underneath and paint with the beaten egg all over. Cut into sections roughly 7cm long.

Line the hot baking tray from the oven with baking paper and put the sausage rolls on top. Brush one more time with beaten egg to ensure a real gloss and sprinkle with the nigella seeds.

Place in the middle of the preheated oven and cook for 40 minutes.

Remove from the oven and shut the door. Crank up the heat to 220°C/fan 200°C/gas mark 7 and brush the outside of the sausage rolls with beaten egg once again. Put them back into the oven for 10–20 minutes, depending on how large they are and how golden. A skewer inserted into the middle should come out warm and the pastry on the outside should be lovely and tanned.

Lard Shortcrust Pastry

There is no doubt about it: lard is wonderful in pastry, especially when it's for a quiche. It provides the 'short' in shortcrust, by which I mean that the lard gives a crumbly, rich, crispy texture to the pastry and enables the bottom of the quiche or pie to remain crunchy, despite being filled. The good news is that this pastry is also very forgiving: you can patch up any holes or cracks with leftover trimmings and no one will ever know the difference. Also, I have found that this recipe produces pastry that doesn't shrink as much as all-butter versions. Proper pastry is so worth the effort because the results are miles more delicious than the shop-bought stuff and, anyway, once you've made this once or twice, it becomes second nature. I've tested this recipe many, many ways and have come to the conclusion that a tiny amount of sugar improves the taste and texture of the pastry, even when using it in a savoury pie.

For a quiche to serve 8–10

You will need a 25cm × 6cm deep, loose-bottomed tin (I like quite a deep-set quiche)

250g plain flour

½ tsp salt

1 tsp caster sugar

60g lard, cold and cut into cubes

80g salted butter, cold and cut into cubes

1 free-range egg, beaten

a little cold vodka (or water), optional

Preheat the oven to 200°C/fan 180°C/gas mark 6 and place a baking sheet in the oven to heat up.

Place the flour, salt, sugar and fats in a large mixing bowl. Cut through the mixture with a round-bladed knife until all the cubes of butter and lard are much smaller. Then, with the tip of your fingers, rub the fat into the flour until you obtain a bowl of what looks like breadcrumbs. You can also use a food processor to do this if you have one.

Once you are at the 'breadcrumb stage', add the beaten egg and repeat the cutting motion until you have a ball of dough. If, for whatever reason, the mixture still seems too dry (this can be because of the size of the egg or the quality of the flour), add a little cold vodka or water, 1 teaspoon at a time, until you have a ball of dough that holds together, without being wet.

On a clean, floured surface, roll out the pastry to the size of the tin. Carefully slide the bottom of the tin (free from the sides) under the pastry and then transfer into the tin mould. Don't worry if it tears as you can fix it later.

cook's tip You can cool the pastry shell and freeze it for up to 3 weeks so long as it's kept in a freezer bag to protect it from frostbite.

Deep set quiche tins are not easy to find (my grandmother had one) and are rather an old-fashioned item. In the absence of one of these, I sometimes use a cake tin of the right diameter. Just remember to cut off any excess pastry neatly once it's cooked and still soft.

The reason I use vodka is that it improves the texture of the pastry because it evaporates more quickly during cooking than water, thus giving you a 'shorter' texture and no vodka flavour whatsoever.

Gently press the pastry into the sides of the tin and trim to fit the top of the tin. Where the pastry is a little thin or cracked, use some of the extra pastry to repair or solidify the crack. It's good to have a decent thickness of pastry around the sides of the tin.

Once the tin is lined with pastry, carefully place in the freezer for 30 minutes to chill right down. Be careful as this is a loose-bottomed tin! Make sure you hold it by the sides and not the bottom.

Once the pastry is really cold, prick all over with a fork and place a sheet of baking paper that's too big for the tin over the top. Fill the tin with baking beans and cook for 20 minutes on the hot baking sheet in the middle of the oven.

After 20 minutes, open the oven door and carefully remove the paper and the beans inside it. (If you have a big sheet of paper you can form a bundle and take it off the pastry without having to take the tin out of the oven.) Once the beans and paper are off, bake for a further 10 minutes to crisp up.

Remove the pastry from the oven and fill as required.

Quiche Lorraine

The trick to achieving that wonderful wobble is to add a couple of extra egg yolks, which enriches the filling and gives this quiche a seductive, soft-set centre. After that, it's all about the quality of the lardons you use. Since the dots of pork throughout the quiche are the only things to distract from the dreamy egg centre, they really need to deliver a decent hit. Ask your butcher for dry-cured, smoked belly of pork, cut into chunks the size of your little finger or smaller and fry them in a large pan so that they get a chance to crisp up. I like to use white pepper and nutmeg, but this is not strictly traditional. I have stopped adding cheese because the fine folks of Lorraine wouldn't approve but I draw the line at the seasoning – *tant pis*!

Serves 8–10

1 × Lard Shortcrust Pastry
    (see page 186), made up,
    chilled and lining the tin
    ready to use
350g smoked belly of pork,
    cut into very fine lardons
    (the smaller the better)
1 tsp sunflower oil
6 large free-range eggs
2 additional free-range
    egg yolks
400ml crème fraîche
a generous pinch white pepper
½ whole fresh nutmeg, finely
    grated (optional)

cook's tip Cutting up the lardons into tiny *allumettes* (matchsticks) will mean you get a better distribution in the egg mixture.

This recipe is also delicious with hot smoked flakes of salmon instead of lardons and lots of snipped chives.

Preheat the oven to 200°C/fan 180°C/gas mark 6.

Bake off the pastry shell according to the instructions on page 187. Leave it to cool for 15 minutes before adding the filling.

Whilst the pastry is cooling, fry off the lardons in the oil. You can get rid of any excess fat at the end but the oil encourages the lardons to become golden and crispy. Once cooked, set aside.

Beat the eggs and egg yolks in a bowl with a balloon whisk to loosen. Add the crème fraîche, white pepper and nutmeg (if using) and mix again.

Spread the cooked lardons over the bottom of the pastry case and pour over the egg mixture, making sure to leave a gap between the top of the filling and the pastry as it will puff up slightly.

Cook in the middle of the preheated oven for 30 minutes, until golden and cooked through.

Set aside to rest for 10 minutes – the quiche will continue to cook as it cools – before serving with a green salad (see page 5).

Po' Boys

My obsession with the American South continues... I have had really amazing Delta shrimp and fried catfish versions of this sandwich in my time but there's nothing like a Po' Boy to use up leftover pulled pork or baby back ribs. In true Louisiana style, I like mine hot hot hot and properly spilling out of the bun. Traditional Po' Boys tend to use baguette-style bread but I actually love them in a hot dog or a hamburger bun. It's probably because I live in France so it's nice to use something different. If you're really pushing the boat out, make a batch of Shoe String Fries (see page 109) and put them right there inside the sandwich... A side of Memphis Mustard Slaw (see page 157) or some other slightly vinegary slaw is also a must, as well as buckets of Barbecue Sauce (see page 155).

Makes 6

6 hot dog buns or 3 French-style baguettes, cut in half

6 squiggles of yellow mustard (1 for each Po' Boy)

4 handfuls of pulled pork, or meat shredded from the ribs, warmed in a low oven

enough Barbecue Sauce (see page 155) to moisten the meat

Tabasco or Louisiana Hot Sauce, to taste

celery salt, to taste

plenty of crisp green lettuce, such as Cos or Romaine

1 large red onion, peeled and cut into thin rings

FOR THE MAYONNAISE

6 heaped tbsp mayonnaise (I use Hellmann's)

1 whole jalapeño, finely chopped

2 garlic cloves, peeled and very finely minced

Mix the mayonnaise ingredients together and slather on one side of each bun generously. Spread a squiggle of mustard on the other side.

Mix the warmed pork with the barbecue sauce and season with hot sauce and celery salt, if you think it needs it.

Pile pulled pork into each bun and add some lettuce and onion.

Serve with fries, slaw and plenty of cold, cold beer.

bring home the bacon

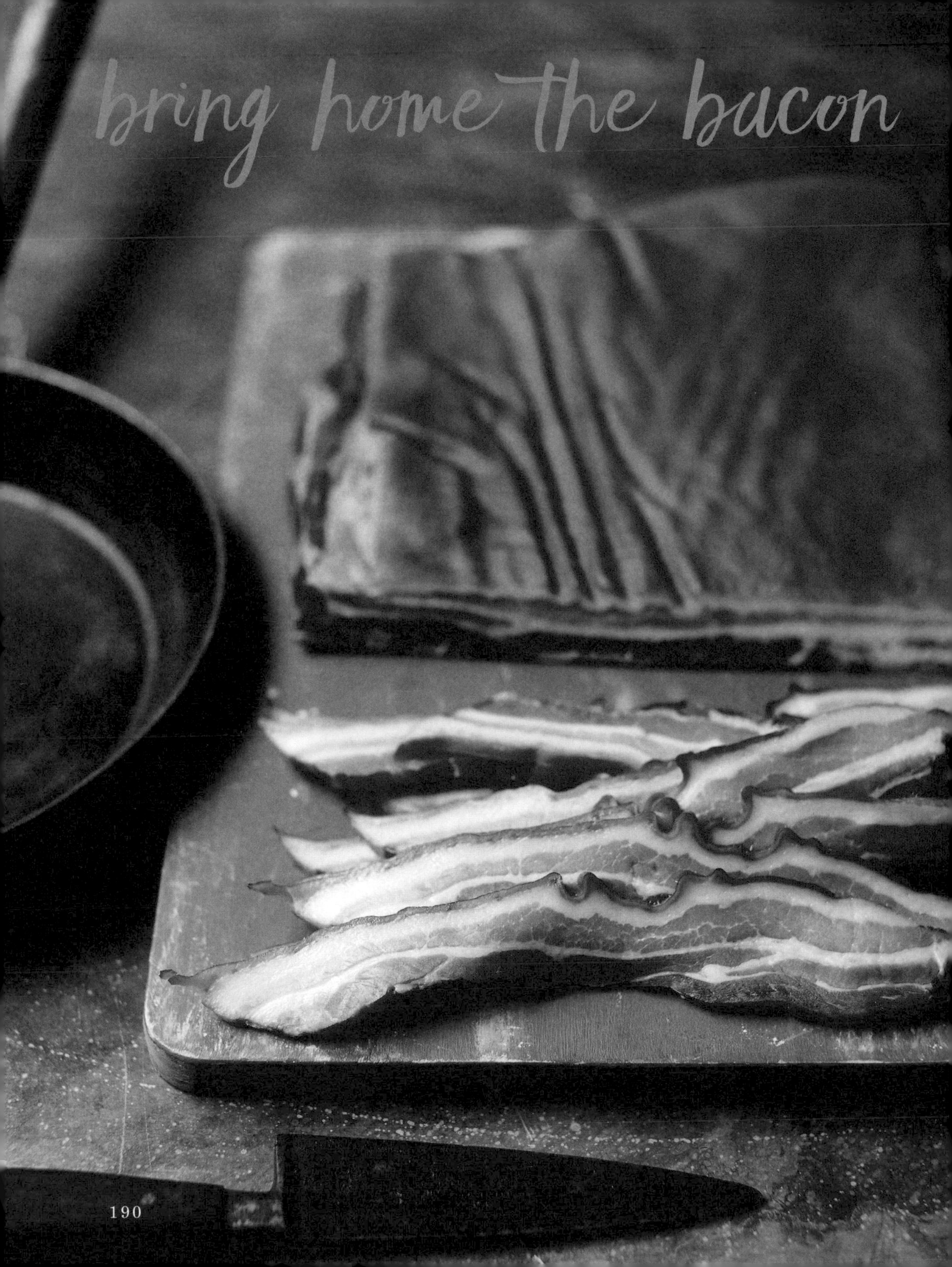

I myself am part of the cliché that vegetarians come back to meat because of the smell of frying bacon. Not only is bacon very popular, it is also a great place to start if you're interested in enquiring about meat. Have you ever wondered why your bacon shrinks to half its original size when cooked? Ever asked yourself what that white shite is? How can you tell what constitutes 'good bacon' by reading the label? If you're busy nodding your head, read on.

why does some bacon shrink in the pan?

The short answer is: because it's full of water. And by water, I mean a water-based solution with preservatives, salt and other flavourings. To understand this fully, it's important to take a few steps back and look at what bacon actually is. Bacon is either brined (wet) or cured (dry) back or belly of pork. It can be smoked or unsmoked but it has to be cured otherwise it's just 'green' pork. It is during the brining process where things can get ugly. If, like me, you accept that industrial food manufacturing is about the bottom line, then it makes sense to buy in a pound of meat, alter the flavour and colour and end up with way more meat than you started out with. I won't go into the fascinating complexities of brining here (see page 71) but different processes of curing can produce bacon that looks vaguely similar in packet form but is in fact very different.

If your bacon came from a slow-raised animal and has been dry cured, it will crisp up in the pan and barely shrink at all. As a rule, dry curing tends to imply a better quality of bacon but, as always, please ask your butcher. You're hoping to hear that it has come from a heritage breed, outdoor-reared animal. Dry curing will reduce the weight of the original meat by around 20 per cent due to the dehydrating effect of the salt on the pork. The dry-curing technique can take up to 30 days but is usually ready within a couple of weeks. On the other hand, a quick and dirty way of 'brining' or wet curing involves injecting or 'pumping' a brine solution into the green pork and vacuum packing it for as little as two days. In this scenario, if you count the water that was naturally present in the pork to begin with, the finished product can contain up to 50 per cent water. Unsurprisingly, this is the stuff that will spit and shrink when it cooks.

My experience suggests that if you're dealing with premium pork, which has taken up to 12 months to raise, there is much less temptation by the manufacturer or butcher to inject it with flavourings and preservatives because the value is in the meat itself. If, on the other hand, you're dealing with low-quality pork from an animal that was raised fast (in 3 or 4 months), it makes sense to make the flesh look as plump and rosy as possible in order to project the impression of a wholesome product. But here's the rub: when that bacon hits the pan, it can't lie.

If all there is in the pan is glossy bacon fat and meat that has barely changed in size, you've got honest, good-quality bacon. If your bacon curls into nothing and leeches out a strange-looking white substance, make a mental note of the product and avoid it in future.

what is that white shite?

For years now, I've been wondering exactly what that white shite is in the bacon pan. I asked a couple of experts and it turns out that it's a mixture of phosphates and water. If you put water into the centre of a piece of meat, it won't stay there. So the manufacturer adds a phosphate to the brine in order to secure it inside the meat and lock it deep inside the muscle so that the meat is cured from the inside out. When this meat hits the heat, a mixture of brine and phosphate is driven out.

in a nutshell

- Always opt for outdoor-reared, slow-raised animals. With pigs, these tend to come from heritage breeds, also called rare breeds.

- Look for British bacon – the standards of welfare tend to be higher in the UK than in other European countries.

- Opt for dry-cured. Although you can buy good-quality wet-cured bacon, it is more likely to have been injected with phosphates.

- Choose a label with as few extra ingredients as possible. Dry curing involves salt, sometimes a little sugar and that's it. Spices, herbs and maple syrup are fun additional flavourings but avoid anything with chemical compounds on the label.

- If you can't find any that you're happy with, cure your own streaky bacon (see page 181). It's easy and can be done within a week.

- Ask your butcher to help you source the best bacon you can find – labelling can be deceiving. (You can call bacon 'dry cured' as long as you don't add more than 8 per cent water to it…)

- If you end up with white shite in the pan, avoid that bacon in the future. It is ALWAYS a bad sign.

- If you can't get hold of good bacon locally, it freezes well (particularly streaky) so you can buy more than you need from a reliable source online (see page 251).

Candied Bacon

This is so wrong, it's right. If you're a fan of the Canadian combo of bacon and maple syrup, then this is going to be right up your alley: sweet and salty rashers of very crispy bacon. I tasted it at a Christmas party in Minnesota and I have wanted to include it in a cookbook ever since, with the small but significant addition of a little bit of Marmite for a British kick. The success of this recipe stands or falls on the quality of the bacon and the very best results I've achieved have involved very thinly sliced pancetta, rather than thicker-cut bacon. If you're making this with pancetta, cut down the cooking time by about half – when they're golden and crispy, they're ready. You'll only need to baste the thinner rashers three times in total. By the way, a BLT takes on a whole new dimension when made with doorstop slices of white bloomer, lashings of mayonnaise and this bacon. Just sayin'.

Makes 15 rashers

15 dry-cured smoked streaky bacon rashers, cut into medium thickness (or 25 very thin rashers, such as pancetta)

50g light muscovado sugar

1 tbsp cider vinegar

1 tbsp runny honey

a pinch freshly ground black pepper

1 tsp Dijon mustard

¼ tsp Marmite

cook's tip The sugar glaze will drip down through the wires of the rack and collect on the tray underneath, which is why I suggest you line the tin with baking paper to avoid mess and ruination of said tray. No amount of candied bacon will make you feel better about having to scrub the life out it.

Preheat the oven to 200°C/ fan 180°C/gas mark 6 – it is best to use a fan oven here, if possible, because it will produce crispier results.

Line an oven tray with baking paper and sit a wire rack over the top. Lay the rashers of bacon on top of the rack – cheek by jowl but not overlapping.

Cook for 10 minutes in the middle of the preheated oven.

Meanwhile, mix together the remaining ingredients until combined.

Remove the bacon from the oven and paint the mixture lightly on to each rasher, before returning to the oven for 10 minutes.

Repeat every 10 minutes, making sure to turn the bacon so that both the underneath and the top get a good basting, until the bacon has had a total of approximately 40 minutes, or is golden and you have run out of the mixture. (The length of time will depend on the quality of the bacon that you're using – the better the quality, the less water, the quicker it will crisp up.) Set aside to crisp up further as it cools.

If making as a nibble, stand the crispy Candied Bacon in a glass to serve.

Christmas or Thanksgiving Turkey Stuffing

This dish is also called 'dressing' in the US and the main difference between 'dressing' and what we call 'stuffing' is that it's much heavier on the bread element. I like mine made with sausagemeat, sage, parsley and onion but it's common to find versions that are totally vegetarian, too, and are high in fruit and nuts instead. This is the perfect recipe to try out in different ways, finding out what suits you best. Much as I adore the turkey part of lunch or dinner, there's something about stuffing that's so more-ish… I always make loads because it's lovely inside Thanksgiving or Christmas sandwiches and great to pick at in the days following the feast. At home, we always stuff the bird's cavity but if you want to make stuffing balls instead, see the Cook's Tip below for how to do this.

Serves 8 or makes 16 balls

1 tbsp olive oil

300g sausagemeat, or the equivalent of roughly 4 best-quality chipolatas

30g unsalted butter

1 medium onion, peeled and very finely chopped

2 garlic cloves, peeled and very finely chopped

1 large stick celery, washed, topped, tailed and very finely chopped

180g white bread (crusty, fresh baguette produces the best results), whizzed in the food processor to make crumbs

1 tbsp each very finely chopped parsley and sage

250ml good-quality chicken or vegetable stock

salt and freshly ground black pepper

Heat the olive oil in a very large frying pan over a medium heat and cook the sausagemeat until separated into golden clumps. Remove from the pan with a slotted spoon and set aside.

Add the butter to the pan and melt. When foaming, add the onion, garlic and celery and cook until the onion is translucent and softened.

Add the breadcrumbs, herbs, stock and cooked sausagemeat. Taste and season, being careful not to over-salt as some stock is already super salty. Mash together with a wooden spoon until combined and set aside.

If stuffing the turkey straight away, use the warm mixture to do this. If using later, then leave to cool and either keep in the fridge for up to 4 days or freeze in an airtight container until ready.

cook's tip If you want to make stuffing balls, simply shape the stuffing into large golf balls. Preheat the oven to 180°C/fan 160°C/gas mark 4 and brush a little olive oil over the base of an oven tray to prevent sticking. Cook the balls for 20–30 minutes until golden.

If making this recipe as part of a big Christmas feast (see pages 206–7), I recommend stuffing the bird as this means one less item to worry about!

game and turkey

Turkey and Chicken Brine

I had to go to America and taste a bunch of different turkeys that had been home brined before I could work out exactly what I wanted flavour-wise for this recipe. I designed this brine solution with Christmas turkey in mind and have therefore given it a winter spice feel. If you want to brine a chicken for a summer roast or smoke a whole chicken (see Smoking Hot page 146), I suggest substituting lemon zest for the orange and removing the cinnamon and cloves. This brine is deliberately under salted so that you don't have to rinse the bird several times before roasting (which is tricky to do when you are only 5ft 2in and the bird is a big old thing). I suggest brining your turkey for roughly 24 hours for a free-range bird that weighs around 5kg. When you've brined your turkey once, you won't look back: the breast meat is succulent, juicy and full of flavour, rather than dry. For a full discussion on this interesting topic, check out Brine Me Tender (see page 71).

Brines a 5kg free-range turkey (for a 2kg chicken, halve the quantities and proceed in the same way)

200g light muscovado sugar

100g table salt

3 tbsp white peppercorns, bashed in a mortar and pestle

4 fresh bay leaves, crushed in your hands to release the oils

2 cinnamon sticks

1 star anise

2 tbsp mustard seeds

4 cloves

2 large onions, peeled and roughly chopped

5 garlic cloves, peeled and bashed

1 large sprig of rosemary, leaves stripped from the stalk

zest of 2 oranges cut into strips with a potato peeler

Heat 1 litre of water until boiling point and then add all the ingredients. Stir until the sugar and salt have dissolved.

Add a further 5 litres of water and transfer to a plastic container big enough to hold the bird and the water. It's important that you don't use a metal container as it will react with the meat. The best kind of container I've found is one of those giant Ziploc bags that work with a hoover so you can suck out the air and pack stuff neatly in the cupboard. The awesome thing about this is that by taking out the air, you're making sure that the bird is completely submerged. If you don't have one of these, I've also used a large cooler bag (like the ones you can buy at the supermarket checkout). Make sure the bag is secured shut once you've added the bird to the mix.

Brine the bird breast down for no more than 24 hours, overnight at a minimum.

When you are ready to cook the bird, rinse the insides out with clean water and pat it dry. Set the bird out, breast side up uncovered, on a clean board to dry at room temperature, which helps to achieve crispy skin during cooking. You do not need to add salt to the skin before roasting but feel free to season it once it's cooked and you've tasted it. The bird will have picked up lots of the flavouring from the brine solution so the seasoning is definitely best done after tasting.

cook's tip Here are some flavourings that you can substitute for both chicken and turkey if you don't want something so seasonally spiced – take out the star anise and cinnamon and replace the sugar with honey, add dried dill, dried tarragon or dried basil, dried shallots, lemon zest, instead of orange, and lots of fresh thyme.

Almost all herbs work well with chicken and turkey except for dried mint! And I prefer using dried herbs – except for rosemary and thyme – because they have a stronger flavour.

When brining a whole turkey, don't brine the giblets or liver – save them for the gravy, see page 202.

It's OK to brine your bird 2 days before using it and, once brined, just let it sit in the fridge unwrapped on a clean platter until needed.

Always Tender Turkey

This is it: the holy grail of turkey recipes for Christmas or Thanksgiving! Why is this turkey always tender? 1) Brine; 2) Low temp then high temp; and 3) Plenty of flavoured butter under the skin (which produces the best gravy on the planet). The key with turkey, as with all meat, is *sourcing* an outdoor-reared, slow-growing, naturally fed bird. The cooking is fairly straightforward – the only thing to remember is that you need to soak the bird for 24 hours before cooking – everything you need to know about this is in the Turkey and Chicken Brine recipe on page 196. I've really gone to town on flavouring the turkey but you could just as easily rub the brined skin with olive oil, a crunch of salt and some black pepper if you can't be bothered with the extra hassle of making a flavoured butter or prefer a less rich recipe.

Serves 10

1 × 5kg brined turkey (save the neck and giblets if you have them for gravy)

1 × quantity of Stuffing (see page 194), cooked and at room temperature

2 carrots, peeled, topped, tailed and cut into rough chunks

2 sticks celery, washed and cut into rough chunks

2 medium onions, peeled and each cut into 6

6 garlic cloves, bruised, peeled and roughly chopped

4 bay leaves

2 leeks (white part only), cut in quarters lengthways and cleaned

2 tbsp olive oil

900ml good-quality chicken or vegetable stock

a little extra olive oil to rub all over the bird

250ml dry white wine

3 tbsp cornflour, mixed with 2 tbsp softened butter until you get a paste

Remove the turkey from the brine solution and pat dry inside and out. Leave to dry at room temperature for at least 2 hours to dry the skin. This will help it to get crispy later on.

Preheat the oven to 160°C/fan 140°C/gas mark 3.

Stuff the turkey with either your own stuffing or the recipe on page 194 and truss the legs with some kitchen string.

To make the flavoured butter, beat the butter and all the other ingredients together in a bowl with a wooden spoon until combined. You want the butter to be of 'spreadable' consistency.

Carefully place your fingers under the breast skin to loosen. Take three-quarters of the flavoured butter and spread under the skin on both breasts. Do the same with the remaining butter on the thigh meat, at the cavity end of the bird. Tuck any loose skin down so that the butter is securely contained and put the bird breast side up back on the board.

In a roasting tin large enough to hold the turkey with plenty of space to spare, place the carrots, celery, onions, garlic, bay leaves, leeks, turkey neck and giblets. Toss with the olive oil and arrange them in a criss-cross pattern so that the bird can comfortably sit on top. Pour over 200ml of the stock to prevent sticking or burning.

100ml double cream

salt and freshly ground
    black pepper

FOR THE FLAVOURED BUTTER

100g softened butter

1 tbsp garlic granules

1 tsp smoked paprika

¼ tsp ground nutmeg

½ tsp ground coriander

freshly ground white and
    black pepper

Put the turkey in the roasting tin on top of the vegetables and rub the skin all over with a little olive oil to make it glisten. Place the turkey in the middle of the preheated oven and cook for 3½ hours. You do not need to baste this turkey as the breast will be tender from the brine and I find that opening the oven is very unhelpful because it messes with the temperature and cooking times.

Remove the bird from the roasting tin and transfer to a clean wooden board. Take out the vegetables, garlic, neck, giblets and bay leaves and put into a medium saucepan. Pour in all the buttery juices from the roasting tin and return the turkey to the now-empty tin. Crank the heat up to 220°C/fan 200°C/gas mark 7 and place the bird back in the middle of the oven to crisp for 30 minutes.

Whilst the turkey is getting a tan at this high temperature, make the gravy. Add the wine and the rest of the stock to the saucepan with the vegetables and bring to the boil. Simmer gently for 30 minutes to reduce, cook out the wine and give the ingredients a chance to impart their flavour.

Remove all the vegetables, bay leaves, neck, giblets and garlic with a slotted spoon and discard. Whisk in the cornflour and butter mixture. Gently bring back to the boil, whisking all the time to prevent the cornflour from clumping. Simmer until thickened and glossy, around 10 minutes. When piping hot, add the cream and season to taste with salt and pepper. You can heat this through again at the last minute, if necessary.

Once the bird has had its full cooking time (4 hours), insert a knife into the thigh to make sure that the juices run clear. Leave to rest for 30–60 minutes uncovered.

Serve the rested turkey on a warmed serving plate, with the gravy and all other side dishes piping hot.

turkey day countdown

The only enjoyable way I know to do Christmas with all the trimmings is to prepare the 'eck out of it and plan your sides very carefully – what goes into the oven when and what can be made ahead. I decided to include a Turkey Day Countdown because I realised that every year I make a planner with a to-do list for each day. I literally couldn't think straight without it AND be ready with all the dishes piping hot AND wear a party dress AND have time for a vodka martini before kick off. So this is straight from the colourful timing and recipe map in my head, that then sits on my wall come December. If you've never done this before, you'll be surprised how fun it is to plot in this way…

This plan presumes that you have pre-ordered your turkey from the butcher (I tend to get this done 4–6 weeks before collection). I'm not including a specific pudding or dessert recipe since this tends to vary wildly from home to home. I'm going to assume that the dessert is either ready or else made before the below starts. (I tend to make my mince pies anytime from the beginning of December, and my pudding is usually finished and ready to be steeped in brandy by the time October rolls around. Saying that, between you and me, some supermarkets sell really good puddings – go for the most fruity, luxury one you can find – if you can't be bothered to make it yourself.)

Feel free to replace or re-jig recipes according to what you're making, swapping like for like. The key is to mentally divide dishes that go into the oven (*roasted*) from dishes that are cooked on the stovetop and can be reheated later on (*stovetop*). These represent the two different categories of cooking and need to be thought of as vying for space in the kitchen. Here is a list of what I would consider to be the 'whole nine yards' in terms of a Christmas menu that feeds roughly ten people:

roasted

- Beef Dripping Roast Potatoes (page 43)

- Sweet and Salty Roasted Parsnips and Carrots (page 212)

- Always Tender Turkey (page 198)

- Cocktail Sausages (follow packet instructions)

- Bacon Rolls (or Candied Bacon – page 193)

- Christmas or Thanksgiving Turkey Stuffing (page 194 – inside the bird makes life a lot easier so this is what I've assumed here)

stovetop

- Nena's Mashed Potatoes (page 25)

- Brussels Sprouts (or Wilted Brussels Sprout Salad with Lemon and Honey Walnuts – page 211)

- Ruby Cranberry Sauce (page 208)

- Bread Sauce (page 208)

- Gravy (page 20)

7 | Turkey Day (T.D.) minus 7

Draw a visual plan of all the dishes, showing the different categories: MEAT DISHES, SIDES, SAUCES.

For each recipe, make a list of the ingredients with quantities. This helps to make sure you don't forget any recipes or ingredients. It doesn't matter if you have the same ingredient twice – you can accumulate them at the end. ☐

Match each recipe with a dish to make sure that you won't get caught short on the day, doubling up sides if needs be. I suggest also plotting what flowers (if any) you're going to use and earmarking vases for them. The big job tomorrow is to tackle the shopping list so make sure you add any flowers to your list, as well as any candles, disposable napkins, tablecloth and table ornaments you might need to get. ☐

T.D. minus 7 is a day to feel organised and get ready for indoor things to come.

6 | T.D. minus 6

Today we're going to shop for and make a few things ahead, so that the rest of the week is all about doing bits and pieces, rather than one BIG BLITZ. ☐

SHOP FOR THE FOLLOWING:

recipes

Cranberry Sauce ☐

Roast Potatoes or Mashed Potatoes ☐

Bread Sauce ☐

items

- Shop-bought puddings and nibbles that won't deteriorate, like crisps. ☐

- Table decorations, disposable napkins and roasting trays (if using). ☐

- Wine, beer, Champagne or whatever it is you plan to drink with the meal. ☐

- Container to brine the turkey. It needs to be made of plastic – or at least not be made of metal or any other material that will react. My favourite vessel is a large, vacuum-sealed Ziploc bag you can buy online. Otherwise a plastic bin or crate is good, too. ☐

If you have a smallish kitchen (like me) then you might want to make some space in both the fridge and relevant cupboards so that you have somewhere to put all the stuff that's about to come into your home… You may consider this taking it too far but I section off a 'Christmas space' in both so that all the relevant items are in one place.

5 T.D. minus 5

If you're making a tart or pie that includes pastry (homemade mince pies, for example), today is the day to make the pastry, line the tin and freeze it until T.D. minus 1. If you're having brandy butter, make that today, too, and store it in the fridge. If you're not bothering with any of the above, take a day off from the kitchen. ☐

4 T.D. minus 4

Boil the potatoes for your roasties. Shake (see recipe page 43) and freeze in Tupperware. Or else boil them for the mash and make the mash (see recipe page 25). Once cool, cover mash closely with clingfilm and put in the fridge. That's your first side done! ☐

Make the Ruby Cranberry Sauce and, once cooked, put into an airtight plastic container. Cool and store in the fridge. ☐

Infuse the milk for the Bread Sauce. Once cool, refrigerate until T.D. minus 1. ☐

Make ice. For cocktails and for cooling down blanched vegetables – you can never have too much! ☐

3 T.D. minus 3

Shop for the ingredients to make the other sides (vegetables, stuffing and also small meat items). ☐

Make the stuffing (see recipe page 194). Once cooked, set aside. Once cool, place in the fridge, tightly clingfilmed until it gets used inside the turkey on T.D. ☐

Prep the devils on horseback and bacon rolls according to packet instructions (remember to stretch the bacon with the back of a knife before rolling and securing around the prune with a cocktail stick). It's surprising how much time it takes to get these small items ready. ☐

2 T.D. minus 2

Prep your sprouts (see recipe page 211), peel and cut your parsnips and carrots (see recipe page 216) or any other kind of veg that you're serving. ☐

Finish making the Bread Sauce. Once cool, store it in the fridge in a covered plastic container. ☐

Prep any garnishes, like caramelised nuts or fresh parsley or coriander, by which I mean put the ingredients into Ziploc bags or small plastic boxes and label them so you know what they're for on the day. Put in the fridge along with the dishes they're garnishing. ☐

Lay the table… I know it sounds mad to do it two days before, but believe me, T.D. minus 1 is going to be a busy day! Lay everything out exactly as it's going to be on T.D. – except for the flowers. ☐

Prep the butter to put under the turkey's skin and also the veg to go underneath it (see recipe page 198). Store in a labelled Ziploc bag until T.D. ☐

1 T.D. minus 1

Pick up the turkey. Remove the giblets and neck and set aside for gravy. ☐

Pick up the flowers and anything that you may have forgotten. When you get home, arrange the flowers in the vases you earmarked earlier in the week. ☐

Make the brine and place the turkey into it. Make sure that the bird's totally covered, so weigh it down if necessary. Keep in a cool place for up to 24 hours. It doesn't have to be the fridge: a cold room or corridor will do fine. If you put it outside, make sure it's protected from foxes or that it's not so cold it will freeze! ☐

Heat the hot fat and roast the potatoes until cooked and crispy. These will reheat beautifully so no need to worry. Once the potatoes are roasted, roast off the parsnips and the carrots (see recipe page 212). ☐

Organise all items in the fridge with their respective garnishes, washed, fried or chopped as the case may be. I like to put post-its on the lids so I know what's what and don't forget anything. The idea here is that it will only take a few minutes to finish these off and all the messy knives and boards can be avoided altogether. ☐

Cook the devils on horseback, cocktail sausages and other small meat items that you're serving with the turkey. Once cooked, cool and keep in the fridge in an ovenproof dish – all together is fine. ☐

TURKEY DAY!

You want to hear the good news? All you have to do today is roast the turkey, make the gravy and reheat a few sides whilst the bird is resting. THAT'S IT.

If you want to have a nice long bath and give the house a quick tidy, you can! No stress, no pressure.

Think backwards: it's no longer T.D. but Turkey Time (T.T.). Make sure you leave enough time to cook and rest the bird according to its weight.

- -

T.T. minus 6 hours

Take the turkey out of the brine and pat it dry inside and out. Leave it to air dry for a couple of hours at room temperature. Take the stuffing and the flavoured butter out of the fridge and let them stand in the kitchen. ☐

When you're ready and the timings fit your plans, stuff the turkey and prep it according to the recipe, including putting the butter under its skin. Put it in the oven and set a timer. ☐

Check the table and get yourself ready. It's time to have a cocktail and start enjoying yourself! ☐

T.T. minus 1 hour

When the turkey has had its time, remove it from the oven and rest the bird under a clean tea towel. It wants 30–60 minutes resting time. As soon as the bird is out of the oven, it's time to make the gravy according to the recipe on page 199. ☐

Use the now empty oven to reheat the roast potatoes and any meat items that are already cooked but want to be served hot. After 20 minutes of reheating the meat and roasties, add the roasted vegetables to the oven for a warm through as they don't take as long – 180°C/fan 160°C/gas mark 4 is usually a good temp to get things moving fast without burning. When they're hot through, turn off the oven but leave the door shut. Remember to put the turkey serving dish in the oven to warm, too. ☐

Whilst everything in the oven is warming, finish the gravy with any juices from the cooked turkey. Taste and season well. The gravy wants to be piping hot. ☐

Reheat the Cranberry Sauce, Bread Sauce and Mashed Potato, if using. I like to use the microwave (less mess) but you can do it on the hob if you prefer. Garnish the now warmed vegetables and any other dish that needs it. ☐

- -

TURKEY TIME!

Plate up the turkey on a warmed dish and add all the little meat bits around it. Set all the veg, sides and sauces on the table. Dig in!

Ruby Cranberry Sauce

This is traditionally served with turkey (see page 207) but it goes amazingly well with game (whether venison or fowl) and also with Swedish Meatballs (see page 66) if you can't lay your mitts on any lingonberry jam. Super easy to make, this is a wonderful staple to keep in your fridge for when you fancy a hit of scarlet.

Makes roughly 500ml

600g fresh cranberries
400g caster sugar
finely grated zest of 1 orange
100ml ruby Port
juice of 1 lemon
1 star anise

Put all the ingredients into a small saucepan. Warm over the lowest heat possible, until all the sugar has dissolved and the fruit is swimming in juice. Turn up the heat a tiny bit and simmer gently until all the fruit has started to burst and release its seeds. Take off the heat, remove the star anise and transfer to a sterilised jar.

Keep in the jar in the fridge for up to 3 months.

Bread Sauce

I have tested many different versions of this recipe and it really matters what bread you use. I recommend a white bloomer, rather than 'plastic' bread or sourdough, both of which impart too much flavour (the first is too sweet, the second too savoury).

Serves 8

1 very large white onion, peeled
    and cut into quarters
6 cloves garlic, peeled and
    finely chopped
4 whole cloves
4 fresh bay leaves, crushed in
    your hand
1 blade mace
freshly ground black pepper
1 tsp salt
1 litre full-fat milk
400g white bread, crusts
    removed, torn into pieces
30g unsalted butter
100ml double cream
½ fresh nutmeg, finely grated

Place the onion quarters, garlic, cloves, bay leaves, mace, pepper and salt in a large saucepan with the milk. Bring to the boil and then leave to infuse off the heat for at least 2 hours.

Strain the infused milk, discarding the aromatics. Place the bread in a medium saucepan and pour the milk over. Add the butter and cook for about 5 minutes over a medium heat, until the milk has been absorbed by the bread and the butter has melted.

Finally, take off the heat and stir in the cream and nutmeg. Serve hot (see page 206).

Spiced Winter Jelly

I really love this ruby jelly with game of all kinds and especially with Christmas turkey. The acidity of the redcurrants, the spices and the sweetness of the pomegranates marry really well with turkey and liven up the stuffing. This jelly works beautifully with pâtés made from liver, terrines or with hard sheep's cheese.

Makes 1 × 400ml jar

250g redcurrants, rinsed under the tap (no need to take off the stems)

juice of 3 large pomegranates (roughly 300ml)

2 star anise

2 cinnamon sticks

2 cloves

juice of 2 lemons

400g jam sugar (with added pectin)

cook's tip To sterilise jars, place them and their lids (beside them, not on top of them) in the middle of an oven preheated to 180°C/ fan 160°C/gas mark 4 for 15 minutes. Remove and set aside until needed.

If you can't get hold of pomegranates or don't fancy juicing them, you can also use Pom Wonderful 100% pomegranate juice.

Combine the redcurrants, pomegranate juice, star anise, cinnamon, cloves and lemon juice in a pan and bring to the boil. Spoon off any foam that rises to the surface and discard. Simmer gently for 15 minutes then pass through a fine mesh sieve.

Add the sugar and simmer gently for a further 20 minutes. Repeat the removal of any foam that forms on the surface, as this will help the jelly to be clear.

Once the jelly has been bubbling for just under 35 minutes, decant into the sterilised jar. Put the lid on and set aside to cool for at least 2 hours, or overnight. If you want to give this jelly an extra Christmassy look, suspend a star anise in the jelly by pushing it down the side of the jar when the jelly is starting to set.

Wilted Brussels Sprout Salad with Lemon and Honey Walnuts

Hmmm… Tricky things, Brussels sprouts. I've never really gone for them as a whole. They're dense and just too, well, Brussels sprouty. A mouthful is a big commitment to the flavour of cabbage. Done this way, however, they're light and lovely with a nutty aftertaste that marries well with lemon and walnuts. If you don't much like Brussels sprouts, then give this recipe a go.

Serves 8–10 as part of a Christmas dinner, or 4–6 as a side

100g walnut halves

3 tbsp clear honey

sea salt

1kg Brussels sprouts

2 tbsp olive oil

50g butter

finely grated zest of 2 unwaxed lemons

ground white pepper

cook's tip Chopped fresh sage and smoked bacon bits are the other way to go with sprouts if you don't fancy the lemon vibe. In this case, simply fry off the bacon first in the olive oil with the sage, then remove when crispy. Use the fat in the pan to fry off the sprouts and proceed as per the recipe, replacing the walnuts and lemon with bacon and sage.

To make the caramelised walnuts, place a large frying pan over a medium heat and toast the nuts until golden and smelling nutty. Add the honey and quickly turn to make sure all the nuts are coated. Sizzle in this way for just over 30 seconds, then tip out on to a plate covered with waxed baking paper and sprinkle with a little salt. Cool completely before using – this is what makes the nuts crunchy. During the cooling time, you can turn your attention to the sprouts.

Put on the radio and start preparing the sprouts. Begin by chopping off the base of one sprout and peeling away the first few leaves. Cut each sprout into slices of roughly the thickness of a pound coin, going from the base to the top, as opposed to through the waist.

Once all the sprouts are ready, heat a large frying pan over a high heat. Add the olive oil and stir fry the sprouts until lightly tanned around the edges but still crunchy, roughly 4 minutes. You will need to do this in batches to avoid them overcrowding and steaming.

Once they are all golden, add the butter and lemon zest to the pan – and return any sprouts that you have set aside from previous batches. When the butter has melted, cover with a lid, turn off the heat and leave to steam for 3 minutes.

Toss the sprouts with the lid on, tip into a serving dish, sprinkle with the walnuts, a little bit of salt and ground white pepper and serve straight away.

Sweet and Salty Roasted Parsnips and Carrots

I'm that weird breed of person who likes to have a mixture of salt and sweet popcorn when I go to the movies (first a layer of salt, then sweet, then a final layer of salt – they mustn't mingle). Same applies to this recipe. What appeals to me here is the mixture between the sticky sweetness of these root vegetables once glazed and the crunch of the salty sea flakes. It's absolutely essential not to overcrowd the roasting tray otherwise the vegetables will steam rather than roast and get crispy. To this end, this recipe only feeds 4 as a side dish but would stretch to 8–10 folks as part of a Christmas feast.

Serves 4

2 tbsp olive oil

1 tbsp clear honey (acacia is my favourite)

1 tbsp maple syrup

400g carrots, peeled, topped, tailed and cut in half lengthways (try and find carrots that aren't too thick if possible)

600g parsnips, peeled, topped, tailed and cut in quarters (roughly the same width as the carrots)

a generous crunch of salt flakes and freshly ground black pepper

Preheat the oven to 220°C/fan 200°C/gas mark 7.

Whisk the olive oil with the honey and maple syrup in a large bowl. Add the vegetables and toss to coat completely.

Lift the vegetables on to a large roasting tray. You want them to have enough space so that they don't overlap – this is important otherwise they won't go crispy but will steam instead. Roast at the top of the preheated oven for 40 minutes until golden and sticky.

Sprinkle with salt flakes and a generous crunch of black pepper before serving (see page 206).

cook's tip If you plan to make these the day before (as instructed on Turkey Day Countdown – see page 200), then cook them completely, leave to cool (do not sprinkle with the salt) and then reheat when you need them for 5 minutes in a very hot oven, spread out on the tray as they were when they were cooked. Sprinkle with salt and a crunch of pepper before serving.

Thanksgiving Turkey Sandwich with a Moist Maker

Those of you who are familiar with my very silly sense of humour and long-lasting love of the television series *Friends* will be surprised it's taken so long for me to include this recipe in one of my books. If there's one category of food that the US really excels at, in my opinion, it's the sandwich. And a great sandwich is not an easy thing to pull off… Some of my favourite sandwiches include ones that I've had the day after Thanksgiving, when the fridge is heaving with leftovers. Lashings of mayonnaise and a little bit of everything is a good start but this sandwich also includes a layer of gravy-soaked bread, a flavour airbag of juicy deliciousness in the middle of the turkey and all the other yummy stuff. It's a game changer. And I owe it all to the fine folks who came up with Monica Geller's infamous creation in Season 5. This recipe works brilliantly with leftover Sunday roast chicken, too. The stuffing is an important component of the sandwich so hold out for a time when you have made some of that, too. As with most sandwiches, this is not so much a 'recipe' as a list of ingredients to assemble (and, in this case, a crucial way of highlighting the virtues of a moist maker).

Serves 1

3 thick slices fresh, wholegrain bread, cut from a loaf (the soft and supple kind)

plenty of gravy, brought to the boil then cooled slightly before using

salt and freshly ground black pepper

mayonnaise (I use Hellmann's)

roast turkey breast, sliced

cranberry sauce

stuffing

crunchy lettuce, such as Little Gem (even Iceberg works well)

Toast one of the pieces of bread and then soak it in the warm gravy until it has absorbed some but not for so long that it starts to disintegrate. This is the moist maker and needs to be seasoned with salt and freshly ground black pepper.

Spread a generous layer of mayonnaise on the other two slices of the bread.

Add the turkey to one slice, followed by the cranberry sauce and the moist maker.

Place the stuffing and the lettuce on top of the moist maker and finish with the other slice of bread slathered in mayonnaise.

The sandwich is now ready to be enjoyed with a side of crisps, if you want to go all out. Just remember not to wear a white shirt… And, in case you're wondering, this is *not* date food. This is best friend food, when schmearing is allowed and even encouraged (for the sake of humour).

hang in there

Dry ageing, or hanging, means to hang freshly slaughtered meat on a hook or a shelf in a temperature-controlled environment, for a prescribed period of time, to tenderise it and develop its natural flavour.

how does it work?

To understand how ageing works, it's important to realise that meat muscle is nothing more than bundles of fibres, of varying sizes, held together by thin but sturdy sheaths of connective tissue. I find it helps to visualise meat muscle as a thick rope that is made up of filaments going in the same direction. Each muscle is a different rope (some big, some small) that are separate but all linked by tendons and bone to form the carcass. Right after slaughter, the rope is full of moisture (blood, water mostly, some fat). If you cut the muscle fresh and put it in a frying pan or a hot oven, it will react by shrinking and releasing its juice all at once. What you will obtain, therefore, is tough, dry meat. If, on the other hand, you hang the meat, you will give the volatile elements that make up the muscle a chance to settle down, adapt to their new form; rest, if you will. The longer you hang the meat, the more moisture it loses until eventually it starts to break its internal structure down. In other words, it starts the decomposition process. This is nothing to be alarmed about – on the contrary. It's because the muscle is breaking down very slowly during ageing that it becomes tender and acquires deeper flavour. The aforementioned rope starts to disintegrate. It starts to be less rope-like and become silky, buttery. That transition into fully flavoured velvet is the melt-in-your-mouth factor.

Depending on the animal, this settling phase that starts the ageing can take as little as 3 days but butchers like Peter Hannan of The Meat Merchant, prefer to rest the carcass for a minimum of 5 days by bringing down the temperature slowly. As he so beautifully put it, 'Freshly slaughtered meat is still a living piece of flesh… it needs to settle into its new state.' Temperature is crucial during hanging and will dictate how long you can hang a piece of meat in order to encourage the good bacteria to get to work and hamper the bad bacteria from deteriorating it. Pete is a master when it comes to the art of handling meat and he has devised a unique salt room where he ages beef for up to a year. Under the right circumstances, there is no limit to how long you can hang meat (nor is there any legal limit at time of publication). Of course, it loses weight as it hangs, which is why so few butchers hang their meat for more than 3–4 weeks. By way of example, you can expect that a rib of beef will lose between 12–15 per cent weight over the course of 28 days.

We've talked about beef but it's also worth mentioning game when it comes to dry ageing. Being lean and rather tough to begin with, wild game are particularly well suited to hanging. Again, maturing them in a cold, dry place will mean that the meat acquires added flavour and, crucially, tenderness. It's a fine balance, though – pheasants, partridges and other small birds can be hung for a week or more but the flavours get too strong for me after about 3–4 days. I don't love those high, gamey notes but lots of people do.

The final thing to say about hanging is that intensifying the flavour of the meat is an excellent way of guaranteeing a feeling of satiation. In other words, a little bit goes a long way. **I am and have always been a believer that quality removes the need for quantity.** Even if I wanted to, I can't eat lots of cured ham, dry-aged beef, or gamey pheasant.

Another point to mull over is that the better the quality of the meat to begin with, the more dry ageing it will be rewarding – it enhances the qualities that are already there in potential form within the meat. Reversely, it also doesn't make any commercial sense to dry age poor-quality meat, so most dry-aged meat is likely to have come from the kind of meat you want to eat. Don't be surprised or put off if a rib of beef that has been aged for a long time comes with a black crust. This is normal and is in fact a sign of maturing. *That's* the piece of meat you want.

beef

You can call beef 'dry aged' if it's hung for a minimum of 12 days. There is no limit to how long you can dry age beef, providing you are in expert hands. Pete's beef is aged for an average of 45 days.

lamb

A minimum of 7 days; 10 is ideal.

pork and chicken

A minimum of 5 days.

game

From 3–10 days, depending on how high you like the flavour of your meat.

a note on wet ageing

Harold McGee defines wet ageing in the following terms: 'Most meat is now butchered into retail cuts at the packing plant shortly after slaughter, wrapped in plastic, and shipped to market immediately, with an average of 4 to 10 days between slaughter and sale. Such meat is sometimes wet-aged, or kept in its plastic wrap for some days or weeks, where it's shielded from oxygen and retains moisture while its enzymes work. Wet-aged meat can develop some of the flavour and tenderness of dry-aged meat, but not the same concentration of flavour.'

The benefits of wet ageing are almost all aimed at the producer and not the customer. Wet ageing is better than no ageing but it's not the same process at all and produces very different results. If the animal was well reared and therefore has good natural flavour and some intramuscular fat, you won't notice it as much but you're always better off with dry-aged meat.

Cheating Peking Duck

The real thing is an absolute nightmare for the home cook: a 48-hour ordeal of hanging ducks to air dry them after glazing repeatedly, roasting them in an oven from a hook so that they cook 360° to get the skin crispy – and I haven't even started on the bicycle pumps and the hairdryers. OK, so I'm exaggerating a tiny bit but I've devised this recipe so that you get the *experience* of Peking duck without robbing you of your will to live. If you fancy pushing the boat out (duck always makes me feel feast-ish), you can make your own Peking Pancakes (see page 219). I can't tell you how many tests I've done to get this recipe right but I felt that a meat book without a Peking duck recipe was somehow wrong. Done well, nothing beats it. It's important to leave the duck uncovered in the fridge the night before in order to achieve a crispy skin. Apart from that slightly annoying planning ahead bit, the rest is really straightforward. I need to emphasise that this recipe is a *cheat* and it's not exactly the same as a real Peking duck but cooking it like this will ensure crispy skin all over and juicy meat. For the legs to be cooked through, the breast is not pink in this version but it will still be tender. Come to think of it, Peking duck in the best restaurants in Beijing isn't served with pink breast meat so I think I'm off the hook. Literally and figuratively.

Serves 4

1 whole free-range duck
    (weighing roughly 2kg)
roughly 2 tbsp table salt
    (not flakes)
1 × 500ml can of beer

The day before, remove the duck from any packaging and scatter over a generous amount of table salt and rub into the fat. Open the can of beer and drink half of it. Place the salted duck on top of the can so that it straddles it securely. Move the duck and the can on to a baking sheet and place in the fridge. I sometimes need to remove a shelf in order to accommodate the height of the duck on the can. The important thing here is to leave the duck uncovered so that the skin can dry out for 24 hours at least. Two days is even better. During this time, occasionally wipe off any moisture and re-apply more salt. This is what makes the skin crispy. Don't be surprised if the skin goes several shades darker during this time.

Take the duck out of the fridge and bring it to room temperature for at least 2 hours.

Preheat the oven to 220°C/fan 200°C/gas mark 7. You do need a fan setting to get really crispy skin

cook's tip There will
be time to make the
pancakes during the
duck's cooking time so
that they are super fresh.

here. If you don't have a fan setting on your oven,
the next best thing is to turn it to 240°C/gas mark 9
and cook it for the same amount of time.

Cook the duck at the bottom of the preheated
oven for 40 minutes, until it is crispy all over.

Once cooked, remove from the oven and rest
on the can for a further 15 minutes. I recommend
puncturing the can with a carving fork to let out
the hot liquid, before easing the duck carefully off
the can and carving the meat.

Serve with cucumber, spring onions, hoisin
sauce and pancakes.

Peking Pancakes

This is a recipe to go with Cheating Peking Duck (see page 216). You can buy these online but a) it's such a hassle to think that far ahead, b) they're not difficult or expensive to make from scratch, and c) they taste about a million times nicer homemade. Oh, and d) it's good fun.

Makes 20

250g plain flour
125ml boiling water

cook's tip These pancakes keep well for at least an hour, providing they are safely wrapped in clingfilm.

They are also a crafty way of using up other leftover meat you might have – try it with Garlic and Fennel Crispy Pork Belly (see page 161) or Pulled Pork Tennessee (see page 174), for a different take on a flour taco.

Pour the flour into a medium mixing bowl and make a well in the middle. Slowly pour in the boiling water, mixing with a fork, until all the water is absorbed and you have a slightly flaky-looking dough.

Turn out on to a clean, lightly floured surface and knead for 5 minutes until the dough feels elastic and has come together.

Roll into a sausage shape and cut into 20 discs roughly the same size. Wrap them in clingfilm to avoid them drying out.

Generously flour a clean surface to avoid sticking. Roll each disc into a very thin circle. Imagine you are trying to read the newspaper through it – that thin. Repeat with all the discs – you may need to flour between rollings – and cover with clingfilm again.

Heat a frying pan and cook them one or two at a time, flipping when the first side is cooked, coloured and has started to blister. This will take 15 seconds to 1 minute tops.

Once cooked, put on a plate, cover with a clean tea towel and repeat until all the pancakes are done.

Cinnamon-roasted Duck Breast with Fresh Orange and Spiced Syrup

I really dislike that old French classic of *Canard à l'Orange*. The combination of duck and oranges (or cherries or figs or any other very sweet and slightly sharp fruit) is a good one, though usually it's a huge faff and the oranges are gagged in a thick sauce, rather than being left to be fresh and vibrant and well, orange. The cooking technique for the duck comes from David Tanis in *A Platter of Figs*. The reason I love his method of cooking the breasts in a pair is that it really helps keep the meat perfectly pink and it also avoids the dreaded searing of the duck on the stovetop, which will stink out your kitchen for two days. His idea is very simple: you tie two duck breasts together top to toe and fat side facing outwards and roast them like a pair of slippers held together by butcher's string. No fuss, no mess – and beautifully cooked duck every time. Remember to salt the meat generously when you take it out of the fridge, at least an hour before cooking and pat it dry before it goes into the oven. This is wonderful with a light spinach and pomegranate salad with thinly sliced red onion and toasted pine nuts (a little balsamic, lemon and olive oil dressing is perfect). It's also great on the side of a big plate of blanched and pan-fried green beans with garlic and toasted almonds with the sauce acting as a dressing.

Serves 2 as a main or 4 as a starter

2 duck breasts (weighing roughly 350g each), pricked with a fork hither and thither over the fat

plenty of salt and freshly bashed pink peppercorns

FOR THE RUB

1 tsp ground cinnamon

½ tsp ground ginger

½ tsp ground coriander

a tiny pinch ground cloves

1 tsp table salt (not flakes)

At least 2 hours before cooking (the night before is ideal), combine the rub ingredients on a plate and then cover both duck breasts in the mixture. Tie the breasts together with butcher's string, making sure the fat is on the outside of the bundle. Leave uncovered in the fridge until an hour before you are ready to cook, sitting them on their side so that the fat is exposed on both sides. This will help it to crisp up later on. Salt the meat generously.

Preheat the oven to 200°C/fan 180°C/gas mark 6.

When the oven is hot, pat the duck breast dry and put the bundle in a roasting tray and then into the oven with one fat side down and the other facing up. Cook for 15 minutes, then turn them over so that the bottom goes on the top and cook for another 15 minutes.

FOR THE ORANGE AND SPICED SYRUP

2 small juicing oranges (choose a variety with sharp flavoured juice)

2 tbsp aged balsamic vinegar

3 tbsp runny honey

1 star anise

2 tbsp fat from cooking the duck

cook's tip If you don't fancy the rub or just want to try a plain version, follow the cooking instructions and just remember to take the meat out of the fridge and salt it 2 hours before cooking.

If you want to serve more people, just multiply the amounts in increments of two.

Meanwhile, slice the peel and pith from the oranges, going from north to south. Do this over a plate so you can catch any juice that runs out. When you have two 'bald' oranges, slice them thinly going across the waist to create delicate, thin wheels. It's best to do this with a serrated knife. You need 100ml of juice for the syrup so, if you don't have enough, crush a couple of slices in your hand to give you the juice required.

Place the juice from the oranges in a small saucepan with the balsamic vinegar, honey, star anise and a couple of strips of orange peel, having first removed any white pith you can see. Bring to the boil and boil for 3 minutes to reduce by half. Take off the heat and remove the star anise and the orange peel.

When the duck has had its cooking time, take 2 tbsp of the fat from the roasting tray and whisk into the orange sauce until the mixture has emulsified. Taste and season with salt. Leave the duck breasts to rest in the remaining fat for 15 minutes before removing from the pan, undoing the parcels and slicing the breasts against the grain. Pour away the remaining fat into a container and save for dripping. Any meat juices (these are the dark juices under the slick of fat) should go into the saucepan with the orange, vinegar and honey reduction.

If the sauce has cooled down, give it a final heat up and whisk before serving the duck with the orange slices and a little of the spiced syrup spooned over the top. Season with pink peppercorns and salt, if needed.

Foie Gras Maison

The pressure was firmly on when I did a version of this recipe live with my father on the France 2 show I sometimes present... Foie Gras done by an English cook: *sacrilège*! The thing is: this recipe is absolutely amazing and they loved it. People would stop me in the street to tell me how good it was when they had tried it at home, no joke. It originally comes from my father's downstairs neighbour, a wonderful little lady called Danielle. When going for dinner at her apartment, you can expect anything from boiled head of veal (done well, this is a triumph) to monkfish cheeks in a cream sauce. She is one of the best French cooks I've ever come across. Dad sometimes makes this recipe at Christmas. It works like a dream, with almost no wasted *foie*. There is a duck farm up the road from him in Normandy where they fatten the ducks the natural way. This means that the livers are smaller but there is none of that horrendous and inhumane treatment you can expect on industrially produced foie gras farms. I'm extremely selective when it comes to where I buy my livers and, this way, I can enjoy foie gras in tiny doses once or twice a year with a clear conscience. More on the prickly subject of foie gras on page 225. For a crash course on how to remove the veins without damaging the flesh see below.

Makes 500g

1 whole duck or goose foie gras (divided into lobes), raw

2 tbsp fine sea salt for the exterior, + a pinch for the inside

2 tbsp freshly ground black pepper for the exterior, + a pinch for the inside

3 tbsp Port, Madeira or Sauternes

Melba toast (see Cook's Tip, page 224), or toasted sourdough, to serve

You can either watch a Youtube video on how to devein a lobe of foie gras or you can do this: gently creak open the two lobes and follow the vein that goes into the smaller lobe. Carefully tug it free from the lobe and then follow it into the larger lobe with your fingers. I find it's much easier to open the large lobe as you would a book, in a couple of places. The vein is then easily accessible. In any case, it doesn't matter if you make a bit of a hash of this because you are going to re-form the pâté later anyway, so just focus on the most important task, which is to catch all the veins, whether they be the small ones or the main large one. You need to be gentle or they will snap and become impossible to remove. This is surgery! The reason it is so important to remove the veins is that it's extremely unpleasant to find one in the pâté later on.

Recipe continues

Fois Gras Maison *continued*

cook's tip To make Melba toast, place thick, sliced, white bread in the toaster on a low setting. Once it pops up, carefully slice in half widthways. Toasting the bread makes it much easier to cut. Remove the crusts and cut each half into two triangles. Bake in the oven at 170°C/fan 150°C/gas mark 3 until golden and crisp on both sides.

When you have a pile of deveined raw liver in front of you, season it generously with salt and lots of black pepper.

Next, compact the liver together in your hands to form a log about the width of a French baguette.

Lay out a sheet of clingfilm on the prep surface and sprinkle the 2 tablespoons each of salt and pepper on to the clingfilm.

Roll the log of foie gras on to the salt and pepper, making sure that all the sides are coated evenly.

Tightly wrap this in clingfilm and set aside in the fridge for exactly 4 hours.

When the foie gras has had its time, carefully remove the clingfilm and scrape off the salt and pepper layer on the outside of the liver and discard.

Next, brush the liver with the Port, Madeira or Sauternes and re-wrap in clingfilm. This time the liver needs to go back in the fridge for at least 6 hours or up to a week.

It's ready! You can either use it all now or freeze some for up to 6 months. When you defrost it, you have about 5 days within which to consume it.

Let the foie gras sit at room temperature for 30 minutes before piling on to toast and seasoning with a little salt and black pepper (taste it first). You can also add a little dab of Spiced Winter Jelly (see page 209) – it's a beautiful combination, especially at Christmas. But on its own, it's truly wonderful, too.

foie gras

I live in France, which is the country in the world that produces the most foie gras and where the culture, for the most part, is behind this culinary delicacy.

When and where did foie gras originate? What goes into making it? Is it possible to buy an ethically acceptable version of this product?

To my surprise, I discovered that foie gras (or some version of engorging the livers of geese for harvesting) has been around for centuries – there are copies of frescoes hanging in the Louvre that are thought to have decorated the tomb of Ti (2500 BC), showing scenes of geese being force fed by hand. It's generally accepted that the reason it's even possible to 'gave' (force feed) a goose or a duck is because they are both migratory birds that have a natural tendency to fatten up before travel, enabling them to cope with the distance and potential bad weather. Not only are these fattened geese and ducks used for their livers, but the external fat is rendered and used to 'confit' foods, helping to preserve precious meat for several months after cooking. This technique is still going strong today, most famously seen in the French classic, Confit de Canard.

During my research, I have found that there is a very small but growing number of breeders of what we could reasonably call 'ethical' foie gras. They produce tiny amounts of livers that are free-range and fattened without force feeding. And by 'force feeding' I'm talking about the use of *force* to feed the animals, or anything that constitutes '*gavage*' with tubes or pipes. The livers are much smaller and the flavour is different: less rich, in terms of texture, but with a more pronounced flavour of the liver itself. If meat is a luxury product, then ethically produced foie gras is a platinum-plated luxury product, a bit like sustainable caviar. As such, it's for very, very rare enjoyment. And if you do happen upon a farm when you're on a road trip somewhere down in southwest France, or the Extremadurian countryside, or in Québec where they sell the livers vacuum packed straight from the farm, then you can turn the raw material into a beautiful pâté using my recipe on page 222. It freezes well so you can eat tiny amounts when the occasion calls for something really rich and special. Everyone agrees that there will never be enough demand for so-called ethical foie gras to support a whole industry. But the key is to enjoy it very seldomly (as in, almost never) and be scrupulous as to where you source it. And if you don't love it, then just avoid it completely because it's going to be very expensive.

What I don't understand is why for so many people foie gras stands out as being more cruel than any other kind of mistreatment of animals. I refuse to be lectured for eating carefully sourced foie gras by someone who is comfortable consuming an industrially produced chicken tikka massala on a Friday night. Same abject cruelty – it's just that one is more convenient to rail against and has received more press attention than the other.

Southern Fried Quail with a Spice Shake

I experience fried chicken cravings about twice a year when I long for the comfort of a plate of hot crispy chicken spiked with a little cayenne and maybe some Dr Pepper Baked Beans (see page 152) or Nena's Mashed Potatoes (see page 25) on the side. I have found, however, that I prefer using game rather than chicken because there's more flavour in a quail or a piece of rabbit and it works even better with the simple, crunchy batter. It's also easier to fry quails because they're small and cook through without drying out, especially if you marinate them for a day as I suggest below. So, over the years, I've traded fried chicken for fried quail and have come to prefer it. In some parts of the American South, there is a tradition of hunting quails and other small game birds on Christmas Day. You then go home and have a big brunch of 'Chicken Fried Quail', which is what this recipe is also sometimes called. Finishing the quails in the oven is a handy way of making sure they're cooked through and it also gives you time to change out of your fried food clothes if you have people over. I nearly forgot to mention another neat little tip: I love having a fresh green salad with a lemon and oil dressing after fried quail. Don't change plates and you'll find little bits of fried crust that have fallen off the quail to eat as croutons. Less washing up and, food wise, it's awesome.

Serves 2 as a main or 4 as a starter

4 quails without giblets, weighing around 160g each
1 x 284ml tub buttermilk
140g self-raising flour
1 litre sunflower oil

FOR THE SPICE SHAKE
2 tsp garlic granules/dried ground garlic
½ tsp celery salt
¼ tsp ground cumin
¼ tsp smoked paprika (the sweet kind that isn't hot)
¼ tsp cayenne pepper
a pinch freshly ground black pepper

The day before you want to serve the quails, marinate them in an airtight container with the buttermilk, making sure they're more or less covered.

Once the quails have marinated, shake them free of any excess buttermilk (it's fine to have some still sticking on, so no need to wipe them) and dip them in the self-raising flour. Coat them thoroughly.

Preheat the oven to 200°C/fan 180°C/gas mark 6 – a fan oven is best for crispiness – and cover a baking tray with baking paper.

Heat the oil in a large pan over a high heat until shimmering. Cook the buttermilk-and-flour-dredged quails two at a time until golden and with a puffed-up crust on all sides. This takes around 4 minutes, depending on how hot your oil is and the size of the pan. Place on the prepared baking tray.

Recipe continues

Southern Fried Quail with a Spice Shake *continued*

cook's tip I have also made this recipe with farmed rabbit and found that it worked really well. I'm not a fan of very gamey game, which is why I prefer quail, but if you love that slightly high flavour then opt for wild rabbit and use the recipe as above.

You can easily double or triple this recipe if you have more people to feed. I would change the oil after having cooked about 8 quails, as it will start to colour the crust too quickly and taste old.

Once all four quails are cooked and sitting on the baking tray, transfer to the preheated oven and cook for a further 15–20 minutes. Check that they're done by looking between the top of the thigh and the body for any remaining pink-coloured flesh.

While the quails are finishing in the oven, combine all the Spice Shake ingredients in a bowl. Sprinkle the shake mix all over the quails and serve straight away with some Dill Pickle Fries (page 229).

Dill Pickle Fries

I first had these in a steakhouse in Chicago a few years ago and loved them. It's such an ingenious idea to replace potato with pickles, as they deliver a wonderful sweet and sour taste, whilst remaining crunchy and vaguely French fry-ish to look at. Having sampled a lot of different variations (they make them differently wherever you go in the US), I prefer them made with a light batter. In Memphis, they tend to cook them with a cornmeal coating and I avoid these as they make the pickle soggy inside. I suggest you seek out a slightly sweet, giant pickle with a pronounced dill flavour when you make these – and stay away from cornichons. They are way too sour and small for this purpose.

Serves 3–4 as a side

300g dill pickles, roughly cut to look like French fries

120g self-raising flour, + 100g for dusting

a generous pinch salt and freshly ground black pepper

1 medium free-range egg, lightly beaten with a fork

150ml fizzy water

1 litre sunflower oil

a pinch paprika

cook's tip You can place them in a hot oven (200°C/fan 180°C/gas mark 6) to crisp up again if you make them slightly ahead.

It makes a big difference to the result if you go for pickles that are sweet and make sure that they're crrrunchy. It's worth investing in a couple of different jars to find out which brand you like best.

Dab each dill pickle with kitchen paper. The less surface moisture there is underneath the batter, the more crispy the result.

Tip 120g of the flour into a medium bowl and make a well in the middle. Season with salt and pepper.

Gradually incorporate the beaten egg with the dry ingredients using a balloon whisk, to avoid lumps. When the egg has gone in and the dough has begun to come together, loosen with the fizzy water, adding it little by little and mixing in between additions so as not to knock out too many bubbles.

Heat the oil in a medium saucepan over a high heat until shimmering.

Add the pickles to the batter and coat them well.

Before placing in the oil, dip each battered pickle in the 100g loose flour to give it a dry coat on top of the wet one.

Fry each pickle off in the oil until puffed up, golden and crispy. This won't take more than a couple of minutes and I tend to fry only 3 or 4 pickle fries at a time to avoid crowding the pan and making the oil temperature drop too much.

Set the cooked fries on to kitchen paper to drain off any excess oil. Repeat until all the fries are done. Serve hot with a little salt and some paprika sprinkled over the top (see page 227).

Pigeon and Pistachio Pastilla

This recipe is a cornerstone of Moroccan cuisine. It might seem weird, when you've read the recipe, to have scrambled eggs in the dish but it's just the most heavenly combination with the pigeon, herbs, nuts and spices. I have tasted many versions of this classic in France where excellent Moroccan food is easy to come by and have sometimes found it slightly too sweet for my taste, which is why I have taken down the amount of sugar by quite a bit. I've also omitted the orange blossom water, which I find overbearing. There are two phases in this recipe: the first is the cooking of the pigeon and scrambled eggs; the second is the assembling of the pastilla. You could absolutely stop after cooking the pigeon and serve the meat over couscous or alongside vegetables for a delectable winter casserole. You could make this pastilla with lots of other kinds of meat, such as chicken, black pudding or even vegetarian options like goat's cheese and courgette. Pastilla is simply the name of the *galette*, or filled pastry. Here in France they tend to use a pastry called *feuille de brick*, which is like an elasticated version of filo pastry with lots of holes in it, like a very thin buckwheat *galette*. I have tested this recipe with filo and it works well, too, so you can use either.

Serves 6

2 tbsp olive oil

25g butter, + extra for greasing

3 plump pigeons, without giblets, weighing around 300g each

2 medium red onions, peeled and very finely chopped

1 large cinnamon stick

¼ tsp ground ginger

a pinch saffron strands

1 handful of parsley, stalks removed and leaves finely chopped

1 handful of coriander, stalks removed and leaves finely chopped

250ml chicken stock

salt

2 large free-range eggs

Heat the olive oil and butter in a large, deep saucepan over a medium heat. When the butter has melted, add the pigeons and sear the skin, until golden on all sides. I find it takes about 10 minutes to brown the birds all over. Remove them from the pan and set aside.

Turn down the heat and add the onions, cinnamon, ginger and saffron. Cook until the onions are translucent, around 10 minutes. Add the parsley and coriander stalks to the onions now, too.

Return the pigeons to the pan, laying them on their backs, and add the stock. Place the lid on and simmer over a very gentle heat for 1½ hours. Turn the birds over in the sauce halfway through the cooking time so they are on their breasts.

Once the pigeons have had their time, remove them from the sauce to cool and turn the heat up under the pan. Bring the sauce to the boil and reduce the mixture by half.

100g shelled pistachios, roughly chopped and toasted in a pan until golden

2 tbsp icing sugar

2 tsp ground cinnamon

1 × 270g pack filo pastry or *feuille de brick*, if you can find any

When the pigeons are cool enough to handle, remove and discard the skin and shred the meat off them with your hands.

Once the mixture has reduced by half, remove the cinnamon stick and then gently tilt the pan and pour or spoon off any surface fat that has risen. Set the fat aside (I normally get about 150ml) and return the meat to the pan with the now-concentrated juices. Taste and season with salt if needed.

Preheat the oven to 180°C/fan 160°C/gas mark 4 and grease a cake tin measuring roughly 20cm diameter.

Place a small saucepan over a medium heat and add half of the fragrant fat from the pigeon sauce (if for some reason you didn't get any fat, melt 130g butter instead and use half of that now). Beat the eggs with a fork and then add them to the pan to scramble over a gentle heat. Once cooked, remove from the pan and add the chopped parsley and coriander leaves.

Mix the pistachios in a bowl with the sugar and cinnamon and set aside. You should have 3 separate bowls or pans: one with scrambled eggs, one with pigeon and one with nuts.

Layer the filo sheets into the prepared cake tin, keeping 2 sheets back, remembering to brush over some of the remaining pigeon fat or butter in between each layer. You're aiming to enclose the filling completely so overlap the pastry sheets in a north/south, east/west, southeast/northwest sort of fashion to prevent any gaps and make sure that the filo sheets rise above the edge of the cake tin.

Pile the scrambled eggs into the base of the cake tin, spreading them out to make an even

Recipe continues

Pigeon and Pistachio Pastilla *continued*

cook's tip I love serving this with a fresh baby spinach salad with a light, yoghurt-based dressing (one part Dijon mustard, one part yoghurt, one part cider vinegar, one part olive oil) and some thinly sliced radish.

Traditionally, you would create a criss-cross pattern on top on the pastilla with icing sugar diamonds cut with cinnamon stripes. Not only is this really difficult to get to look perfect, it also adds more sugar and cinnamon, which I don't particularly like.

layer. Place a single layer of filo pastry on top of the eggs and then top with three-quarters of the pistachio nuts and sugar, then another layer of filo, and finally add the pigeon layer.

Fold the top edges of the pastry over the filling, remembering to brush again in between each addition. If you've run out of fat, use some more melted butter at this point. Once the filling is totally enclosed, place the cake tin on a baking sheet.

Cook in the middle of the preheated oven for 20 minutes until the pastry is golden. Remove from the oven and carefully turn the tin upside down on to a serving dish or board to release the pastilla.

Scatter over the remaining nuts and sieve over the sugar. Cut into wedges and serve.

Rabbit and Rosemary Casserole with White Wine and Cream

Although I made this recipe up because I was craving a warming, white-wine-based rabbit dish, I suspect that the Italians are behind the pairing of rabbit and rosemary. A little celery, some onion and the white wine are the main players here and they work together to create a rich, pale sauce that is completely wonderful. I tend to buy farmed rabbit because that's what I can find more easily but, by all means, give this a go with full-flavoured wild rabbit if you want to. The only change to the recipe with the wild version is that I might soak the rabbit in water or milk for 24 hours, changing the liquid before going to bed and then again at breakfast time. This will help calm down some of the very top gamey notes if you're not a fan (I'm not). Piled on top of fresh pappardelle or gnocchi and with a little finely grated lemon zest, this is the most fabulous casserole dish and can easily be made ahead for a dinner party.

Serves 4

1.2kg rabbit, jointed

2 tbsp plain flour

30g butter

2 tbsp olive oil

1 stick celery, washed, topped, tailed and very finely chopped

2 small white onions, peeled and very finely chopped

1 garlic clove, peeled and minced

200ml dry white wine (Italian makes sense here)

500ml good-quality chicken stock

2 sprigs of rosemary

1 tbsp Dijon mustard

100ml crème fraîche or double cream

salt and plenty of freshly ground black pepper, to taste

a little finely grated zest of an unwaxed lemon and some finely chopped parsley, to garnish

Toss the rabbit pieces in the flour until well coated.

Heat the butter and olive oil in a large saucepan over a medium heat until the butter has melted. Add the rabbit pieces and fry off until golden on all sides. Don't let the rabbit get too dark at this point as you don't want the butter to burn – blond is good but dark brown is too far. You may have to do this in batches, depending on the size of your pan. Once all the rabbit has been browned, remove from the pan and set aside.

Add the celery, onion and garlic to the pan and sweat over a low heat, making sure to scrape up all the little bits on the bottom of the pan with a rubber spatula. Cook for 10 minutes until the onion is translucent and then pour in the wine and stock, and add the rosemary and the rabbit pieces back to the pan.

Bring to the boil then turn the heat down to reduce to a very slow simmer. Cook with a lid on for 1½ hours, until the rabbit is falling off the bone.

Remove the meat from the casserole carefully with a slotted spoon or tongs and set aside.

Recipe continues

Rabbit and Rosemary Casserole with White Wine and Cream *continued*

cook's tip If serving with pappardelle, I tend to take the meat off the bone with the help of my hands or two forks. If I'm serving with gnocchi, I dish it up as it is.

A different version of this could be made with 6 free-range chicken thighs if you hanker for the comfort of the dish but can't get any rabbit.

A final thought: if you're unsure how to joint a rabbit, you can look it up online. There are a couple of good videos – I've checked. The easiest of all is to ask the butcher who sold you the meat to do it for you, though. Another reason to shop for meat at the butcher's!

Discard the now-bald rosemary stalks. Boil the liquid and vegetable mixture to reduce and thicken by a third. Take off the heat and add the mustard and cream. Stir to dissolve. Taste and season generously with black pepper and as much salt as you need (beware – some stocks are quite salty).

Return the meat to the pan, garnish with a little lemon zest and parsley to serve.

Coq au Pheasant

The title for this is completely inaccurate but I like it because it implies what it is: a Coq au Vin made with pheasants. The truth is that it's better to make Coq au Vin with older birds – although they are drier, they have tons more flavour. This recipe would also adapt well to a large older chicken, if you're able to lay your hands on one. I can't think of anything better in the colder months than this with a pile of piping-hot Celeriac Winter Mash (see page 163) on the side. And if you happen to have any left over, I like to strip the meat from the bones and mix it with crème fraîche and mustard. I then either top it with puff pastry in a pie or enjoy it on top of fresh pasta.

Serves 4

250g smoked lardons, cut into strips

2 tbsp olive oil

1 large or 2 medium carrots, peeled, topped, tailed and finely sliced

1 medium red onion, peeled, halved and very finely sliced into half moons

4 large garlic cloves, peeled and very finely sliced

200g chestnut mushrooms, wiped clean and quartered

30g butter

2 whole pheasants (roughly 750g each), giblets removed

250ml tawny Port

200ml chicken stock

2 bay leaves

a few sprigs of thyme

salt and freshly ground black pepper

cook's tip If you want to make this ahead, stop cooking after 1½ hours and finish off with the mushrooms a day or two later.

Preheat the oven to 220°C/fan 200°C/gas mark 7.

Place a very large ovenproof casserole dish over a medium heat, and brown the lardons in half the olive oil until they start to go golden.

Add the carrots and turn down the heat. Cook for 5 minutes and then add the onion and garlic. Cover with a lid and cook for about 10 minutes, or until the onion is softened. Remove everything from the pan with a slotted spoon and set aside.

Turn up the heat, add in the remaining olive oil and fry off the mushrooms. Cook for about 10 minutes, or until they are golden and slightly softened. Remove them with a slotted spoon and set aside on a separate plate.

Melt the butter in the dish and brown the pheasants on all sides. Once the birds are golden, pour in the Port and stock, and add the bay leaves and thyme. Return the vegetable and lardon mixture to the pan and give it a stir. Cover with a lid, place in the middle of the preheated oven, and cook for 1 hour.

After an hour, add the mushrooms to the dish and cook for a further 30 minutes.

Remove from the oven and season with plenty of fresh black pepper and some salt, if needed (lardons can be quite salty so it may not need any more). Fish out the bay leaves and thyme before serving with a pile of steaming mash.

Venison en Croûte

If I'm being cheeky by giving this Wellington recipe a French name, it's because I think they have understood this recipe better than we have. Somewhere in the universe, the competitive spirit of Napoleon Bonaparte is rubbing his hands with glee, I know. Beef fillet is not the right cut to use in my view because it lacks flavour. The texture is tender at best but the mushroom duxelles and the pastry crust don't give it enough oomph to make it interesting beyond that. In fact, the only way that I enjoy fillet of beef is when it's dressed in something gorgeous and independently rich, whether a Sauce au Roquefort or Sauce aux Morilles (see pages 51 and 56) – in short, something with nuts and guts and umami to pump up the jam on the slightly *bof* flavour of the meat itself. For the price per kilo, it's a scandal to have meat that is so lacking in inherent flavour but such is the meat market at present that we prize the cut that is the leanest, easiest and quickest to cook over the ones with more flavour… This is a conversation that I develop in more depth on pages 45–7. Coming back to the matter at hand, though – *flavour.* Venison fillet is *stuffed* with flavour and just as tender as beef fillet. In other words, it is perfect for a Wellington, or a Venison en Croûte.

Serves 6–8

60g butter

800g venison fillet, trimmed, roughly the same thickness at both ends

300g chestnut mushrooms, wiped clean

1 large red onion, peeled

2 garlic cloves, peeled

100ml ruby Port

salt and freshly ground black pepper

1 tbsp Dijon mustard

a bunch tarragon, finely chopped

6 large slices prosciutto

1 × 320g pack all-butter puff pastry

2 free-range medium eggs, beaten with a fork

Warm up 20g of the butter in a very large frying pan and, once foaming, add the meat. Sear over a high heat until the meat has browned on all sides, including the ends. I like to really push the colour at this stage as this is a great way of adding flavour to the recipe. Remove from the pan and set aside to cool.

Blitz the mushrooms, then the onion and garlic, in a food processor until very finely chopped.

In the same pan, melt the remaining butter and add the chopped mushrooms and onion mixture. Cook over a medium heat until the onion is softened and translucent.

Pour in the Port along with a good crunch of salt and black pepper. Turn up the heat and cook until all the Port has disappeared from the pan. Add the mustard and tarragon and set aside to cool right down.

Recipe continues

Venison en Croûte *continued*

cook's tip If you can't
find one 800g fillet, you can
use two 400g fillets and lay
them together top to toe –
which will also give you a
very consistent thickness.
I tied them together tightly
before the searing stage
of the recipe to help them
stay in place, cutting away
the string only at the last
minute before placing in
the pastry.

It's best to use a serrated
knife to carve this neatly.

Lay a very large sheet of clingfilm on your
work surface and place the prosciutto slices
slightly overlapping on top so that they create a
base layer. Spread the cool mushroom duxelles
over the prosciutto and top with the cooled meat.
Wrap tightly in the prosciutto and then the layer
of clingfilm, so that it resembles a tightly packed
salami.

Put in the fridge for 2 hours or overnight to set.

Preheat the oven to 220°C/fan 200°C/gas mark 7
and place a baking sheet in the oven to heat up.

Roll out the pastry on a lightly floured surface
so that it's big enough to cover the meat cannon
totally.

Unwrap the meat, taking care not to tear the
prosciutto. Place in the middle of the pastry
and bring the pastry over to create a sealed
parcel, pressing down on the seam to secure
it shut. Turn the pastry so that the seam is
underneath and then brush the top with egg and
criss cross the top in a pretty pattern.

Place on the hot baking sheet and cook in the
preheated oven for 35 minutes for a thick fillet
(the width of a takeaway coffee cup). This will be
rare at the thickest end and better cooked as you
taper to the thinner end. If the pastry is browning
a little too quickly, place a sheet of tin foil loosely
over the top to protect it. The best way to test if
it's perfectly cooked inside is to insert a skewer
into the middle of the fillet – if the tip comes out
warm when placed just under your lower lip (this
is a very sensitive part of your body for testing
temperatures – the chocolatiers use this technique
for tempering) it is done; if it is still cold, put it
back in. Check again in 5 minutes.

Once cooked and golden, leave to rest for
15 minutes before carving and serving.

Venison Sausage Casserole

I had a venison casserole about 12 years ago in Scotland and it was so good I can still taste it. I did a fair bit of research before setting off into this recipe and it turns out that there are almost no recipes for venison sausage casseroles out there... This is a mystery to me since I think there's something so warming and comforting about this dish and the great thing about venison sausages is that they are bursting with flavour. Not that I don't love a sawdust banger on the barbie once in a while. For anything that's remotely slow cooked like this, I prefer to use sausages with more character that can stand up to the other ingredients. This is a lovely winter or late autumn recipe and can be made a day ahead so is wonderful for dinner parties or family suppers when you want to take the stress out of the situation and actually enjoy yourself.

Serves 6

12 venison sausages (they will be mixed with a little pork)

2 tbsp olive oil

30g butter

2 red onions, peeled and finely sliced

1 fennel bulb, very finely sliced

1 sprig of rosemary

2 bay leaves

$1/3$ whole fresh nutmeg, finely grated

3 tbsp redcurrant jelly

300ml strong veal or chicken stock

400ml good red wine (I tend towards Burgundy because Bordeaux can go purple and deliver too many tannins)

salt and freshly ground black pepper

1 handful of fresh parsley, stalks removed and leaves finely chopped, to garnish

In a frying pan over a medium heat (but not so hot that the sausages burst their skins), brown the sausages with the olive oil until golden all over, then remove them from the pan and set aside.

Melt the butter in the same pan and cook the onions, fennel and aromatics (rosemary, bay and nutmeg) over a very low heat. Give the pan a good scrape and use the vegetables to 'mop' up the juices on the bottom of the pan. Don't rush this stage, it is the basis of the casserole flavour and will take around 20 minutes with a lid on. When the onions and fennel are translucent and completely softened, add the redcurrant jelly to the pan. Stir to combine.

Return the sausages to the pan and add the stock and wine. Turn up the heat until you reach a slow simmer. Cook uncovered for an hour, turning down the heat if it bubbles too hard.

Adjust the seasoning at the end of the cooking time and serve piping hot with the juices spooned over and parsley scattered over the top.

cook's tip I love Yorkshire Puddings (see page 33) and Celeriac Winter Mash (see page 163) with this casserole but fluffy mashed potato (see page 25) would work beautifully, too, or a steaming bowl of fragrant lentils. And mustard. Obviously.

Crispy Chinese Seaweed

I want to love kale, with its deep, dark green colour and vitamins bursting from every curl… but it's so *bitter* when blanched or even stir fried. When I first had kale chips (this was a big food craze about two years ago), I thought *bingo*! Crunchy and light and still stuffed with green goodness; plus it reminded me of the crispy appetiser you get at Chinese restaurants that I have loved since I was a child. So this is a recipe for seaweed using kale and giving it only a light seasoning of sugar and spices, rather than the often fried, overly sweet flavour it can have (and which is no doubt why I loved it so much when I was little).

Serves 6

400g kale, washed and spun dry
    (this is important as it needs
    to be very dry)
1 tbsp cider vinegar
1 tbsp sunflower oil
2 tsp caster sugar
a generous pinch salt, to taste
a very small pinch cayenne
    pepper

cook's Tip If your first batch of kale comes out of the oven looking crispy but brownish, your oven probably runs a little hot, so turn it down a tiny bit. You're looking for a rich khaki green colour on the leaves once cooked. Equally, if the leaves in the middle of the baking sheet are still limp, then toss and put back in the oven to crisp up for another couple of minutes.

If you don't finish all the kale, store it in an airtight container and reheat in a hot oven for 2 minutes to give it back its crunch.

Preheat the oven to 180°C/fan 160°C/gas mark 4 – it is best to use a fan oven with this recipe if possible – and line a baking tray with parchment paper.

Cut out the hard stems from the centre of each kale leaf. Roll and then finely chop the leaves so that you have very fine green ribbons. Toss them first with the vinegar, then massage the leaves with the oil. I know it sounds mad but believe me: rubbing the kale with your fingertips enables the oil to go further (helping to achieve the right texture later).

Lay out flat on the baking sheet, in a thin layer. It's better to cook the kale in 2 or 3 batches rather than crowding the baking sheet, otherwise it won't crisp up. Bake in a hot oven for 12 minutes then set aside whilst you bake off the rest. You can do this hours in advance if you want and it won't affect the crispiness of the kale.

Toss with sugar and salt and serve with a pinch of cayenne sprinkled over the top (see page 160).

index

guacamole, holy 83
Guinness: beef and Guinness pie 80–1

H

ham
brining 71, 72
carving 38
ham hock risotto with asparagus and peas 171–3
ham hock stock 170
redcurrant glazed ham 177–8
hanging 214–15
hummous 116

I

industrialisation of food x–xi, xii, xvi–xvii, 65, 72, 191, 215

J

jelly, spiced winter 209

K

kale: crispy Chinese seaweed 242
kibbeh 110–11
kidney beans: bowl o' red 84–5
kidneys: veal kidneys with Madeira and mustard sauce 89
knives 36

L

labelling viii–ix, xvii
lamb
brain fritters with Middle Eastern spices 137
carving 37–8
cumin, chilli and garlic chuanr rub 119
environmental issues xvii
gourmet lamb burger 107
hanging 215
kibbeh 110–11
mincing 131
moussaka 126–8
Rue des Rosiers lamb shawarma kebab 135
shepherd's pie 132–3
slow-cooked shoulder of lamb – 3 ways 102–3
steaks 47

tandoori butterflied leg of lamb 121–2
lamb stock 104, 105
lard shortcrust pastry 186–7
latkes 75
leek confiture 21
lemons
salade verte 5
wilted Brussels sprout salad with lemon and honey walnuts 210
liver
calves' liver with shallot and sage crisps 97
chicken liver pâté with port and prunes 2–4
foie gras maison 222–4

M

marinades
cornflour 166
cumin, chilli and garlic chuanr rub 119
dry rub 148
Hawaiian pineapple pork 159
methods 123–5
Middle Eastern 102
tandoori 121–2
white wine, garlic and fresh herb 30
matzo crackers: chicken and matzo soup for the soul 10–12
mayonnaise
celeriac en remoulade 179
gourmet lamb burger 107
po'boys 189
Russian dressing 78
meatballs, Swedish 66
Melba toast 224
Memphis mustard slaw 157
mighty salt beef 74
milk
béchamel sauce 128, 163
celeriac winter mash 163
poaching 137
ragu Bolognese 69
veal ethics 88
Yorkshire pudding (via Japan) 33
mincemeat, homemade 98–100
mincing 62, 130–1
morels cream sauce – sauce aux morilles 56
moussaka 126–8
mushrooms
beef cheeks Bourguignon 39
coq au pheasant 237

bibliography

The Complete Meat Cookbook Bruce Aidells and Denis Kelly

A Girl and Her Pig April Bloomfield

Adventures of a Bacon Curer Maynard Davies

Shark's Fin and Sichuan Pepper Fuschia Dunlop

Offal Nina Edwards

Pig Tales Barry Estabrook

Whole Beast Butchery Ryan Farr

The River Cottage Meat Book Hugh Fearnley-Whittingstall

Hawksmoor at Home Huw Gott, Will Beckett and Richard Turner

The Butcher's Apprentice Aliza Green

Charcuterie and French Pork Cookery Jane Grigson

The Complete Book of Butchering, Smoking, Curing and Sausage Making Philip Hasheider

The Essentials of Classic Italian Cooking Marcella Hazan

Nose to Tail Eating Fergus Henderson

Beyond Nose to Tail Fergus Henderson

Salt Sugar Smoke Diana Henry

Slow Fire Ray 'Dr BBQ' Lampe

Lobel's Meat Bible Stanley, Evan, Mark and David Lobel

On Food and Cooking: The science and lore of the kitchen Harold McGee

Cooking on the Bone Jennifer McLagan

Fat Jennifer McLagan

Odd Bits Jennifer McLagan

Basic Butchering of Livestock and Game John J. Mettler Jr

Beef Lorna Piatti-Farnell

The Cookbook Pitt Cue Co.

The Omnivore's Dilemma Michael Pollan

Planet Carnivore: Why cheap meat costs the Earth (and how to pay the bill) Alex Renton

Pork Katharine M. Rogers

Charcuterie Michael Ruhlman and Brian Polcyn

Eating Animals Jonathan Safran Foer

Steak Mark Schatzker

Fast Food Nation Eric Schlosser

Hamburger Andrew F. Smith

Jack Ubaldi's Meat Book Jack Ubaldi and Elizabeth Crossman

Ginger Pig Meat Book Tim Wilson and Fran Warde

suppliers

I have a little surprise for you. I'm not going to provide a traditional supplier's list because, after some debate, I decided it was more useful to give you helpful tips on how to recognise a good butcher instead. This idea and The Butcher Test below come straight from my friend Pete Hannan, a wonderful butcher (and person), whose advice and outlook on meat matters I trust and respect.

First of all, a good butcher won't get offended by someone who asks them questions about the meat they're selling – quite the reverse. A good butcher *wants* you to ask him or her questions. It's also an excellent way to start this very important relationship – your butcher will learn your likes and needs. Showing the butcher you mean business will give them the incentive to offer you the best they have. In other words – the stuff they're saving for themselves or other discriminating customers. **A good butcher wants to feed you well. They want you to come back and give them good feedback.** A good butcher will never sell you something that he or she wouldn't want to take home themselves; it's not in their interest to do so. After all, a good butcher is your meat dealer. He or she should know everything about the meat they're selling: the breed, the feed and the animal husbandry. You can't be expected to know all the information about the meat in front of you – you rely on their expertise. The hallmarks of a good butcher are: integrity, transparency and honesty.

Be firm and tell your butcher that you're happy to pay for the best (good meat should be expensive) but it must be **outstanding**. Be flexible. You may have gone in for sirloin steaks but be prepared to come out with a rack of lamb. Plan the menu around the meat – exquisite meat will always be the centrepiece on the table. Beautiful meat speaks for itself and turns even a beginner cook into a masterchef. As Pete says, 'If the meat is great, the dinner is done.' Ain't that the truth?

The Butcher Test

1 Be firm and tell your butcher that you're happy to be guided in terms of what you buy and that *you're willing to pay for it*, but you want something very good.

2 Ask questions such as: 'What is particularly good today?' 'Can you tell me about the breed of that piece of meat?' 'Has it been aged and for how long?' A good butcher will be able to give you the answers. If they don't know what they're selling, it's not a good sign.

3 Always give feedback, whether positive or negative. This will encourage them to go the extra mile in future.

4 A final and extremely practical thought is that anyone who is looking for a good butcher should know about the Q Guild (**www.qguild.co.uk**). It is a slightly elitist group of butchers that have set themselves apart as having very high standards or, as they put it, 'skill, craftsmanship, and above all quality'. What's more, the website lists butchers from all over the British Isles. It doesn't mean that all great butchers are listed – your local might be outstanding and not feature – but it's a good starting point.

Finally, I can't recommend Pete's company highly enough. I could wax lyrical about their salt chamber dry-aged beef all day but my editor is busy red-penning out the waffle so I'll just say this: go to **www.themeatmerchant.com** and take a look.

acknowledgements

This is always my favourite page of a new book to write. I love saying thank you. And in this case, it's been a project that has meant so much to me for so long that I have lots of lovely thank yous to dish out.

Transworld and **Doug Young** continue to believe in me and my ideas for books. I consider it a privilege to do work I love. You enable this to happen. Thank you.

To **Becky Wright**, thank you for helping me to get this project off the ground and for being there for the crucial first half. **Jo**, they were big shoes to fill but you slipped effortlessly into them and you have brought so much to *Carneval* and to me in the process. Thank you both for such an intuitive understanding of what this book is about and what it meant to me. Jo, thank you also for saying '*carne*' on that drab Monday morning… It was an inspired hunch. Magic moments like that don't come around often.

To my work family: **Tab**, Loop, **Annie** – the book became itself on the shoot days, the result of your combined visions. Thank you for pushing for more, for better. And for such hard work. **Super Cooper**, thank you also for giving me a crash pad during the shoot, especially the week before your weddin'. I'll pay you back in cheese. That's a promise.

Kathryn, Kendal and Laura – thank you for assisting with enthusiasm, for the best polenta I've ever had, for magically disappearing parsley from my teeth in portrait shots and for great energy on the shoots.

Thank you Phil Lord for stepping in and saving the day. Thanks to Sarah Whittaker, Katrina Whone and Sarah Harwood from Transworld.

Thank you to Felicity Blunt and Emma Herdman for being my allies over at Curtis Brown. And Jon Fowler for taking such good care of me and all things telly. Zoe, you parachuted in last minute. Thank you for such great energy and drive.

My real life family: **Mummy**, thank you for your support, especially in 2014–2015. Thank you for helping me get *here*. Dato, you're always on my team. You and Souphie were responsible for taking me to butcher my first lamb and to visit Kintoa Pig Farms in the Pays Basque fifteen years ago. You've never tired of conversations about my work. Thank you.

Thank you to **Rob** for letting me write and even live at yours when I needed it; for brilliant strategy and for having my back.

Un grand merci to the following Parisians who have supported, tasted, encouraged, discussed meat matters and taken me out for a drink when I needed to put the work down and just get out of the house: Nor, Michael, Imo, Gretchen, Mark, Emma G, Annabelle, Rom, Amy, Camille, Pierre *et* Brigitte.

From London and beyond, for your friendship and for all the years of putting up with my obsession with meat and butchery, I want to thank: Joss, Sarah T, Jo McGrath, Herbie, Luce, Jax, Tina and the scoobies, Ultan, Alli and Aaron. Thank you to John at Smithfield for giving me a shot all those years ago and to Evan and June Baillie for putting me up on your farm in New South Wales back in 2005.

Pete Hannan, you've been a saint. I can't believe your patience and generosity. Thank you for editing and improving my Meat Geeks. You embody everything I hope the meat industry will become. Thanks to Cannon & Cannon for taking the time to talk to me about bacon and Andrew Cavanna for foie gras.

Lastly, I want to thank my sister, Georgie Parr. Even from Beijing, you continue to deliver the best advice, send me light and always find a minute to talk despite your crazy schedule with the winks and work. By the way, the coolest dungarees and kids's clothes in Britain can be purchased at www.dottydungarees.com. If all of this wasn't enough, you're responsible for introducing me to three of my favourite people on earth: Maximum, Otto and Eloise Parr. This book is for you.

ANNIE   HARRY   JO   KATHRYN

KENDAL   LAURA E   LAURA U   TABITHA

Harry Eastwood first came to the public's attention in 2007 when she co-presented Channel 4's popular prime-time television series *Cook Yourself Thin*. She later went on to present the 20-part US version of the show on Lifetime network and is the author of three other cookery books: *Red Velvet & Chocolate Heartache* – which has sold nearly 50,000 copies; *The Skinny French Kitchen* – which was nominated for the prestigious Guild of Food Writers Miriam Polunin Award for Healthy Eating; and *A Salad for All Seasons*. Famous for her imaginative and unusual approach to food, Harry's focus remains the creation of original and reliable recipes that work every time.

Her most recent TV series have included Fox's *Baking Good, Baking Bad* and *Sinful Sweets*, which aired on Cooking Channel USA.

Harry is especially well known for successfully sneaking vegetables into cakes. What may come as a surprise is that she has also been researching meat in all its aspects for more than 15 years. Her passion for butchery and all meat matters even took her to Smithfield Market where she moonlit as an apprentice butcher in her early twenties. *Carneval* is the result of this colourful journey.

Harry lives in Paris.